Nicole Nobody

The autobiography of the
DUCHESS OF BEDFORD

W. H. ALLEN
London and New York
A Division of Howard & Wyndham Ltd
1974

Ex Libris

KEITH
and
JUNE
BOARDALL

FIRST PUBLISHED 1974

REPRINTED 1974

NO REPRODUCTION OF THIS WORK IN WHOLE OR IN PART OR IN ANY FORM WHATEVER
IS PERMITTED WITHOUT AUTHORITY FROM THE PUBLISHERS.
PRINTED AND BOUND IN GREAT BRITAIN BY
BUTLER & TANNER LTD, FROME & LONDON
FOR THE PUBLISHERS W. H. ALLEN & CO. LTD.
44 HILL STREET, LONDON WIX 8LB.
ISBN 0 491 01472 4

Contents

[v]

Contents

1950–1957

1957–1960

1960–1974

Illustrations

Executive Duchess; happy families.

Their Graces!

Chef de cuisine, David, with his crew; amethysts and ancestors.

Riding a rhinoceros; 'I love animals'; Melchior; room with a view.

Bertrand Russell and Freddie Ayer; Barbara Cartland and the Duchess of Leeds; Miss New Zealand with Paul Getty and Nubar Gulbenkian.

Between pages 278 and 279

Common Market: Highland Gathering: the Japanese grand master.

Two beautiful human beings.

Caterine, Mati, Serafine; Gilles, Galaad, Manuella; with Andrew and Robbie; la belle Anyes.

Persepolis and the Shah's beautiful wife; with ex-King Umberto of Italy.

With Lady Fairfax and Charles Lloyd Jones in Sydney; with the Begum.

Paul Getty learns the twist; at the zoo party.

St. Trinian's in Paris; with Twiggy and Mary Quant.

Nicole Nobody.

To IAN

Didier, Caterine, Gilles, Anyes
Serafine, Galaad

Robin, Rudolf, Francis
Andrew, Robbie

I   *'She's so ugly'*

THEY STOOD AROUND the shrivelled, strawberry-coloured new-comer, stunned by what they saw. For a few moments no-one dared speak.

'She's so ugly.'

My Aunt Cécile at last put into words what the whole family must have been thinking. 'She is so fragile. Will she live?'

'Do not come too close,' the nurse ordered, 'and don't pick her up. She's very feeble.'

My mother's love for my father was possessive and mystical and in her eyes as pure as the passion of Héloise for Abélard. She vowed to herself that she would never have any children so that she could serve him with a devotion that would be complete, whole, single-minded.

My mother was distraught when she discovered that she was pregnant. This inconvenient accident only became tolerable to her when she convinced herself that her first child would be a lusty, beautiful son whom she could show off at her daily bridge party. For nine months she did her utmost to ignore the fact that she was having a baby at all. But then came two days of labour . . . a sickening experience.

Relatives and friends had gathered, as was the custom in France, for a first look at the baby. Like my mother, they had anticipated an arrival worthy of such an esteemed and attractive couple.

Finally the nurse had opened the door and said:

'Come and see the baby.'

[1]

And there I was—premature, underweight, so weak I was unable to suckle, ugly, and the wrong sex.

But stubborn as I already was, I had decided to live. And this I did with all the passion and life force that a small baby can summon. To be born at all was just what they came to expect of Nicole Marie Charlotte Pierrette Jeanne—as the baby was called—and to be a girl instead of a boy was just like her, too. Impossible.

I was given the name Nicole because my parents liked it; Marie because of the Virgin Mary to whom I was dedicated; Charlotte because my godfather was called Charles; Pierrette because the father of my cousin Marie-Thérèse was called Pierre and had died gassed at the war, and Jeanne after my grandmother.

My mother was so distressed by my sex and appearance that my father brought her a doll dressed as a boy to soothe her. I remember that doll clearly. It haunted my childhood. It was pretty with pinkish suede skin that looked real. He had clear, blue eyes and blond curly hair. 'It,' for I never thought about it as anything else, wore brown taffeta pantaloons with a pale beige shirt and black patent leather shoes.

When I was twelve years old I threw the boy-doll into a blazing fire the day before Christmas. Let the psychiatrists make of that what they will.

My parents had the kind of romance that early film scripts were made of—dashing, imaginative, flamboyant. It was a product of the First World War.

My grandmother, Jeanne Durand, was an officer in the Red Cross, and in 1917 asked for volunteers to shred sheets because there was a shortage of bandages. Her daughter, Marguerite, who had offered her services along with other debutantes, was assigned to a hospital in the Place de l'Arc de Triomphe. The most distinguished and cherished patient in that hospital was the aviator-ace Paul Schneider.

He had been born at Carignan in Lorraine, an area that produces some notably stubborn people. He was only 17 when he piloted a plane for the first time, a friendly rival of Blériot, who first flew over the English Channel, and of Guynemer who became the greatest French ace of the First World War.

Paul Schneider was of medium height, blue eyed, generous and good humoured, and wildly attractive to women.

He was also the most pampered patient in the hospital, for the aces of the First World War were a race apart to the generation who had just witnessed the incredible birth of the flying machine.

With millions of foot soldiers mired in the mud of the battle-fields, the fighter pilots soared aloft in the clean blue skies, turning history back to the days of single combat between knights in armour. They fought each other in flimsy planes of wood and canvas. They dropped wreaths over the funerals of vanquished foes. They challenged each other to sensational duels. They were gallant and glorious—a new breed of hero—and children collected postcard photographs of them, as they had gathered souvenirs of athletic heroes in peacetime and today collect pop stars.

Schneider had been admitted to hospital after one of those spectacular ordeals that made those aces so much larger than life. With a shattered shoulder and only barely conscious, it seemed for certain that he would spin to his death. With his right hand he had raised up his useless left arm and gripped the thumb in his teeth.

Somehow he brought his plane down with the control stick between his knees, only to find that he was inside the German lines. With the last of his strength he pulled back on the controls, gained altitude, and bounced safely back to a landing field in French territory. Then he fainted. But a new hero had been born.

The doctors shook their heads at the terrible wound and said that they did not think that the shoulder and arm could be saved. But they were—at that time a remarkable piece of surgery. However, the operation could not restore the use of the arm, and he was finally turned over to a blind doctor who specialised in acupuncture —the Chinese method of using needles in the body to re-establish the nerve pathways. Over months this doctor worked with his sensitive fingers, re-educating the nerves and muscles. To my mind this was, in its way, just as notable an achievement as the war hero's adventure.

Paul Schneider was honoured with the Croix de Guerre with seven palms and the Légion d'Honneur with the rosette on gold.

Since he was handsome as well as brave, it was not long before my mother was spending more time chatting with this patient than she was tearing up sheets. And so they fell in love. True love —for it survived even the armistice.

My grandmother, a member of the haughty Crouzet des Roches family, was not convinced that in choosing a husband the heart should rule the head. She made it quite clear that such matters were better arranged by practical parents than by impetuous young people.

My mother decided to elope—the most important, independent decision of her life. The date was June 24, 1919. Later her parents relented and after the secret civilian ceremony gave the young couple a church wedding.

Three hundred and seventy days later I was born.

For my impudence in being conceived, and for compounding it by being born a girl, I was sent by my parents to live with my grandmother while mother went back to her full-time occupation of adoring my father. Fully recovered from the war years, he had begun to assemble business interests all over Europe. They led the respectable bourgeois life that was expected of them. This lasted until the birth of my brother Pierre, in 1925, when I was five years old. Since he was a cherubic *boy* with enormous blue eyes, round, pink, healthy cheeks, and beautiful brown curls—everything I was not—my father and mother decided to become active parents.

They called me home to their apartment on the Avenue Malakoff near the Bois de Boulogne from my grandmother's big apartment at 12 Boulevard Péreire and her rambling manor house at Chantilly-Creil, 50 kilometres from Paris. I brought back with me memories of some of the happiest years of my childhood and a way of life that was then passing in France as surely as the stately homes are now drifting into history in Britain.

My grandfather, Louis Durand, had a huge cast-iron foundry, Les Fonderies de Creil, which made all the machinery for stamping and printing the coins and notes of France. He was a good businessman but in his personal life there was a touch of unreality. Over the years he recognised me and my brother Pierre and my cousin Marie-Thérèse as relatives of one sort or another and as regular residents of his houses, but he never quite managed to grasp all our names or relationships.

I see him now—quiet, reserved, with a humorous mouth half hidden by a bushy grey moustache, thick eyebrows and pince-nez spectacles.

He called me 'Coco' simply because he called all the children in the house 'Coco'. It saved him the embarrassment of a more exact identification.

Some mornings we would be playing in the gardens when he came out to get into his limousine to ride to his office. With a grand sweep he would occasionally wave to the front seat and we would rush to pile in next to the chauffeur. But the best treat of all was to be taken to the factory and allowed to walk round with him. I have never forgotten the great buckets that poured molten metal into the moulds in cascades of sparks, like so many dazzling fireworks, and the ferocious heat.

Today I have an unquenchable passion for fireworks. For my fiftieth birthday my husband gave me the most fabulous fireworks display that I have ever seen—except the one put on by the French Government to mark the official visit to France of Queen Elizabeth in 1958.

That birthday present had everything—from 'Happy Birthday Nicole' in the sky to a bouquet of flowers and even an elephant walking in a meadow to remind me of the animals in our safari park. Friends who had joined us for the celebrations were puzzled that I preferred stars in the sky to actual jewellery. They did not have my childhood memories—and they do not really know me.

At home grandfather spoke little, except to business or family equals, simply because he realised he was living under a matriarchy. He was quite resigned to it.

My grandmother ran their considerable establishment as an absolute dictatorship, and not a detail escaped her of what went on. She must have had her own private intelligence system. The main house was three storeys tall with many rooms as well as garages and stables for the coaches and horses and, of course, the gardens. But grandmother knew everything—as I discovered many times when she chided me for what I thought were secret escapades.

Grandmother was small and, like many small people, sat and walked tall. She looked stern, but we children soon learnt that her austere façade concealed a soft inner being. At the first hint of illness or unhappiness she would bring us gifts and sit by our bedsides, telling us fairytales which she ruthlessly adapted to end as she thought they should.

She was a born hostess. She had a genius for arranging meals that took not only many hours to prepare but almost as long to eat. Every Thursday brought the unchanging ritual of market day. At mid-morning grandmother would appear in her special shopping clothes—a brown skirt, with a long jacket, a high-collared blouse boned to cover the neck, beige gloves and a small toque perched on her high-piled hair. She held herself so erect that when I first saw a photograph of the late Queen Mary of Great Britain in one of her famous toques I thought how much my grandmother looked like her.

When we left the motor at the market a picturesque procession would form up. My grandmother led the way. Directly behind her, in single file, came her red-cheeked Breton chambermaid, Corentine, holding a bag of money; then the cook, Marie; then the chauffeur, Robert. Next came our governess, and strung out behind her whatever children were in the house.

As we approached the market square my grandmother became as alert as a Red Indian scout. She enjoyed getting a bargain, but only when the goods were of the highest quality.

When she spotted something interesting on the butcher's slab she would turn her head meaningfully to the cook and motion her with her eyes to examine it. It could be anything—chicken, goose, duck or pheasant. The cook would take the bird and in complete silence look it over carefully, smell it, touch it, press it, shake it. Once satisfied that it was suitable for our cuisine, she would utter a short 'oui' and step back into line.

Grandmother would then turn to her chambermaid and take charge of the bag of money. All the time the money would be held tantalisingly close to the face of the butcher as she began her astute bargaining.

Grandmother always won. Shrewd tradesmen realised that it

was good business to give into her price because she was the best hostess in the district, and other shoppers frequently followed her lead.

With the purchase of any item completed, the chauffeur would step forward and open a capacious wicker basket for the cook to put in the poultry or game. Then we would all move on to the next stall.

We children also had our own tiny baskets, and we would be rewarded by carrying perhaps six bananas or some pears. Grandmother would never allow anything to be mixed. She would never dream of placing a chicken on top of vegetables or fruit. Every basket had its own designation and way of being handled.

My grandmother claimed to have a special nose for melon, and not even the cook was allowed to choose one. She would go to the counter herself, pick up the fruit, squeeze it and smell it, searching for the fragrant bouquet that belongs to a ripe Charentais melon. Often the ones she rejected would be so tortured and bruised that they could no longer be sold as top quality. But she was adamant. Maybe the stallholders were furious, but as she bought in large quantities, they suffered silently.

I always think of my grandmother when I pass an English fruit stall and see the warning sign on melons: 'Don't squeeze me till I'm yours.'

Grandmother would have torn it up!

We children loved the dramas . . . the unexpected market-place dramas that invariably occurred. Like the day my brother, dressed in a sailor's suit and eating a banana, stopped to watch a tinker mending a saucepan. The man had a monkey on a chain which, on seeing the banana, first hopped on to my brother's arm and then promptly bit him in the leg.

The monkey's eye-teeth were long, and sunk into the flesh. Dripping trails of blood, my brother had to be taken to the chemist. The story was on the front page of the papers. We children were fascinated.

I was always up to mischief, encouraging my cousin Marie-Thérèse to join me. One day, seeing all the ripe peaches hanging from the espalier trees, I challenged her to eat more than I.

Marie-Thérèse started—one, two, three. I went up to 47 and was violently sick for the rest of the week.

Corentine, the Breton maid, was responsible for one of the most bitter disappointments of my young life. I was so young and trusting that I still feel the hurt today. For many months I had watched Corentine sitting sewing. She would sit with her strong shoulders tensed, only the thick shining plait on top of her head visible as her coarse fingers created the most exquisite dolls' clothes. Everything from lace-edged underwear to ribbon-bedecked dresses. They were beautiful. I watched fascinated because in my heart I knew she was making them for my doll called Bluette. I was so happy as I pictured how Bluette would look in all those stunning clothes.

Christmas came and went. Bluette did not get her new clothes. They were for the daughter of the concierge.

I was too proud to cry.

At the age of ten I lost my appendix and my good friend, Maurice Griffe, the son of my grandmother's gardener, at the same time. My Latin teacher saw me trying to hide tears and was so surprised at this display of emotion—no one had ever seen me cry—that he personally took me home to my mother. A doctor was called and ordered me into hospital for an emergency operation. My mother and grandmother were in my hospital room, waiting for me to come out of the anaesthetic, when I began to mumble.

'Maurice . . . Maurice . . .' I called in the soft, dreamy voice of semi-consciousness, punctuating my words with vivid and profane expressions.

My family were quick to deduce who had been my teacher! Maurice was forbidden to talk to me after that.

There is a curious coincidence about my operation. My father was in Eastern Europe on business and was taken ill at almost the same time while flying in a plane. We received a telegram from Rumania telling us that he had undergone an appendectomy just as we were about to send him one saying that I had been operated on successfully for the same thing.

My grandmother was also a collector of porcelain. She had

several sets of great beauty which were kept in a special room. She washed them herself and dried them with pieces of old linen sheets to give them a special shine.

These services were taken out only for special occasions like Christmas, New Year or Easter.

When the first bomb fell on the house during the war it crashed straight through this room. Not one dish, not one Sèvres cup, not one Meissen plate for asparagus, was saved.

There and then, when I heard this, I decided that I would use my pretty things every single day, because one does not know what the future holds.

And this we have done at Woburn. Apart from the Sèvres dinner service and other special porcelain, I have always seen that our table was arranged beautifully.

Life is alarmingly short.

2 *'Not as stupid as she looks'*

I MOSTLY REMEMBER my grandmother at the stone mansion at Chantilly-Creil in the lush countryside outside Paris. You could set a clock by her morning review of the staff, and probably my passion for organising and efficiency stems from these early impressions.

Grandmother's official day began at 9 a.m., at which precise time she would come downstairs to inspect the row of servants. She had the all-seeing eye of a sergeant-major. There they stood at attention with grandmother calm and unsmiling. They loved this indomitable little woman because she was kind and good, but her orders were never questioned. That is except by Monsieur Griffe, the head gardener. Grandmother had an idea that the soil of Chantilly-Creil was as lush and fertile as in the tropics, and she was constantly demanding that Monsieur Griffe attempt some exotic cultivation.

Mémé, as we called my grandmother, would say, pointing to a photograph of a flower or shrub, 'And now this will go on the west side, next to the Katalpa.'

'It will not grow there,' the gardener would reply.

Grandmother's fine, youthful brown eyes would narrow—a storm signal no-one ignored. Except Monsieur Griffe.

'I know it will grow,' she would say in a low, menacing voice. 'Plant it all the same.'

'No,' he would insist. 'It would be a waste of time.'

But grandmother won—absolutely. The plant would be procured, planted and tended—and sometimes it would flourish.

Monsieur Griffe and grandmother were fiercely proud of the flowers, hedges, shrubs and trees that swirled around the house in a wide semi-circle. And although Monsieur Griffe could not and would not reproduce the vegetation of the Congo in this French garden, he managed to get more out of the soil than anyone else could have done—and grandmother knew it.

Her first orders of the day went to the cook, Marie. They constituted a loving recital of menus for lunch and dinner, with a bit of culinary advice thrown in. I find myself today doing just as my grandmother did when we have a houseful of family or guests. Her influence on me is indelible.

'A tiny pinch more tarragon in the sauce, Marie.'

'Do not fatigue the lettuce so much.'

'See that the butter is brown but not burnt.'

A nod of grandmother's grey head and Marie would fall out of line and return to the kitchen. Then it was the turn of the maids. Grandmother would instruct them where to put any arriving guests and which rooms to give special attention to. The maids would duck their heads and depart.

Next came the chauffeur, Robert, and his wife, Madeleine, who was an extra maid. Madeleine did all the mending. Grandmother had one unusual system—all linen was marked with a different-coloured ribbon to denote the year it was acquired. So in giving instructions for making up the rooms, she would say:

'Take two of the 1919' or 'We will use two of the 1923', as though linen had its own special vintage. There were no sheets before 1919 because grandmother had had them all torn up for wartime bandages and dressings.

With the working day thus organised satisfactorily, she would retire for a few minutes to a large green tapestry Louis XIII armchair. It was strategically placed so that without moving she could see the garden, the front porch and the service entrance and, if she left the door open, she could also keep the big iron gates and steps under observation.

Grandmother sat on several cushions, her small body stiffly rammed against the back of the chair. Around her throat she always wore a ribbon, white grosgrain edged with black early in the day, if she were in mourning for someone. In France you always seem to be in mourning for some distant relative. Her evening ribbons were exquisite and delicately set with marcasite or small black seed pearls, which were called 'widow pearls'.

She made an attractive picture in her chair, and knew it. On one side of the chair was a copper table-lamp—a tall lamp with a green shade. Carefully arranged on the large table were also all the things she needed to while away the morning, if she had nothing else to do. There were packs of cards, boxes of sweets, knitting or embroidery materials in a bag, books to read, writing paper, swatches of materials from fashion houses, a tray with a bottle of water and a little three-legged antique porcelain jar of biscuits—a crackling variety called Crêpes Bretonnes—the only kind she ate. If I was bent on some sort of mischief round the house, I could judge how safe I was by the sound of the crunching biscuits. On the tray was a mat of fine starched linen with two or three rows of scalloping round the edge. It took the femme de chambre three hours to iron it, with special ironing tongs, to my grandmother's taste.

My grandmother invariably wore a hat when she received friends at home. She always referred to someone she did not wish to have anything to do with as 'une femme en cheveux'—a woman without a hat. This was a terribly derogatory description.

In the provinces of France, even today it is not extraordinary to find your hostess wearing a hat. The late Coco Chanel was never seen in public without one.

Some mornings my grandmother would order the chauffeur to bring the motor-car round, and she would visit her cousin, my godmother, Jeanne Laroche. She was a wonderful old lady whose garden was a menagerie of dogs, cats, tortoises and birds.

On other days she would visit the cemetery to inspect the flowers on the extraordinary family tombs. Extraordinary because they were all made of cast-iron and most of them had been designed by their occupants. The tombs deserve an explanation. Since grandfather and his family for more than a century had been foundry owners, it was a matter of family pride to have the tombs cast in iron. I was too young to be deeply interested in a final

resting-place but for the elders in the family the design and en-
graving of their tombs was a matter of frequent luncheon conversation.

'I would like a square tomb—rather large, I think,' one relative
would say.

'Sketch it the way you want it,' grandfather would reply.

'Personally,' someone else would remark, 'I'd prefer mine to be
high and rococo.'

'As you wish,' said grandfather.

I remember one relative who went to the foundry to see his
tomb being cast. He paced it for size, and complained:

'Well, I'm much longer than that. Can't I have a bit more space
for my feet?'

Grandmother, who was fond of the Empire style, had her tomb
designed with fluted pillars linked with chains.

All the tombs were kept immaculate, and grandmother actually
had a special garden just for 'cemetery flowers'.

When my grandmother was 72 she had what her doctor and
family considered to be her final illness. She sank into a coma. All
the preparations were made for the funeral and even her tomb was
ready. The family took the mothballs out of their mourning
clothes. But grandmother woke up and decided to live another 15
years.

Her liver, however, was in a terrible state through overeating
all her life, and the doctor recommended that she should be kept
on a strict diet of nothing but boiled vegetables and fruit. Father
arranged to have her taken with a private nurse to her country
house. As the weekend approached, father said to mother 'We
should go and see Mémé', and the family left in the car with much
concern about the state in which we would find her.

Father did not telephone, so we arrived unexpectedly at tea
time. I shall never forget my parents' faces when they entered the
drawing-room and found my grandmother eating a large cream
praline cake which she was washing down with thick chocolate
topped by crême Chantilly. Mother was furious. We children were
laughing.

Grandfather's tomb was formidable—the size of a chapel. As a child I found the constant talk of death somewhat boring, and after one visit to the cemetery I remarked that I wanted to be buried in the 'fosse commune'—the potter's field. This earned me the lecture that not only was I expected to live in the style of the family but that I had to die in it as well.

My grandfather spoke in clipped sentences on the rare instances when he spoke at all. Consequently my grandmother developed the habit of holding conversations with herself. We children, in the blessed age when children were seen and not heard, dared not interrupt this monologue, so we developed a sign code for conveying our own thoughts during luncheon.

There would be grandmother chatting happily away to herself, with occasional grunts from grandfather, and we children signalling each other by placing one or two fingers to mouth, ears and eyes. It always ended the same way. As grandmother continued her soliloquy, grandfather would steal glances at her and secretly begin piling butter and cheese on tiny slivers of bread. Eventually grandmother would run out of one-way conversation and pounce on grandfather:

'You are breaking your diet again.'

Grandfather was so absent-minded that when he went by train to Paris from Chantilly-Creil, a one-hour journey, the chauffeur went with him to keep an eye on his briefcase.

After my grandfather's death my grandmother decided to taste the life she had been missing all the years of her dull, secluded, marriage. She began to spend money as she had never done before.

She took herself to such places as the Folies Bergère and the Bal Tabarin, and I could not help giggling when friends remarked:

'Guess who I saw at the Lido last night? Your grandmother . . .'

She lunched at Maxim's every day.

Her daughters began to worry, not only about her growing eccentricity but perhaps also about her growing extravagances.

Suddenly her world changed. She became an embarrassment to her daughters.

She had been a rich woman, with a house in Chantilly, a house in the south of France, a large apartment in Paris. She had a motor-car and a chauffeur and many servants. God knows why it happened, but her daughters suddenly removed her from all this and put her in an old people's home in the Pigalle district.

There was only one tree, no birds to sing, no green lawns, no sweeping rosebeds, no tangible beauty. None of the things that she had surrounded her life with during all those years—those years when she had given us all so much love and understanding.

In the old people's home she had a pokey, dark room with only a hard bed, a single chair and a small table in front of the window. All her life she had lived with beautiful pictures: now there was not even one in her room. A cupboard with a tiny stove served as her kitchen. She did not even have her own bathroom.

Her younger daughter never visited her, but she inherited the house, the money and her possessions. She died last year, leaving everything to my brother, and I only hope he will be kind enough to let me have some of the furniture that so reminds me of my early childhood.

For much of the time my grandmother was in the home, I was immature and fully occupied in bringing up my own family of young children. I could not begin to understand why she was treated as she was, nor could I interfere as no-one sought my advice. My only practical contribution was to send parcels to her from the various tradespeople.

She did not deserve her treatment. It was not right. She had been a good wife, married to a dull man, and she had run her household well. She was kind to her daughters, taking over their children during the long summer months so that they were free to travel or do what they wanted. She was loving and comforting to her grandchildren.

She was everything a woman should be.

She died in her mid-eighties. The immediate cause was that she had never been able to resist the pleasures of a good table. Loneliness may have been another.

During her last days doctors ordered that she should have only stewed fruit. But grandmother pined for fresh fruit . . . the delicious fresh fruit she had eaten all her life. When the maid arrived with stewed fruit, grandmother declared:

'I shall not have this. I want fresh fruit.'

The maid became petrified by her tone, and was frightened to move. My grandmother then became cross and motioned her to go, again demanding fresh fruit.

The maid returned with fresh fruit and found my grandmother dead . . . a smile on her lips.

My father's mother, Berthe Schneider, was even more extraordinary. I have a painting of her—pale skin, dressed all in white with a large white hat framing her enormous deep, dark eyes. She was a romantic and beautiful woman, and her tragedy was that she did not marry again after the early death of her husband. She came from a military family but when my father enlisted at 17 years of age, the shock turned her into a recluse. She had planned an entirely different career for him.

She conceived the idea that the country was riddled with German spies and tried to turn her apartment into a fortress. She bought large quantities of putty to seal the windows. She drew the curtains tight closed, and they were never opened again until after her death. She refused to use gas, electricity or central heating, and burned candles or oil lamps.

Grandmother Berthe, who spent all her time reading magazines and books, never threw one away. Year after year, as the papers and books filled one room, she moved to another. And then another. Finally when she died, she was found to be living in a small space not much more than a few yards square. She must have stood up most of the time because there was little room to lie down.

After her death, when my father went to catalogue the apartment and let fresh air sweep through it for the first time in nearly half a century, almost everything inside crumbled into dust.

I have my own special memories of grandmother Berthe. My father was so worried because I was skinny and small—although physically strong—that he sent me in her care to Berck in the cold and depressing north of France where there is a special beach for children suffering from tuberculosis and diseases of the bone. It was a wretched holiday. The only other children there were lying on cots or in irons and I had no one to play with. We were both cold and miserable.

My only happy memory of that desolate beach was that the

children were asked to enter a competition to make animals out of sand. I spent laborious hours trying to make a donkey, and for days I collected shells in my little bucket.

I had such a collection that I was able to adorn the entire donkey in various coloured shells, and I won the competition. The first prize was a wrist-watch, my very first.

My father always worried about my lack of size, even when years later, in 1935 and 1936, I trained for France in running, swimming and diving. Fortunately, he never bothered about my capacity for mischief, which was infinite and ingenious.

Our cook, Marie, at Chantilly-Creil was enormous and bad-tempered and had a coarse voice and a laugh that sounded like a whinny. We children decided that surely she must have a tail like a horse. To confirm this suspicion we caked our shoes with mud, rushed through the back door and began an argument while treading mud all over her kitchen. Marie came out with a broom to brush the floor, too angry at our antics to pay much attention to anything else. It was my job to look under her dress to see if there was a tail.

Everything went according to plan but just as I lifted Marie's dress, my grandmother arrived. Naturally I was punished.

My Aunt Cécile taught me manners, but she never succeeded in turning me into the little fashion-plate her own daughter Marie-Thérèse always seemed to be. She wore a pretty silk or broderie-anglaise dress with white socks and black patent shoes, and a large taffeta ribbon round her waist to match the one in her hair. My brother was often dressed in a velvet sailor-suit with a silk shirt. They were the pretty, neat, well-behaved children that parents like to show off, and whenever we had visitors they were put on show—I was always banished to the nursery.

Every time I wore a white dress, I ended up looking like Robinson Crusoe's Man Friday. Every time they tried to keep a ribbon in my unmanageable hair, somehow it became crooked or torn. They finally stopped trying to make a lady out of me and dressed me most of the time in a gingham pinafore like any village girl. Perhaps to this day I have remained exactly that—a peasant girl at heart.

Mischief was my game. I relished it like other children enjoyed chocolates. I remember the ghost scare vividly. In the billiards-room adjoining the drawing-room my grandmother had a harmonium with which she rehearsed the girls for the church choir. It was placed behind a silk Chinese screen when not in use. While some friends were gathering to await my grandparents, I slipped into the room, popped behind the screen and began pedalling furiously without playing the keys, so that an eerie hissing sound issued. I fled before anyone had time to investigate. When my grandmother heard the story of the ghostly noises, she uttered the one-word solution: 'Nicole!'

Then there was the incident of my grandfather's precious glass photographic plates. He was an amateur photographer and treasured his enormous camera and tripod, such as were used in those days. Whenever there was an unusual gathering of relations or friends, he insisted on committing it to posterity. He would spend hours getting everyone grouped properly. He would then disappear under a black cloth while Robert, the chauffeur, would shake a handkerchief to distract us from the lens so that the picture would seem more natural. Of course the burst of magnesium flare always gave us that startled, bulgy-eyed look.

These plates, trophies of his prowess, were kept in a fifteenth-century wooden cabinet which stood on four unsteady legs. From time to time grandfather brought out his precious plates to show his friends.

I was scuttling under the table one day in a game of hide-and-seek when the door of the cabinet slid open and the plates shattered on the floor. This was a major disaster. With the help of my cousin and brother I swept up all the broken glass and buried it in a corner of the garden. I pooled our allowance money and asked Robert if he could get me some glass cut exactly to size. The chauffeur never understood why we needed the glass—at least he pretended not to. And my grandfather claimed till his dying day that he was unable to work out how his photographic plates had become transparent glass.

My Aunt Louise and my Uncle George—Aunt Louise was my mother's sister—were a flamboyant couple. He was extremely intelligent and sure of himself and very handsome. My Aunt Louise, whom we called Tante Lou, was extremely elegant, tall, distinguished, good looking and had a mane of copper hair.

My aunt and uncle were very exotic and travelled round the world. When they returned they always brought back presents which evoked far-away countries—a dress from the Argentine, loukoum from Turkey, beads from India, amulets from Egypt. We children loved all this and were always longing for their strange and exciting presents.

When I was thirteen they came to see my grandmother. To our dismay they came empty-handed. As they were about to leave my uncle said:

'Children, I did not bring you any presents this time, but ... and into each of our hands he pressed a banknote.

I thrust mine angrily back at him.

'I am not your employee,' I said.

My uncle looked at me for a long moment.

'You know,' he said, 'that one is not as stupid as she looks.'

He spoke kindly, and raging though I was, I realised that in his voice was respect, not criticism. 'Not as stupid as she looks.' This was better for me than any present, and I decided then that, just to prove him right, I would make something more of my life than simply being a wife or mother. At least I have always tried to do more than the wives and mothers I saw in my own family—and I still try!

Today Chantilly-Creil seems so far away—another land, another age. The last time I visited the place was towards the end of the war. Five bombs had destroyed the house and churned my grandmother's cherished gardens into desolate craters.

3   *'My daughter a ballerina, never'*

MY MOTHER WAS never, throughout her life, maternal to me. She was in love with my father—it was as simple as that. When I was a baby her life was a triangle, herself in one corner, my father in another and bridge in the third. I failed to stretch her imagination or interest into a square. So I gave up. We were friendly, and that is the most that can be said.

When my brother was born five years later, it was different. She adored and worshipped him and indulged him all his life. He lived with her until he was almost forty. As my father was always travelling and had many business interests, I think she transferred to my brother all the love that she had for my father. I was the intruder.

My relationship with my mother never improved—there was nothing in common. When she was alive I wrote to her on her birthday and sent her presents at Christmas. She was not even interested in her grandchildren, and seldom asked to see them.

On Didier's third birthday I invited her to come to the children's party. After their noodle cake and their ersatz milk (it was wartime) they went to play, as all children do.

The few young mothers, my mother and I sat while the children played. I was knitting for my future baby Gilles. My mother noticed the white ball of wool, and asked:

'Did you get that wool with your coupons?'

'Yes, I did,' I replied.

'Very nice wool,' she said.

She looked at the little coat I was knitting, and asked for some

[20]

wool. I thought at last she had come to terms with being a grand-mother. I smiled at her and handed over the wool. Some time later we went with the children to visit her in Neuilly, and sud-denly she said:

'I must show you what I have knitted.'

I waited with expectation until she appeared carrying a pair of gloves that she had knitted for herself!

When I had lived at Woburn for some time I asked her to come and stay. After three days, as she had not yet made any comment, I said:

'Don't you think the place is beautiful?'

She answered in a detached manner:

'Ce n'est pas mal.'

The translation of that remark, I knew, was 'Why did you ever go and marry a foreigner?'

When she died unexpectedly in February 1971, of course I went to the funeral. I knew she loved flowers, so I asked specially for a beautiful wreath of sweet-scented white and mauve lilac.

Before the funeral we all sat huddled together in silence in a small room near the chapel. A nun came and asked if we wanted to see my mother before they closed the casket. I thought that I had not seen my mother for several months, but I was paralysed, and kept looking at my feet without answering.

Father went to the casket with my cousin Marie-Thérèse, but I still did not move. During the funeral ceremony I stood in the church, saying to myself: 'I should feel something. She is my mother.' I was glad when it ended.

Exactly a year later Daddy died in Paris, having lost most of his money in the aftermath of war. He had given his body to science, which in itself was remarkable as nothing like this had ever been done before in our family. My brother was against doing any-thing at all but I decided to have a memorial service in the small chapel of the building where my father had lived. We put a notice in the newspaper *Figaro*, thinking that some of his old friends who were all in their eighties might come. I had expected a handful, but over 400 people arrived. They were squashed, standing on the stairs, in the aisle. It was extraordinary.

They were all old and emotional. Five of them spoke so movingly that all the congregation was in tears, including me. I always knew Daddy was loved by everyone and this proved just how much.

My father was one of the pioneers who cut man's chains with the earth, but when it came to raising a daughter his moral outlook was bogged down somewhere in the age of the horse and carriage. He would censor the books I read even in my teens, and I would often find the pages pinned together. Since even his unseen presence was so strong, I never did dare unpin the forbidden text, with the result that there were vast areas about life of which I was totally naive. I approached my first marriage with absolutely no knowledge of what it involved—other than living with a man in the same house.

My grandmother had taken me to have ballet lessons since I was five. I was extremely good, and after several years the ballet teacher had approached my parents to let me join the Opéra ballet school.

My father was aghast at the suggestion. 'My daughter a ballerina, never.' And that was the end of my lessons and joy. To this day I regret it, and whenever I go to Covent Garden I always sit right at the front so that I can hear the sound of the dancers' feet on the floorboards, and the hard breathing, and watch the perspiration pouring.

Like many people who have had luxury at their fingertips, my father never paid much attention to it. He did not collect paintings, was uninterested in clothes and jewellery, and drove a functional car. Money as such meant little to him and he gave away fortunes.

On the other hand he was intensely devoted to good food and good wines and must have had one of the best cellars in Paris. He spent two months of every year in the vineyards, selecting his own wines. They were shipped to Paris to a specialist, who came to our cellar to bottle them.

As a child I found the ceremony as solemn as Mass. We children were not permitted to interrupt the day-long tasting, the taking of the temperature, the careful examination of the cork. It went on like a liturgy until my father emerged with a light in his eyes akin to love.

For several months of the year my father was more a signature on a postcard than a parent. It used to amuse me to note the postmarks—Château Neuf du Pape, Château Latour, Château Haut Brion and so on—all the great vineyards. Daddy was on his annual rounds.

I saw my father only at his request, and then I had to be brushed up and clean. Although I was barely at the 2 × 2 multiplication stage, he would demand that I solve problems in higher mathematics. Or he would remark:

'Her legs are not straight.'

With a mother who practically ignored me and a father who appeared out of nowhere at long intervals, it was no wonder that I grew up longing for affection and attention.

4   *'She will marry a peer'*

WHEN I WAS summoned back to the family from grandmother's house after the birth of my brother, I was sent to school—the Cours St. Honoré Eylau, near the Place Victor Hugo. I was taken by my English governess, a tall angular woman. She would hurry along, taking one step to three of mine, roughly pulling my arm to keep me in step. To this day my right arm is still a little longer than my left. I was so intimidated by her constant warnings to be a good girl, to behave well, not to speak, not to move, not to laugh, that on my first day at school I was too timid to open the books in front of me.

This was duly noticed by the supervisor, whom I found terrifying because she glared at us, holding a metal ruler and banging it on her desk to attract the attention of the offending pupil. Her thin hair was parted in the centre and pulled back so tightly that I feared her scalp would split open and her brains fall out.

On that first day she noticed that I was not looking at my books, although I did have a look inside one book at the pictures while the teacher and supervisor were speaking, but not knowing what to do, I put the book back on the pile in front of me.

'Have you opened your books yet?' the supervisor asked.

'No.' I answered shyly. This was my first lie.

She turned to my teacher and said loudly:

'Well, it looks as though we've got another idiot on our hands.'

She immediately sent me to the back of the classroom, where I sat bewildered and terrified.

I had told my first lie. Until then I had been completely truthful, but I had lied now out of fear and awkwardness in my anxiety to be what they expected of me. It served as a fantastic lesson to me because it was probably not only my first but almost my last lie. It was a very white lie, a little lie, but to me it was extremely important, and when people now find me direct, always truthful to the point of abruptness, I think it all stems from that day.

Until then I had been brought up in the country with my grandmother and gardeners and maids. It was a world I knew, understood and trusted. Going to school was the first experience I had of the outside, hostile world.

The school uniform was a black pleated apron with long sleeves, and a stiff white collar with a big blue satin bow beneath. I hated it because the black dye in the material had an unpleasant smell. After my marriage to Ian he came to bed one night in black pyjamas. My mind jumped right back to those awful school days.

'I am not going to sleep in the same bed with you until you change those pyjamas,' I said. 'They remind me too much of school.'

Fortunately for me, my governess agreed to take the daughter of one of our neighbours to school as well, and this girl became my first good friend apart from my cousin Marie-Thérèse. She was Marie-Victoire Alphand, the sister of Hervé, who has served with such distinction as the French ambassador to Washington.

I envied most Béatrice Guichard, the little girl who had the desk next to me. I was an ugly, skinny child, always badly dressed outside school. Béatrice had the face of a cherub, with long blond ringlets. Her dresses were the prettiest of all, with flounces and ribbons.

One day somebody came to fetch her from school in the middle of the day. Our teacher told us that her mother had died and we were all going to church to pray for her. Béatrice did not return for a week. I do not know who committed the sacrilege, but all her curls had been cut off and now she was like me, with straight hair and a pin, and she wore a black dress in mourning.

I hated the world for doing that to a pretty little girl.

My third friendship with a girl almost cost me my life. We lived on the third floor of an apartment house where I became friends with Madeleine Gaillard, a chestnut-haired girl, whose family lived on the same floor. I was fascinated by her curls, so thick and springy that when I pulled them out they coiled back into place with a snap. Madeleine admired my tomboy daredevilry, but her mother did not share the same appreciation for muddy shoes or an untidy human whirlwind in her home. She tactfully barred me from the apartment. But I was undaunted; I discovered that the narrow ledge outside my window led to Madeleine's apartment. Every day after homework I climbed out of the window, edged around the building and spent the rest of the day with her.

This went on until our coalman arrived with two gendarmes and the concierge. They had found me calmly moving along the ledge, which was only seven inches wide, some 40 feet above the pavement.

I remember their cries:

'Mon dieu . . . she will fall to her death . . . go back in at once, mademoiselle!'

When I was eight years old I inherited from my godfather Charles Schneider, the ownership of a technical college for students of electronic engineering, the Ecole Bréguet. I had to attend a gathering of the eminent technicians and businessmen who directed its destiny.

How does one dress a spindly little educator for such an occasion? My mother bought me a black dress with black shoes and stockings and a tartan tam-o'-shanter with black ribbons hanging down my back. I thought unhappily that I looked like a beetle.

In later years when I was a film producer I often recalled the scene. It must have been pure Hollywood—a little girl lost in a big red velvet chair, sitting solemnly among the adult members of the board of the college whose ages ranged from my father's to nearly 90. I also remember the kindly faces and the shiny, bald heads nodding deferentially.

After the session I was taken to the auditorium where I dutifully handed out the end-of-term scholastic prizes to grinning young men of 20 to 22 years of age. After this we all retired to the apartment of a huge man called Monsieur Faust, the Director, who I found most attractive. He had a metal leg and a strange, jerky walk. As a well-brought-up child I had always been told not to look at this sort of thing, but of course little girls' eyes are drawn to such strange sights. Altogether there was a kind of devilish look about him. He had a housekeeper who was well known for her skill at organising superb food. That day there was a complete luncheon for about 20 people. I was sitting with the housekeeper, Madame Octobre, at a small separate table while all the men, in their late fifties, enjoyed their fine meal. Among them was one who had recently returned from India. With great relish he related how he had become interested in the occult, and had studied how to foretell one's destiny. Of course they were all fascinated, but suddenly he turned and said:

'I am not going to predict for any of you. I am going to read the future of that little girl.'

I remember well that he took me on his knees and began staring at me with his fantastically clear, piercing blue eyes. For what seemed to me an eternity he said not a word. Then he began to tell me things I have never forgotten . . . that I would marry very young . . . that I would have several children. He then said, so that everyone could hear:

'She will travel a great deal and she will marry a peer of England.'

In French a peer of England is a 'pair d'Angleterre'. 'Pair' and 'père' (father) sound exactly the same in French; being a child and never having heard of a peer of the realm, I remember asking my father afterwards why I would have to marry him.

This fascinating man then took my hand into his and told me I had a very lucky hand that would make everything in my life come right; he said I had a one-in-a-million gift of bringing luck to whomever I first touched each day.

5   *'A naughty little girl'*

I APPROACHED MY teens with my parents apparently resigned to a daughter who would always be plain and undersized and in no way the adornment they had hoped I would become. They knew very little about me and seemed to care less.

My body was small, it was true, but it was very strong, and already I was gaining a considerable reputation as an athlete. We moved, in my twelfth year, to Neuilly, a residential district on the outskirts of Paris, and I was transferred to a new day-school near our home, the Cours Secondaire de Neuilly. This faced the Lycée Pasteur, a boys' school, and for the first time I became aware of boys.

At that innocent stage, boys to me were like a marvellous new kind of girl. They did not care if your hair was untidy or your dress was crumpled. And they ran and swam faster than ordinary girls too. So I began to think more about the students of the Lycée Pasteur than about the girls of my school.

Boys, I decided, were obviously more fun than girls. I have never had any reason since to change that opinion.

I was reasonably happy at my new school as I had found out for myself that I could lead people and could, therefore, command respect. This was most important for a child coming from such an insecure family background. During one of his infrequent visits, my father noticed for the first time that the opposite building was full of boys. I do not know what dangers he fancied that this exposed me to, but I was immediately taken away and entered in

a convent, Sainte Marie, only 100 yards from home. This breaking
of ties with my very first real friends was cruel enough, but partly
because my grandfather was seriously ill, my parents decided to
enter me as a boarder. I was now completely cut off from everything that I knew.

From the garden of my convent I could see the windows of our
apartment, more often than not through eyes that had to fight
back tears. Boarders were allowed to leave the convent from
Saturday at 4 p.m. till Monday morning, but I seldom went. My
parents were too busy. . .

It was a very cruel experience for a child to see the warm
lights of her home, or watch her parents and their friends laughing
on the terrace, and know that she was not wanted there. I am glad
now for their sakes that they could not see the lonely little face
staring out across that forbidden hundred yards. Nor did I have
many visitors. The convent was built on the principle of a
monastery, which means a square building with a lot of cloisters
surrounding a central courtyard. At some time in the school's
history this area had been walled in with glass and made into a
parlour for parents and friends to meet their children. It was a
dismal room with wicker armchairs, languid, green plants and a
centre table filled with goody-goody magazines and literature
about church affairs. But for the girls who went there, it was a
joyful experience. In the afternoon, if you were lucky, your name
was called to go down to the parlour, perhaps to see your mother,
your godmother or an aunt, but in any case somebody just for
you—a breath of the family, of home and the outside world that
was now denied you.

My name was seldom called. I would wait and listen, facing up
to the truth long before it was a reality that my name would not
be called that day. My grandmother who lived in the country
came once or twice a month. My Aunt Cécile had become a
widow and was now directrice of Jean Patou, the fashion house.
Aunt Louise lived in Brussels and, of course, could not come over.
My sweet godmother was living in the country and never travelled and my own mother was less interested in visiting me than
in playing bridge.

A visit not only meant news from home and family contact, but also a packet of biscuits, home made cakes or, perhaps some fruit. It was not for myself that I missed these treats, but I felt desolate when I was never able to have anything to share with the other girls in the dormitory. In the evenings after dinner we were sometimes invited to the room of one of the housemistresses, the very vivacious and well-learned Mademoiselle Desdouits, to exchange ideas. Sometimes there was music or we had a guest like the young priest, Abbé Potevin, whom I liked very much. Everyone would bring their fruit and biscuits from home. I felt deprived when I had nothing to offer, and bitterly ashamed.

We used to sit around Mademoiselle Desdouits in her long sitting room, and she would suggest a subject for discussion. The arguments raged, and this intelligent woman skilfully manipulated and invigorated our young minds with new ideas on literature, music, politics. She also taught us about Karl Marx because, wisely, she realised even then that his impact on the world through Russia would grow with the years. She is a marvellous woman and I still visit her. She was one of the few people to give me warmth and understanding in my youth.

School routine was strict. We were woken at 6 a.m. and had prayers and Communion at 7. 30. We had services every morning, with a particularly long Sung Mass on Wednesdays. I had such an out-of-tune voice that I was forbidden to sing. In such stringent surroundings I would have thought confession a mere technicality, but we were still expected to make it at least once a week. Abbé Potevin, who heard our confession, was an attractive man, and since none of us ever had anything lurid to report, I invented a whole series of wrongdoings to made his day more rewarding. When he questioned me about boys, I told him verbatim a story I had read in a book as though it had happened to me.

I told him I was a liar, which in itself is a lie as I am far too direct not to tell the truth. I confessed to petty pilfering, to being greedy, in fact anything to make him feel that he had had a worth-while morning saving an erring soul. Not content with myself, I helped and encouraged other girls to think up similar stories.

I genuinely enjoyed my weekly sessions with Abbé Potevin, whom I secretly admired because of his dashing looks. He, in turn, was genuinely disturbed and one day, without telling her what I had confessed, remarked to Mademoiselle Desdouits:

'You have a naughty little girl in your class.'

Mademoiselle Desdouits, who was dark and sensually beautiful and had taken early in life the triple vow of poverty, chastity and obedience, called me to her office and said:

'Well, Nicole, I can't believe that you can be that bad and that rotten. What have you been up to?'

I laughed aloud and confessed:

'Mademoiselle Desdouits, it is all made up. It is all nonsense.'

After that my confessions to Abbé Potevin became truthful— and very dull.

Was it the twinkle in Mademoiselle Desdouits's eye I saw, because I know that I never felt afraid? This marvellous woman had such a human way of handing out discipline. She cautioned me gently that next time I would be sent to the disciplinary committee, which would have been very serious. Instead I was to be demoted by having to sleep for a week or so in the little girls' dormitory.

My natural talent for mischief did not take long to flourish, even in the children's dormitory. It was the fashion in those days for girls to wear their hair in long curls. These were tied up with ribbons during the day, and looked to me like the organ pipes in the chapel. In order to get the curls into shape, they had to be put into curlers at night. These curlers were made from twelve sheets of loo paper rolled around a little string, since the brushes and pliable wire used today had not been invented. I was experimenting with the hair of the little girls when I realised to my delight that if I took only one sheet of paper, and wet the hair thoroughly, it would become so curly that it could not be combed. One evening I curled the hair of the entire dormitory that way, and in the morning the mistress nearly had a fit. All her children looked like sheep on their way to be shorn, and once more I was ordered to the office of Mademoiselle Desdouits for punishment.

I pretended to be frightened, because that was the way you

were supposed to look. I stared at my feet and twisted my fingers, but when I raised my eyes Mademoiselle Desdouits, who had certainly seen the same performance from hundreds of girls, was smiling.

'I can't keep you out of my division too long, Nicole,' she said. 'We miss you.'

I think these were the kindest words I had ever heard till then. I even felt a twinge of regret a few days later when I hooked all the beds in the dormitory together.

I liked being with the little girls, and discovered a gift for inventing fairytales, which I wrote down and read to them. After I was married I read the same stories to my own children. Some day I intend to have these stories published for all the little girls of the world to read.

I found out that I was extremely good at clowning . . . making funny faces, and my quick wit made the girls laugh. As I was good at games I was respected, and those two qualities made me popular and wanted, replacing, to some extent, the love I had missed from my family.

6   *Michel*

MY BEST FRIEND at the convent was Mado Domicent—later the wife of Roger Masson—who attended as a day student and slept at home. She was not as wild as I, but followed me everywhere. Our main occupation at that time was buying coffee éclairs and slices of andouille de Vire—a kind of sausage made from rolled tripe from Normandy—and tins of pineapple. We would go to her home or mine and consume that revolting mixture of food.

Mado and I were the same age, and we were given a joint seventeenth birthday party at the house of a friend, Bernard Rochet, who also had a birthday at about the same time. My friendship with Bernard had been as wholesome and blameless as only friendships can be among the very young and innocent; I regarded him more as a basketball player than as a young man.

Bernard, with another friend, Michel Bouteloup, conspired with Mado to see that I got my first kiss. At one point in the party Mado called me to another room. I thought she had some confidence in mind, but instead I found her with Bernard and Michel. A new game was suggested. I was to be blindfolded and then the rules would be explained. When the blindfold was on, Michel Bouteloup suddenly gripped me in his arms and pressed his lips to mine. Then Bernard grabbed me and kissed me, but more ardently.

'Which kind of kiss did you like best?' Bernard asked.

I fought wildly to break loose, snatched away the blindfold and slapped first Bernard across the face, and then Michel. I hated, hated, hated, what had happened. I rushed out of the house and did not speak to Mado for a month. In some way, I was not quite sure how, I felt I had been defiled and that Bernard had taken what rightfully belonged to my husband—my first kiss. In addition there was the fear that I would now have a baby. I really believed all this—amusing as it may seem today to my daughters Caterine and Anyes.

Bernard is still a friend of mine . . . a very good friend. We ski together every winter at Meribel les Allues, an enchanting village in Savoie in the French Alps. When he is not taking care of Bally shoes, he is very prominent in politics, a fervent de Gaullist. He was head of the Conseil Municipal of Paris, and politics is now his passion.

The other boys in our group were the twins Gérard and Jean de Royer, who became aides-de-camp to General de Lattre de Tassigny and served with great gallantry in the war. And the brothers, Antoine and Michel Bompard. Antoine, who became aide-de-camp to General Leclerc, was among the first French to re-enter Paris; he planted the flag on the top of Strasbourg Cathedral, and was decorated with the rosette of the Légion d'Honneur before he was thirty.

Michel Bompard I met when I was sixteen.

It was a grey November day with fine, cold rain blurring the outlines of Neuilly as in an impressionist painting. I was at home doing homework. Now that I was older, my parents had taken me out of the convent for the All Saints' Day holiday. It was a Monday, and the smell of washday had begun to seep into my room from the laundry. It was an ugly, musty smell, which I hated, so I decided to go for a walk. It was about 6 p.m., and I was walking as usual without an umbrella or a raincoat. Suddenly someone at my side said:

'Would you like to come under my umbrella?'

I turned to see who had spoken. A tall, slender young man, about the same age as I, smiled at me. The street was deserted, but he seemed decent and well behaved and I was not worried. But I did not reply.

'I live near the church of St. Pierre,' he said. 'Are you going that way?'

For no reason at all, I said: 'I am taking the bus.'

I was within a short distance of my house but I thought that if I said I was waiting for a bus he would go. At the next bus stop I paused, and he said he would wait with me under the shelter of his umbrella so I would not get drenched. Then a bus arrived. I nodded briefly to the young man and got aboard.

I did not know then that I had just met the man whom I was going to love for years to come. He was gentle, intelligent, brilliant, and had a charming elegance; but most of all he made me feel that I was wanted.

We did not meet again for almost six months, until May 1, 1937. I was leaving church with Mado when the same young man approached and held out a sprig of lilies-of-the-valley, the pleasant French custom of wishing your friends well on the first day of May. He was with Jean de Royer who offered his flowers to Mado. We were just introducing ourselves when my father, who was passing in his car, saw us talking to boys. In father's eyes this represented moral peril of the first order, and he immediately stopped his car and said to Mado and me: 'You should not be standing around here!'

He drove Mado to her house, after duly reporting to her parents the scene he had witnessed. She spent the day in her bedroom, and I spent the day in mine—copying Latin verses.

I wondered whether I would see the boy again. I did not know then how our lives would be woven together into a tapestry of young love, of renunciation, of war and of death. Looking back from this vantage point in time, I can see how fated we were to meet. There was the chance encounter in the rain, the chance meeting on the first of May. Then Mado asked me to accompany her to a girlfriend's apartment in Neuilly one weekend so that we could help each other with our homework. I was good at French and Latin—but very poor at mathematics, as was Mado.

But her girlfriend said:

'I know a boy who lives here who is wonderful at mathematics.'

We rang the bell. And Michel opened the door!

So we became friends, and my life took on another dimension. Through Michel I got to know others of his group, and we would all meet in the early evening at the Sabot Bleu, a newspaper stand on the Avenue de Roule in Neuilly, where we could chat while pretending to look at magazines.

Michel was my 'date', although we did not put it on so personal a basis. If we went to a party, Mado would naturally dance with Jean de Royer and I with Michel. I would go to the party, accompanied by my mother. He would arrive on his own. After it was over, he would go home on his own, I would go home with my father.

I found Michel terribly romantic, as I understood the term then. He was certainly attractive as a man. His grandfather had been ambassador to Russia, and he used to show us his grandfather's swords and his memoirs. He knew many things about Russia, and I was deeply impressed. Then there was the sympathetic fact that his father had died when he was a little boy and his mother had brought up a family of seven children. I grew to love his mother, Mamy Bompard, and I began to look forward to visiting their noisy, happy home, so warm and friendly. So different from my own.

Madame Bompard's husband, a member of the haute bourgeoisie—the 'establishment'—had been an administrator of the Mines de la Sarre. He was killed in a car crash when she was expecting her seventh child. She not only brought up her own children—six boys and a girl—but she took into her family the young son of a woman who was killed in the same accident, Gérard Sériaux. She was a second mother to him—and to me. I owe much of what I am to her.

Young as he was, Michel was a believer in Nietzsche and he instilled in me what he called 'the great impulse of life'—to care about other human beings. He was tall and slim. He had long legs and long arms and long, elegant hands. Some people might have thought him too slim. I thought he was beautiful. He was the best dressed and most elegant man I had ever known, and I later found all his qualities and looks in my present husband.

Michel was a good swimmer and sprinter and a first-class tennis player. I agreed with him on the importance of sport, but he never succeeded in convincing me that appearance itself was important.

I used to wear my cousin's old clothes. She was 14 months older than I, and taller, so her hand-me-downs were all I was given anyway. My mother took the view that since I never went anywhere with the family and was not glamorous enough to show off to their friends, there was no point in wasting money on unnecessary finery. I realised this and somewhat defiantly adopted the attitude that I did not care what I looked like. Michel cared very much. He wanted me to go to a good dressmaker, to patronise a good hairdresser, and to have manicures. Alas, I found being well dressed too complicated and boring.

Michel was a born organiser and he managed to get most people to do the things he wanted—as the Germans were to learn. But it was not until I heard he was dead that I bleached my hair, put polish on my nails—for the first time, and bought myself the most stylish clothes I could find in wartime Paris. It was my way of paying tribute to him, as others might send wreaths of flowers Michel was not there to see me, but I like to think that somehow he knew.

Our relationship before the war was that of friends. We hardly even held hands—and yet surely we were falling in love. But before we could realise it, my mother played a bridge game that set in train the events that were to make me the desolate bride of a man I did not love and never even came to know after marriage.

7 *'You will be married'*

AT ONE OF the endless bridge sessions at our apartment, my mother discovered that the daughter of one of the regular players, Madame Caradec, was getting married and that they would like me to be a bridesmaid.

My mother accepted for me because I was not yet 17 and the girl getting married was 26. We had nothing in common, I did not know her friends, and the wedding would interfere with my training in swimming and diving.

My mother, who sensed my indecision, said shrewdly:

'All the bridesmaids will have beautiful pink organdie dresses and big pink hats. Now wouldn't you like such lovely clothes?'

The novelty of having something new, not a cast-off from cousin Marie-Thérèse, was irresistible—just as mother had suspected it would be. Besides, I was getting tired of having to persuade Marie-Thérèse to ask her mother for perhaps a sweater, which she would immediately be given, and then after a decent interval quietly pass on to me. I regretted the decision when I saw the bridesmaids' dresses. They were monstrous masses of bright pink tulle, and the hats had clusters of artificial greenish-blue cornflowers at the back. I glanced in the looking-glass and decided that I resembled a dancer in a cheap circus. My straight, dank hair hung under the brim of the hat like the ears of a spaniel. The outfits were hideous enough in themselves but whoever thought them up had made matters worse by giving the

12 ushers buttonholes of natural blue cornflowers and we girls ugly artificial ones.

There we were, the 12 bridesmaids and the 12 ushers, and I seemed to be the only one who noticed or cared about the clash of natural and artificial. I took all the flowers out of the lapels of the ushers, snatched one artificial cornflower from the hats of each of the bridesmaids, and put those into the ushers' buttonholes instead. A great improvement! It drew the attention of a 31-year-old painter, Henri Milinaire, who had been pressed into service at the last moment as chief usher.

The original chief usher had to have a wisdom tooth pulled that morning. The combination of dental surgery and the wind from his convertible car twisted his swollen face into a grimace. When he telephoned the bad news to Madame Caradec the morning of the wedding, she called my mother who said:

'Another of my bridge partners has two sons and I am sure one of them has a morning coat.'

So my mother telephoned Madame Milinaire's home and Henri answered. He was trapped and he knew it and with as good a grace as he could muster he said:

'I will be delighted to come.'

From the moment I switched the flowers Henri, whose hobby was painting, began to follow me about, as though I had done something extraordinary. After the wedding, my father told me that, as usual, I would have to go to bed by 10 p.m., but Henri begged him to make an exception as all the ushers, bridesmaids and attendants wanted to go to Versailles for dinner and if I could not come it would leave one man without a partner. Grudgingly my father said I could go, provided I was back before midnight. I was quite impressed with Henri who made sure I was home on time—with my father grimly waiting up for me.

That weekend Henri telephoned and asked my father if he could take me to the races. Father naturally said no. The next day, just before I left for the convent, the postman brought me a package containing a silver cigarette lighter. I never quite understood what made Henri choose such a gift for a girl who was really still a child. I used no makeup, no nail polish. It should have been obvious I did not smoke and, in fact, I was 27 before I had my first cigarette. My father confiscated the lighter. But I was a heroine at school when I hurried there to tell the others how a grown man was courting me.

My father was furious about Henri's attentions and refused his permission to take me out again, but my mother, always ready to help a bridge partner, said he could. I did not really want to go. I was 17 but with the thoughts of a girl of 12. He was fourteen years older. It was like going out with an uncle as far as I was concerned.

By coincidence I met two of the men who played important parts in my life on June 18—my first husband Henri, and my husband the Duke of Bedford. French and British—at least I have been true to the Entente Cordiale.

On June 29 I reached the age of eighteen, and my father decided to take the family down to Carquairanne, a little harbour in the south of France, for a holiday.

Henri's sudden appearance in the middle of the holiday puzzled me. Obviously a great deal more had passed over the bridge table than cards, and our families seemed to expect that I would be his life companion.

I felt trapped, pursued and helpless.

As always at such times in my life I thought of Michel. He was also in the south of France at a small village which I understood to be Cavalière. I wrote begging him to hurry to Carquairanne and save me from this man.

Michel did not receive the letter. He was actually at a place called Cavalaire, nearly the same sounding name as Cavalière only a short distance from where we were. Thus abandoned, as I thought, I had no one to support me. It would never have occurred to me to disobey or question my parent's decision.

Even today there is a great difference between family life in France and England and America. In France the father is the head of the family and his word is law. In my own case it was unthinkable that I could have questioned my father's decision. Amazingly, I had at that time seen him no more than a few times in my life.

Even now in the French provinces it is an accepted thing that the parents choose their daughter's future husband. And actually it is not a bad thing. At least the girl is marrying into an ambiance and style of living similar to her own and she is, therefore, better equipped to cope.

One day at a family conference my mother said:

'Henri is a very nice man and he would be a very nice person for you to be married to.'

My father was more direct.

He ordered me to walk with him round the island where we had our summer house. There were five or six of these small islands, each with its own house for children or guests. They were linked with tiny bridges and set amid silver birches and rushes. Both my parents were keen fishermen but with my mother I always felt it was only an excuse to sit quietly and look into the lake.

As we walked my father stood beside me and suddenly I knew he was going to say something of profound importance.

'The son of Madame Milinaire wants to marry you. You will, therefore, be married on December 17th.'

Just that. A bald, flat statement that was to seal my future. My father was a kind person, a good person, but still one did not discuss anything with him. Never once did it occur to me that I could say that I did not want to marry Henri.

I looked into the lake and stood silently. Then I began walking with anguish oozing from inside and enveloping me like the fog around the rushes. A kind of panic seized me as if I was going to drown.

I felt chilled all over. All alone.

This was the summer and I had just four months in which to learn what I could about my future husband and his family. From a material point of view it was considered a good marriage. My father-in-law to be—a tall, thick-set, paunchy, blond man— owned a steelworks that made armour for ships, and a mattress factory, and he received a royalty on cigarette-lighter flints; he also owned valuable property, including the building where we lived after Caterine's birth in the Faubourg St. Honoré.

Although Henri was a mother's boy, he had the stubbornness

[41]

of a spoilt child and did not always follow his mother's advice. She thought I was too young for him—she was quite right—and opposed the marriage on that ground. But gradually she came to realise that she could not change his mind. She decided that, since I was young and immature and convent-bred, it would be easy to mould me into the image Henri wanted for a wife and she wanted for a daughter-in-law.

I disappointed them both.

Michel did not realise at first how serious were Henri's intentions. But even if he had, our own feelings at that time were simply those of friends, and there was really no way he could interfere with the relentless approach of the wedding. Besides, he was absorbed in his examinations, and all through October and November we did not meet.

In France there are two wedding ceremonies—the civil and the religious. No convent-bred girl could possibly consider herself really married until after the church service. Henri, as a man of the world, could not have been expected to understand this point of view.

The civil ceremony took place at the town hall, two days ahead of the religious ceremony. My father gave me my first fur coat, a sealskin. My mother let me choose a black hat. Black is worn only by married women in France, and I picked a hat that had an enormous bird with a beak and a tail of brilliant blue.

It must have been ghastly, but I was very proud of it perched on an enormous chignon of my own creation. After the wedding I went home to my parents' house to await the religious ceremony in the church two days later.

The day before the church wedding, which my father was organising on a lavish scale as I was his only daughter, Henri took me to Rambouillet to visit an uncle of his, Maître Jacques Wavrin, a famous notary. He was a First World War hero who had undergone more than eighty operations after being gassed in a German attack.

I only saw a funny man with hair that looked as if it had been pasted on and wearing a tall winged collar that supported his thin neck.

The purpose of this visit was to introduce me and to see a piece of furniture it was proposed to give us as a wedding present. It was an eighteenth-century 'bonheur du jour', a handsome specimen of its kind. Henri's uncle must have thought me very strange indeed, for I wept bitterly all the time I was in their house, and so they never did give us the cabinet—something I have always regretted.

There were good reasons for my tears. On the way Henri had stopped the car in the beautiful, thick Forest of Rambouillet. He must have been very worried about the innocent child he had married because he began to ask questions to prepare me for what marriage was all about. It was so patently plain that I knew nothing about sex.

He could see by my answers that I was not only desperately naïve to a point of stupidity but that I did not know the difference between a man and a woman. Although I had met boys, I did not know that we are built differently. How could I know? My mother had never told me, and in the convent we saw only ourselves.

My brother's bedroom and bathroom were not even in the same part of the flat as mine, so I had had no opportunity even of seeing him in the bath as a baby.

If you do not have the key you cannot open the door!

Poor Henri was getting more and more confused, so he probably decided that the best way to explain to that silent, shy girl was by way of demonstration.

I had only been kissed twice before by boys ... at Mado Masson's party. Henri's kisses were different ... so different I tried hard to keep my eyes, and lips, tightly shut.

I do not wish to condemn Henri for being impetuous before the religious ceremony, since we were legally married, but my agonising and, for me, premature introduction to my duties as a wife clouded our relationship thereafter, and it was only one of many incidents along the uphill road of our life together which eventually brought us to divorce. I tried in every way I could—and I think Henri tried in his own way as well—to save our relationship.

I had not looked forward to the church wedding up to that point, but now I was anxious for it.

In France weddings as elaborate as mine start in mid-morning and run on far into the night. I wore a beautiful white pleated dress, with long pleated sleeves designed to show off my narrow wrists, a bodice tied in a bow, Chanel-fashion, and a long train that swept far behind me. A circlet of orange blossoms, from which floated a long veil of lace, rested on my hair like a coronet.

The dress fitted tightly and there could be no question that my figure was catching up with my 17 years. I had grown swiftly in the last year or two and had reached my full height—five feet four inches. If I had thought of such things I would have been proud of my figure. All this white stretching protectively about me was supposed to emphasise the purity of the bride.

I used to think my orange-blossom crown was unique, but in one of the bedrooms at Woburn Abbey there is a portrait of Queen Victoria wearing one of the same design.

The first item on the wedding programme on the morning of December 17, 1938, was the group photograph, which in France is taken before the ceremony, as well as afterwards. The couturier arrived earlier in the day to help me dress, and the hairdresser came to set my hair in soft waves and curls. When they finished they sat me on a high stool and told me not to move. After ten minutes or so, my back began to ache, and I felt fidgety. I snatched off my head-dress and veil and hooked it over a wooden carving of the Virgin and Child. I took off the dress and threw it over the back of a chair.

I went back to bed and fell asleep.

My parents had arranged a buffet before the church service, and the guests were drinking champagne and munching little sand-wiches and petit-fours when it was discovered that I was not in the room. My mother and Madame Milinaire assumed I must be hiding—probably weeping and nervous, in the fashion of young brides. They could not find me any where. Pandemonium! A search party was organised and only as a last resort did they look into my bedroom.

Not only was I not awed by the importance of the occasion, but

I actually had the effrontery to be peacefully asleep. This was too much! They dragged me out of bed, practically threw my wedding clothes on me and hurried me out for the group photograph, which plainly shows the result of this hasty preparation.

The wedding guests had been asked to be at the Church of St. François de Salle at noon. I was instructed on my arrival, half an hour later, that I was to fix my eyes on the calves of the sacristan and keep them there until I reached the altar. The sacristan met us at the door, a resplendent figure in pink silk knee-breeches, white stockings and silver-buckled shoes, with a long coat of navy blue serge piped in gold. He wore a Napoleonic tricorne hat with fluffy ermine trimming, and a sash of gold. He carried a brass halberd with an enamel-decorated top which he pounded on the floor to mark each pace of our procession.

I took my father's arm and carefully examined the sacristan's calves all the way to the altar, where I was seated in a velvet high chair in a small pew of velvet and gold. I carried a bouquet and a Bible, specially bound in white doeskin with golden edges and a gilt design.

Henri arrived with his mother and sat in the pew next to me. I learned later that on the way to the church, Henri had felt in his pocket for the wedding-ring, and panicked. It was gone. A friend hurried back to his home and found the ring in the ashes of the fireplace, where it had fallen. I often wonder if this was an omen.

Henri and I were not supposed to look at each other in church, but to focus on the altar and pray. I was much too curious about what might be going on behind my back, so instead of staring at the altar I stole glances around me. The walls had been covered with flowers, and my army of bridesmaids looked like clusters of white chrysanthemums in the nave of the great church. For the service father had hired the soprano and chorus of the Opéra, and many musicians, including a violin virtuoso. It went on for what seemed like hours. The ceremony itself was performed by the Abbé Loti, a figure as controversial in the French Church as the Red Dean of Canterbury was in the British. He was noted for his bluntness and frank criticism, and my wedding was no exception. He climbed to the pulpit, looked out over the massed elegance of Paris society and snapped:

'Vanity . . . vanity. Is this what you bring to church?'

After the ceremony Henri and I and our witnesses went to the sacristy while the guests pushed and shoved their way forward to congratulate us. It looked like a football match played in Ascot clothes. We stood side by side to shake hands with those who had done us the honour of coming to our wedding—starting with close relatives and thinning out more than two hours later with people we hardly recognised. My white gloves were black from the handshakes. At one point I slipped my shoes off under my long dress. My sister-in-law, who had recently had an appendectomy, began to feel faint. She staggered back and sat heavily in a chair, right on top of my father-in-law's high silk hat. It was crushed so flat that he had to hold it out of sight when they took the after-wedding photograph.

By now—2.30 p.m.—everybody was hungry, and we adjourned to the Salon George V, a beautiful mansion opposite the Hotel George V. It was pulled down in 1961 to make room for an apartment house. At French weddings there is a big luncheon for the family, the bridesmaids and the bridesmaids' families. Ours was an elaborate affair of ten courses. The reception and dance for those guests not invited to the luncheon was set for 5.30 p.m.

The bride and bridegroom are expected to open the dance before departing for their honeymoon. We did so, but I had no wish to leave. To begin with, I was not looking forward to a repetition of the incident in the forest, even in its proper environment. And secondly I had written to Michel, pleading with him to make every effort to get to the reception. I did not know what Michel could do, once I was married, but I wanted to see him, even if it were only to say goodbye.

Michel arrived late because he had been taking examinations that day. We had a dance together, and suddenly terrified, I said:

'Please save me. I'm frightened.'

He looked down on me as we turned slowly around the floor.

'I can't do anything about it now,' he said, his eyes sad. 'Be brave and be good.'

He bent and kissed my cheek and left, walking swiftly with the easy grace I knew so well.

8   *'You really are too innocent'*

HENRI WAS NOW waiting for me at the door. I turned to look at the room filled with my laughing, dancing friends, and it seemed to me that my youth was over.

I was 18 and I had become a matron. I made a mental resolve to have six children and warn them all not to marry young, not to marry when so immature, so ignorant, so carefree, so full of joy as I had been.

I have kept so literally to that vow that only my eldest son has married, and neither of my daughters has.

That night we slept together like brother and sister. Henri was tired, and I was thankful.

The next morning I was awakened by the doorbell. I could not imagine who would call so early. The maid was out, so I put on my negligée and went to the door. Standing there, all in black, was the small, straight figure of my grandmother.

'I came to see how you are,' she said, her eyes searing my face. 'Are you all right?'

I think she expected me to fall into her arms and weep, as all brides probably did in those days. Instead I smiled my welcome, for I loved to see her, and said brightly:

'Of course. Why not?'

Grandmother left, shaking her well-coiffeured head, and muttering something about how times had changed.

The day after our marriage Henri announced we were going to Nice and Monte Carlo—by coach. Why he chose this method of travel I was never able to find out. It was not lack of money, because he had plenty. It was not lack of a car, because he had one too. There was no shortage of fast, comfortable trains. Perhaps he thought a coach more fun.

Along with 40 other passengers, we boarded the coach in the dark of early morning, fighting our way between dustmen and dustbins. Just before 6 a.m., an English couple came aboard, and discovered that their badly placed seats faced the rear; they claimed that they had been promised seats that faced the front. Henri had reserved seats, but since I was very sleepy and wanted only peace and quiet, I gave the woman my seat and took hers. As soon as the coach started I fell asleep, a black chiffon scarf over my face.

I remember awakening several times and being uncomfortable and unhappy on the long ride down. We ran into a snowstorm in the mountains, which meant we had to navigate very carefully on the winding Route Napoléon.

Everything would have been all right except that a car, driven by a young couple ahead of us, had stalled on a hairpin curve with a sheer drop below.

Our driver swung wide sharply to avoid a collision, but the road was so icy that the coach skidded out of control. With locked brakes we slithered over the brink of the cliff.

I was instantly awake—my whole body, every nerve.

'I don't want to die, I don't want to die,' I kept saying to myself.

There was a sickening drop before the coach struck the side of the cliff with a terrible jar and bounced over and over down 100 feet to a stream that ran between a cluster of rocks.

I was nearly suffocated in a tangle of bodies as we scattered about the falling bus. The final, shuddering impact on the rocks tossed me out through a window. The coach rolled over on top of me and I escaped being crushed to death only because I had fallen between the rocks which held the coach a foot from my body. There were cries and moans and hysterical confusion, and some of the men started fighting, from sheer fright. An Italian who had lost his spectacles tried to punch Henri and get out first.

The coach driver was killed. An old lady lay seriously injured with her ear nearly severed. I noticed her coral earring flapping down against her neck. The Englishwoman to whom I had given my seat had her eyes gouged out—which might have been my fate if we had not changed places. Finally they dug me free. I was black, blue and cut all over. My fur coat was in shreds. I had lost my shoes. Painfully I hobbled round, looking for my husband, whom I found, miraculously uninjured.

I found a first-aid box in the glove compartment of the coach. This may seem a small thing in itself but it was the first time in my life I had acted on my own in a serious situation.

I date myself as an individual from that accident.

I made a ball of snow, poured the iodine over it and rubbed down my body wherever I was cut and bleeding. Soon I was stained all over. For others I did what I could. We had to wait and wait. Two hours after the accident a car carrying some Dutch people stopped and took the most seriously injured to a hospital. Another coach was sent to pick us up.

The accident was reported in the newspapers, and the next day the telephone rang every few minutes. Our friends and relatives thought we were dead.

My own first-aid measures, and my youth, combined for a quick recovery from my injuries, and on Christmas night Henri took me to a ball at the Negresco.

The menu was printed on white satin, all the women were dressed in white, and all of them were given pretty white party hats. The setting was extremely beautiful, but mass parties did not appeal to me then, and do not now. I was delighted to return to Paris and the first home I could call my own.

Henri had leased an apartment at the top of Montmartre, near the Basilica of St. Pierre, with the most fabulous view of the city. From the balcony at night it shimmered below us like a permanent Christmas tree. I was enchanted.

I even accepted the Empire-style sitting-room with its ornate furniture. In my heart I hated it but I was taught at the convent that the rules for a good wife were: be obedient, always cheerful and attend to the welfare of your husband.

For a while I was happy in the new freedom of being able to go around and look in the shops without a chaperone. When I decided to get married I had bought my freedom. I know that by doing so I was at last going to build a life for myself as a person.

I was discovering myself.

Henri was out during the day, and in the evenings he would come home for dinner. Most of the time he buried himself in a newspaper and said very little. I was soon bored. We did not go out much, and hardly anyone came to visit us. Henri appeared to have only one close friend, Raymond Pommier, and he and his wife Madeleine were practically the only people we saw. Henri's favourite phrase, which he repeated again and again, was 'Pas d'amis, pas d'ennui'—no friends, no trouble.

Henri and Raymond had been companions of pleasure and most of their conversation was, understandably, on the level of 'Do you remember that blond?' or 'Do you remember the night we never slept?' I decided not to introduce Henri to my own friends who were of a younger generation. He would probably not have appreciated their talk of classical music and philosophical books. Henri considered the theatre 'arty', and preferred operettas to anything more serious.

We had little in common.

To a man of the world the process of moulding me more to his liking must have seemed an unnecessarily long and tedious affair —particularly if there were short cuts available. One day he brought me a suitcase and said:

'Look through that, keep what you want and throw the rest out.'

I opened the suitcase to find bundles of letters and photographs. But what letters! And what photographs! At first glance I thought the subjects might be acrobats. Henri, after all, had been an athlete of sorts. Then I dropped the pictures as though they were red hot. There were men and women in strange poses, revolting and bestial to my young mind.

Whatever effect Henri hoped to achieve, he got the frigid opposite. The whole affair repelled me. Doubtless he had wanted to broaden my horizons, in what he thought was my own interest, but he had misread my character.

I had barely recovered from the shock of this experience when Henri stopped the car one night while we were returning from dinner.

'You really are too innocent,' he said. 'So I am going to take you to a very interesting place.'

Paris was full of fascinating places I had not yet seen, so I was quite willing to be surprised. We drove to the Left Bank and pulled up before a building that I assumed was a nightclub. Henri led me into a large, somewhat garish room, and there the surprise turned into shock. Although I looked like a woman physically, I still was a very young girl. My husband's attempt to educate me in the ways of the world, therefore, shocked me more than he could have suspected. We were at The Sphinx, the most notorious brothel in Paris before the war. I knew nothing about such places. I sat stunned and disbelieving at our table, and then I desperately fastened my eyes on the bottle of champagne a waiter brought— but it was impossible not to notice what was going on.

There were girls leaning against the bar. Some wore tiny, pinkish-peach pleated aprons with a cerise border. These garments flapped like G-strings, revealing more than they concealed.

A row of assorted half-naked girls—blonds, redheads, brunettes, white girls, orientals, negroes—sat in the middle of the room on a red velvet banquette, chatting away and laughing. Occasionally a man would saunter by, appraise them like so many cattle, and disappear with one. Some of the girls walked about perhaps seizing a man's hand and plunging it down their aprons.

I felt physically sick. I was close to tears, trying to make sense of what my eyes could not comprehend. My husband poured me a drink, which I refused, feeling that it was dirty. Suddenly he summoned two girls who were sitting at a nearby table, and introduced me to them as his wife.

I got up to leave. I could not stand another second of that whole terrrible experience.

I suppose in retrospect, that there is nothing really very terrible about a husband showing his wife one of the notorious places of the city in which she lives, but only now do I realise the full impact of this episode on me. Henri did not realise that I was a child.

I had the innocence and mentality of a 12-year-old. Today, through television and the popular Press, children are exposed to vulgarity and sordidness which they accept as part of the pattern of living. But in my day I was catapulted into a world with which I was totally ill-equipped to deal.

I hated what I saw.

I DID NOT know anything about sex when I married. I did not even know about having a baby, simply because no-one had bothered to tell me and I was not interested enough to ask. When, therefore, I could not keep any food down I merely thought I had eaten something wrong, and sent for the doctor.

It never entered my head that I could be having a baby.

Suddenly everyone around me knew. As Henri could not sleep at night because I was constantly rushing to the bathroom, he suggested that we go to his family home at Meaux in the Seine-et-Marne district east of Paris.

I was glad that the child was coming as I felt it would give me something to occupy my mind. But I was worried at the feeling of emptiness—my inability to make any mental contact with my husband. We seemed like strangers to each other.

The Milinaire home was a grand house with a private park. This was the first occasion I had been with my mother-in-law for any length of time, and although I tried to be as dutiful to her as I was to Henri, we proved to be just as incompatible as I was to become with my husband.

One of the first things Madame Milinaire did was to examine the wardrobe in my bedroom and count my nightgowns. As I was not expecting to stay more than a fortnight, I had brought six with me, which I thought would be enough. In the middle of dinner Madame Milinaire remarked in her high-pitched voice:

'Only six nightdresses. How ridiculous. This is no trousseau. These flimsy things won't last.'

I suppose she wanted me to wear the solid nightgowns with a modest flap or trapdoor over the pelvis which I saw around the place. I thought my mother-in-law's examination of my wardrobe rather an invasion of privacy, but I did not protest.

Then later Madame Milinaire said:

'You take a bath every day. Are you feeling ill?'

She took a full bath only once a year and then went to bed for a day to recover. During the rest of the year the bath was covered by a board, on the top of which she stood plants, cologne and so on.

The French were very funny in those days. They washed in bits. They considered it unhealthy to bath all over. In the cities it has of course changed today but in some parts of the countryside old habits still prevail.

Some time afterwards I was watching a bicycle race from the windows. I was only 18 and not far from my own cycling days. The excitement of the contest outside helped to offset the bleakness of the house.

'One does not look through the windows,' Madame Milinaire said. 'Only low class people do that.'

We were always being served over-ripe pears for lunch. One day, with no malicious intent, but with a good deal of logic, I said:

'What about jumping one or two days and starting with fresh pears, and then we will always have fresh pears?'

My mother-in-law replied that I was unreasonable and extravagant.

I spent as much time as possible reading in my room, but even there I had no refuge. She would come barging in without knocking, with remarks like:

'You reading again? That's bad for your sight. Soon you will have to wear glasses.'

This became more understandable when she confided:

'I have never read a book in my life and I am proud of it.'

I sometimes wished she had never had a singing lesson in her life, either. One of the nightly chores was to sit and listen to her attack the few helpless songs in her repertoire.

My stay at Meaux stretched on into the long summer.

Now, suddenly, it seemed to me that something of great importance was happening which I had not fully understood. I began to recognise words and phrases that kept repeating in the headlines ... Maginot Line ... S.S. troops ... anti-Jewish atrocities ... conscription ... Chamberlain ... Anschluss ... Munich.

One night in mid-August I had one of the vivid dreams—always premonitions of tragedy—that I have found in my life always come true. I came downstairs deeply disturbed, still trying to shake off the visions of trains and soldiers, of battles and wounded men, of Hitler, and Benito Mussolini of Italy.

'We will have war in September,' I said.

This produced the loudest laugh I had heard at the breakfast table since my arrival. It was just after Munich and Prime Minister Neville Chamberlain's promise of 'peace in our time'. Everyone was feeling more secure than for many months. They told me I was a fool, unsettled by approaching motherhood, and that I had undoubtedly eaten something the night before which had given me indigestion. But my heart was heavy. I read the papers every day, convinced nothing could halt the holocaust.

War broke out on September 2, 1939. My father immediately hurried to Meaux to transfer me to a place of safety. Madame Milinaire suggested that we all go to a friend of hers in Normandy, which she remembered had been safe in the First World War.

'At least we will always eat there,' said my mother-in-law, putting first things first. She had a remarkable appetite for a woman so thin.

Then a complete comedy started. The whole house was in an uproar. My mother-in-law counted her silver, rolled each silver item in tissue paper, wrapped each bundle of silver in felt, and packed the bundles into crates. The crates were then piled in a room, the door of which was concealed by papering the wall and hanging a family portrait over it with a solid chest of drawers underneath.

The Milinaires forgot only one thing. There was a window out-

side, and anybody counting the windows would have known there
was a room behind the concealed door. But the Germans could
not have been too bright because when my parents-in-law returned to Meaux, they found the room inviolate and all their silver
and other valuables intact.

Henri, meanwhile, had been called up, and went first to St.
Cloud and then to Rheims.

The house in Normandy, at Longueville-sur-scie, near Dieppe,
was charming. But my mother-in-law, along with many others,
was quite wrong in judging the Second World War on the basis
of the 1914 war. For Dieppe was the scene of one of the first big
Allied raids.

We lived in Normandy with a wealthy farmer-businessman,
René Sins, and his family. His daughters became my friends. Martine was a fine pianist and Gilberte had a good voice, and many
nights we sang songs around the grand piano. In the lush countryside the war seemed to recede, and I felt young again, despite my
pregnancy. Being in contact with nature always recharges my
spirit.

In the village I bought a wicker cot and yards of cobweb-fine
voile embroidered with little blue circlets—an exact replica of the
design I had once purchased for my doll, Bluette. My health was
excellent. Gilberte and Martine took me to visit the poor of the
village, and there I saw mothers putting Calvados in the milk
bottles of the new-born.

'It's good for them,' one of them assured me. 'It kills the germs.'

The midwife, who had been chosen for me, Mademoiselle
Masson, did not place her trust in Calvados—but in gallons of
antiseptic. She had delivered about a thousand babies, and as soon
as she took up residence in the house, she began by spraying every
room with chlorine and lavender. She had bales of equipment
with her. Everyone who wanted to enter the room in which I lay
waiting for the birth had to wear a white blouse and white gloves.

As my time approached, my mother-in-law and our hostess,
Madame Sins, were progressing towards hysterics in their own
individual way. My mother-in-law kept claiming that she felt
cold. Our hostess argued that it was getting hotter.

They kept padding up and down the broad and elegant first-floor corridor, and every time either of them came to my room, she would poke her head in to see if I was all right. The first time my mother-in-law looked in, she complained about the cold and put on a scarf. When Madame Sins came by, she was in a sleeveless dress, and explained she had taken off her cardigan because of the heat. The next time my mother-in-law arrived she was wearing a fur coat. Madame Sins next appeared in a petticoat—even a dress was too warm for her. Then my mother-in-law returned. She was wearing a hat with another scarf over the hat. Madame Sins, meanwhile, had removed her stockings and shoes, and was barefoot. At the finish, Madame Sins was dressed only in a short chemise, knee-length with a lace bodice. My mother-in-law was muffled in a fur coat, two scarves, a hat and mittens, and she carried a muff.

'Il fait chaud . . . Il fait froid . . . Il fait chaud . . . Il fait froid . . .'

I laughed so much when I saw these two women—one dressed for the North Pole, and the other for the Riviera—that I give them credit for a nearly painless birth.

We had contacted a doctor in Dieppe, but when the birth became imminent, it became clear that he would not be able to make it. Our host had a thought that seemed practical at the time, if not a little bizarre. He said that he was not convinced a midwife could deliver a baby on her own, and as I was so young and thin, any kind of doctor was better than none. So he summoned the village veterinary surgeon, who arrived in the belief he was going to help deliver a calf.

Instead, the midwife hauled him into the kitchen where she had filled a soup tureen with an iodine solution. She made him roll up his sleeves to the elbow and scrubbed his hands and arms with a brush and soap. Then she plunged his arms elbow deep in the iodine for ten minutes. I had my eyes closed when he entered the room, and when I looked up for the first time, I saw his arms bright red to the elbow, and nearly fainted. The baby—a boy—arrived within minutes.

I named him Didier—in Latin, Deo Datus—given to God.

I looked at the little mite and wept with pride and with love. I was frightened to hold him, but they put him in my arms. How close we were at that moment, and how close Didier has always been to me.

How wonderful to feel in all my children this immediate bond of one-ness.

My father and Henri came to see me on December 17, 1939—the first anniversary of our marriage. Henri was extremely proud of his first son. Two months later he was again on leave and returned to take me back to Paris.

10   *Boiled beef in champagne*

DIDIER WAS NOW three months old and I had learnt with enjoyment how to take care of him myself. The daily contact with this wonderful child filled my heart with joy. Helping me to look after him was Paulette, a nanny as young as myself, who had come with me from Normandy.

It was March 1940, and spring was approaching. The windows were open in the apartment and Paulette and I were playing happily with the child, when the doorbell rang.

'There is a Monsieur Bompard at the door,' Paulette said.

Michel! In the excitement of my baby I had almost forgotten him.

I went to the sitting-room and found him there, tall and graceful as always, standing by the window. We did not say a word. We just looked at each other, then fell into each other's arms. We did not kiss, just clutched. That strange force called love flowed between us.

Suddenly I returned to reality and said:

'I must pack. We are going away for the weekend. Come with me into the bedroom where I am packing.'

I will always remember him standing there in front of the chimney. I remember because for part of the time he had his back half turned to me and spoke to me through the looking-glass over the fireplace.

We were both somewhat shy after the long separation. We talked trivialities.

'You've grown again,' I said.

Michel waved his hand over Paris.

'You have a pretty view.'

I followed him out onto the balcony.

'It's nice to see you,' I said.

We enquired about our friends and how the war was affecting them. He did not ask about my marriage. Personal happiness was not discussed so openly in those days. I showed him my son, and he left. We did not mention meeting again.

A few mornings later Michel telephoned and asked if I wanted to see the Flea Market. I had never been there, so I decided to go. He bought me a pair of brass candelabra.

His visits to my apartment became more frequent. He would bring me books, saying I ought not to sink into the mental rut of the ordinary French housewife, but that I should always keep my mind alive. After I read a book we would discuss it. Patiently, expertly, Michel brought a whole new world of knowledge into my life.

With my interest in learning revived, I enrolled at the Ecole de Louvre to complete the classical education that had been interrupted by my marriage. I went back to ballet classes, which uplifted me spiritually and mentally.

Every time we met I told Henri. I was determined to make a success of my marriage and I would have stopped seeing Michel if Henri had asked me. But my husband seemed happy that there was someone else to take me out, especially to concerts of classical music which he loathed and which put him to sleep. Thus Michel and I saw a good deal of each other, but it was still the old friendly relationship.

On May 31 my father telephoned to say that his factories had been hit by eighteen bombs, that three of his women had been killed and that he was moving his plant from Boulogne-sur-Seine to Blois. He wanted me to leave Paris with him. He told me to pack a few suitcases as rapidly as possible.

My father never acted as though I was married, and thought nothing of trying to organise my life.

I was in the midst of the most incredible disorder—piles of

nappies, the dismantled cot, crates of tinned milk, piles of clothes —when Michel suddenly appeared again.

He could see that I was preparing to leave. I laughed and said, 'I always seem to be packing when you come to see me. My father's coming at 1 o'clock, and I'm going with him to a friend's house in the Loire.'

Michel lit a cigarette and leaned against the fireplace, watching me. I chattered away for a few moments but he said nothing, and I fell silent and buried myself in the packing. Michel lit another cigarette. And another. Finally I raised my eyes.

He was looking at me in a way I had never noticed before. The boyish grin was gone, he seemed suddenly older. But still he did not speak, and I went on mechanically folding clothes for ten minutes, which dragged oppressively by like so many hours.

Then Paulette came in with her bright smile to say that she had prepared a tray of coffee and biscuits. The tension eased. I jumped up, feeling happier, and took Michel by the hand into the sitting-room.

Somehow the room looked even less inviting to me than usual that day, and I took two cushions from the sofa and carried them out into the glorious sunshine on the balcony. I sat on one cushion, Michel on the other, his long legs inside the living-room and the tray of coffee between us.

For perhaps half an hour my invitation to coffee had been the only words spoken. Even the things we normally talked about at our meetings seemed to fail us in the moment of parting. Michel's brown eyes were searching my face, and I knew he was thinking, as I was, that in war all separations may be final. I could see he was gathering himself to make a decision. He reached into his pocket for his fountain pen. Then he took one of my hands, which he always said were so beautiful, and on the unvarnished nails he wrote the letters of the words:

J-E T'-A-I-M-E.

I could not speak. Michel rose and left without looking at me. For the first time I understood what my heart had been trying to tell me about him for so long. I knew I loved him then and always would. Today Michel's memory is as fresh and bright as the day I last saw him.

My father found me unusually quiet, but put it down to worry about the war.

The house at Blois was beautiful, set in the middle of a flower garden with fountains. The food was fabulous and there was an ocean of champagne. The property belonged to one of the champagne proprietors and the entire cellar was stocked from floor to ceiling with fine vintages. We were urged to take our gas-masks everywhere, but I could not get mine to work properly —I learned that it was defective—so I threw it away and stuffed the case instead with gold coins and jewellery. I went about with the baby on one arm and the gas-mask case on the other. My father had a pretty red-headed friend named Marion, who was a lively companion for me when he returned to Paris.

It was hard to believe that France was at war except for the occasional spy scares. I had a French maid of Polish extraction, which made her immediately suspect, and an officer came to see me one day to denounce her for signalling to enemy planes. Signs such as 'The Enemy's Ears are Listening' were everywhere in evidence, and such accusations were not uncommon.

I went into the garden that night to consider what action I should take. And there in the night I laughed aloud with relief. For a breeze had sprung up which caused the blackout curtains of my maid's room to flap in such a way as to make the light in her room appear and disappear like the beam of a lighthouse. I ran upstairs and helped her secure the curtains.

The authorities, quite rightly, had meanwhile decided that ours was too large a house for only two women and a baby, so two officers were billeted on us. One spent most of the night writing long reports about possibly imaginary enemy agents, the other was a charming colonel who loved classical music and sat around with us at night while Marion played records on her gramophone.

On June 9, 1940, Monsieur and Madame Sins, in whose home Didier was born, arrived with their two daughters, a maid and their personal belongings. I put them up as best I could. Then came my paternal grandmother, still beautiful and mysterious and

forced from her strange seclusion in her apartment only by the
war. It was easy to see even then why she was regarded as one of
the great beauties of 'la Belle Epoque'—the golden era before the
First World War. And still they came. The next arrivals were my
mother-in-law with her husband and her two sisters and their
husbands.

The house was big enough for this family colony but there
were problems. For one thing, the electricity supply was erratic.
And for another, a bomb disrupted the water supply and there
followed an hilarious period during which we had to use champagne in place of water.

When the water-pipes went we found it impossible to arrange
repairs—the Germans were across the river Loire only five kilometres away and it was only a matter of time before they constructed a temporary bridge. So we used well water. But this soon
ran dry. Then one day somebody said:

'We've got a cellar full of champagne—why not use it?'

The first day we boiled beef in champagne for lunch. We also
washed the cabbages and leeks in it. It was the most wonderful
meal I have ever tasted.

Then we began to brush our teeth in champagne. I washed the
baby's nappies in champagne, and was disappointed because they
did not come out white. With Paulette's help, I filled a large laundry basin with champagne, put it on the cooker to heat and took
a bath in the best vintage. The bubbles tickled deliciously against
my skin. After this there was no restraining us. We did everything
to the popping of corks, and used champagne for all purposes—
washing windows, bathing, cooking and, of course, drinking.
Everybody in the house was joyful.

One of our house party was my husband's uncle, Maître Wavrin. The old warrior, bless him, was planning a private blitz
against the Germans. The gas attack in the First World War had
left him with silver plates in his system, and he had to be careful
of over-exertion. But it had done nothing to his courage. Secretly
he had hidden parts of two machine-guns among his socks and
shirts, in his gas-mask and even under his hat in the cupboard.

Uncle Jacques was a distinctive looking man who wore his

glasses down on the tip of his nose, affected high stiff collars and black cravats, and had a passion for beige cotton suits. But under the eccentric exterior there was the heart of a lion. We were at tea in the garden one afternoon—the whole motley crowd of us. Suddenly Uncle Jacques charged out of the house with a fully assembled machine-gun cradled in his arms. Perhaps he had brushed his teeth with too much champagne. He marched through us in the garden, brandishing the gun, and announcing:

'I am going to kill two or three of those bastards.'

Before we could stop him, he was on his way to the village, and we all chased behind him, begging him not to do anything rash. He was so excited that I was afraid he would fire at the first stranger he saw, but I could not keep up with him because I had the baby in my arms. My father-in-law was in close pursuit, pleading:

'Jacques, please control yourself.'

My mother-in-law was also in the procession, appealing in her high-pitched voice:

'Jacques! Jacques! Please come back to me.'

Even grandmother Berthe joined the chase, but in her old-fashioned long skirts she could not run very fast.

Didier was quite a weight, so I fell back in the race, but I kept shouting to try to catch his attention.

Fortunately our butcher came along, and after goggling at the sight of his best customers sprinting along the village street, he realised what was going on and helped us disarm Uncle Jacques. The dear, sweet man had tears in his eyes.

'I will strangle the Germans with my bare hands,' he promised, holding them up.

With the Germans closing in, my house guests began to disappear. The Normandy friends moved on, and my mother-in-law and her group departed. Then my father appeared with trucks from his factory carrying his irreplaceable precision machinery and some 15 or 20 of his workers. And also—very precious—a huge full drum of petrol. He said he had rented a twelfth-century château with a moat and drawbridge at Voutezac, near Souceyrac, in the Massif Central, where we were all to rendezvous as soon as possible. He filled everybody's car with petrol, indicated a safe route for us all to drive, and set off. I was left in charge of a 100-litre drum of petrol.

My father tried of course to get me to go with him, but I saw no reason to rush because in any case I did not share the general anxiety about what the Germans might do when they reached us. I thought he was unduly worried because of his experiences in the First World War, and I was not going to let myself be carried away.

I felt no fear, and said I saw no reason to leave until after I had given Didier his morning feed. My father left and I went to sleep. About 5 a.m. I was awakened by a fantastic noise. I put on a robe and looked through the window. Two French soldiers were kicking with their boots at the iron door of the courtyard.

'What's the matter?' I called out.

One soldier said:

'We've come to requisition the petrol.'

'What petrol!' I asked, playing for time to think.

My brother Pierre, who was 15, had now woken, and I told him to go downstairs and talk to the men. I put on a coat over my lace dressing-gown and joined him. The soldiers insisted that we had petrol, and although I admitted that my father had brought some the night before, I said that he had departed, taking it with him. One of the soldiers began to look around for a likely hiding-place. Suddenly I had a thought.

'Have you a search warrant or requisition papers?' I asked.

When they said 'No', I told them simply, 'Go and get one.'

Instead of leaving one to guard the house, both left for the little town of Pontlevoy, a round-trip walk of at least 20 minutes. As soon as they left, my brother and I took the sheets from the beds and used them to bundle everything we could gather together—clothes and clocks, shoes and hats, everything we could lay our hands on. I discovered later that in my haste I had packed 12 belts and only one dress. We threw the stuff into the car and drove off just as the soldiers came running up with their search warrant.

The car was so overloaded that the silencer was ripped off by one of the gate fasteners, and we roared through the village, waking up the frightened residents who must have thought the Germans had finally arrived. I was so afraid the soldiers would follow that I drove without stopping until the petrol-tank ran dry.

This faced us with the problem of transferring the petrol from the heavy drum to the tank. Pierre and I could not lift the drum, but among the outlandish junk we had assembled I found some rubber deck-tennis quoits. I bit one of these in half, turning it into a length of rubber pipe. We tilted the barrel and the petrol sloshed through the quoit and into the tank. A lot of it spilled on the road as well. My shoes were never cleaner, or more inflammable, but at least we had our tank filled again.

Just then a passing car stopped, and the driver came back to us. He seemed quite a pleasant man and I thought how kind it was of him to help us. I thought wrong. Without a word, he punched my brother in the face, knocking him down. Then he knocked me down as well, stole our barrel of petrol, and made off with it.

At that moment in French history, petrol was worth more than gold or diamonds.

We stopped that night in a small village near the top of a mountain. We were so tired, and fell asleep immediately. I was woken by what felt like a wet mop dragging across my face. We had parked near a fountain, blocking the traditional path of the village cows to their watering-place, and one of them was licking my face. Weary as we were, Pierre and I laughed at the sight of the mooing herd gathered thirstily around us, and we moved the car out of the way.

I do not have pleasant memories of the peasants of the Massif Central. I had weaned Didier, and I was short of tinned milk. The peasants charged me 15 francs (about 37 pence) for a little boiled milk, and even 10 francs (25 pence) for boiling water. The baby was ill and he became worse when I gave him some goat's milk. My only hope was to get to my father, and I drove without resting until I reached Soucirac.

At the village post-office I asked the way to the château. A girl

[67]

clerk said she had never heard of a château there and referred me to an inspector. He thought for a while, then exclaimed:

'I have it. You must mean Souceyrac.' My mind had played me a trick. I had gone automatically to that lovely city described by Anatole France in 'Monsieur le Sous-Préfet aux Champs' (which might roughly be translated as "The Assistant Sheriff Goes Back to Nature"), and I was 200 kilometres from my father, worn with fatigue, desperate, and with a sick baby on my hands. With some difficulty we managed to telephone my father, who told me to rest and said he would come to fetch me.

On our arrival at the château, a magnificent structure of soaring turrets like something out of a storybook, I figured in a heart-rending drama. I was getting out of the car when a man rushed out of the house, threw his arms around me and sobbed:

'Oh Cécile, my little Cécile, at last you're well again.'

My father, who was behind me carrying Didier, spoke con-solingly to the man, who turned and went back into the château, still crying. My father explained that the man and his wife and two daughters also lived in the house, that the eldest daughter, Cécile, was dying of meningitis because the doctor could not get the proper medication, that the girl had been delirious for about a week, and that her screams of 'Don't let me die!' had unbalanced the father. I found the incident so tragic that I could not eat my lunch and I went instead into the garden to pick flowers for my bedroom. Again the man ran out and put his arms around me:

'Cécile, Cécile, my little Cécile,' he wept. 'The sun is too hot for you. Don't forget how ill you have been.'

He was trying to drag me into the house when my father hurried over and separated us. After that my father decided it would be impossible for me to stay at the château and took me to look at rooms at a place which called itself a hotel. It was July and the hot summer air imprisoned in the valley was steamy and suffocating. We found that the 'hotel' consisted of several rooms over a shop. The passageway was dark, the floor rotten, and when I tried to balance myself by putting my hand on the wall, I quickly withdrew it because of the unseen spidery insects crawling about.

On the first floor, a large woman waddled towards us, folded her fat face into a grimace, and opened a door.

'This is my best room,' she said.

The window was closed and the air so thick with disgusting smells that I tried to open it.

'Don't strain yourself,' said the woman. 'We nailed the window shut ten years ago because it opened by itself in the wind.'

My father was on the other side of the room, his glasses on his nose, examining the wallpaper. He turned to the woman and said in his courteous way:

'Thank you very much. This is a very lovely room. We will let you know.'

Outside he shuddered.

'You can't stay there—the walls are crawling with bedbugs.'

My father had brought some tents along for his workers, and we agreed this would be preferable to the hotel. I had never camped out before, and certainly not with a five-month-old baby to take care of as well, I spent most nights awake with my head outside the tent, watching the stars.

A few days later Cécile died. We collected cornflowers, poppies and daisies for a wreath. A stranger witnessing the funeral procession might have thought we were on our way to a picnic—except that everybody was crying. We had come away, most of us, with only our summer wardrobes, and there we were, the mourners, in bright red and blue and green flowered dresses, moving across the meadows in a blaze of colour. The only dress I had was pale blue, so I found a small piece of black ribbon which I pinned to my arm.

Sadly my twentieth birthday passed without anyone remembering it, for there was a far greater event on that day—the fall of France.

Germany had cut my country in two, the Wehrmacht legions were in our sacred Paris, and my father decided we must return to find out what was happening to all his workers and his factories.

We had heard terrifying stories of German atrocities, and we did not know what to expect at the demarcation line between Free and Occupied France.

When our car halted at the border of Occupied France, a large and aggressive German officer, carrying a riding crop, led his jackbooted men towards us. He slashed the air to emphasise his orders, and after scowling at us, traced a 'P' with his riding crop on our car, and a soldier painted the letter where he had indicated. Then he tapped my father, none to gently, on the shoulder, and we were allowed to move on.

We had been ready for the worst, for the trip had been a nightmare, with enemy planes—Italian, I think—strafing the roads. My father had ordered us out of the car from time to time to hide in cornfields or ditches as the machine-guns tore up the highways.

A man and woman lay dead, machine-gunned, in one of the motor-cars in front of us. In the back seat their small child was hugging her doll—and staring blankly ahead. Some people from her own area took charge of her.

We passed one of the gaudy 'Paris By Night' sightseeing buses, covered with posters of naked girls and advertisements for strip-tease clubs.

It was filled with nuns.

I saw a man pushing his wife along in a wheelbarrow. She was screaming hysterically. He carefully rested the barrow, walked around to face her, and knocked her out with a punch on the jaw. Then he resumed pushing the barrow, with his wife lying unconscious—and silent—her arms, legs and head dangling like those of a rag doll.

I I   *Caterine*

MY FATHER LEFT me at my apartment and I tried to pick up the threads of life again with Henri. He was supposed to be working for my father, but hardly ever went inside the factory. Everything was difficult. Eighty thousand people were dead, they said, and 700,000 were prisoners. You could not find a potato in the whole of Paris in August 1940. Bread was grey and so was the taste. Butter and meat were scarce, oil, soap and sugar almost non-existent.

In November there were German decrees against selling fresh bread, and butchers had to observe three or four meatless days a week.

I turned to Henri for companionship, trying to convey to him that I wanted to be more to him than a physical convenience.

He put down his paper and said:

'All I want from you is to take care of my welfare. To see that we have food of good quality, keep the baby quiet, and mend and sew like other wives. Nothing else.'

I thought that I had not made myself clear, so I told him of my loneliness and my need for warmth and companionship.

I do not know what inner turmoil this awakened in Henri but he began to cry. I had never seen a man cry before and I blamed myself for being stupid. This ended the discussion but I made a new resolve to forget my own needs and to try to fashion myself closer to the kind of wife my husband seemed to want.

But I still had to occupy my time some way. I took the baby

out in his pram for long walks, and sewed and embroidered all
his little clothes. He was growing into a lovely boy with blond
hair and blue eyes, and he scampered about so swiftly on all fours
that I bought a blue and white playpen.

I went to the Ecole de Louvre to study the arts. I renewed my
reading of philosophy, and registered myself for courses with a
correspondence school. They can never have had so diligent a
pupil. All day long between the nappies and the baby's bottle, I
studied.

I felt compelled to stretch myself mentally to obliterate the
boredom and disappointment of my marriage. I wanted to sat-
urate myself with knowledge and beauty.

I tried experimenting with our meagre food rations and let my
imagination take flight. One was very lucky to get butter, eggs or
meat. For Didier's first birthday I made a little cake, with one
candle, out of dried apricot cooked with shredded carrots and a
light caramel mixture. It tasted quite good, although Didier preferred to eat the candle rather than the cake.

I also experimented with another cake ... pieces of noodles
cooked with jam made from dried fruits until they were soft.
When it was cold I would cover it with a custard sauce made from
dried milk and powdered eggs, flavoured with scented vanilla.

Among the other 'Cordon Bleu' dishes in my wartime cuisine
was cow's udder, boiled or baked and sliced very thinly. It tasted
like foie gras, but the main vegetable was kale, which normally is
given to cows. If I smell it now, all the awful memories come
flooding back.

When I was not stretching my kitchen ingenuity to the utmost,
I studied the teachings of Schopenhauer, Freud and Jung, and
made Jung my master. I went back into sports training. There was
still a club open where I did a lot of running, and soon I was in
very good physical condition.

I also returned to classical ballet again, after a lapse of six years,
at the Salle Pleyel.

I would work at the bar, stretching my body and limbs until I
was exhausted and too tired to remember my problems. I liked
the discipline, the pain, truth and beauty of the ballet class.

My instructress was Vala Bovie, a Russian ballerina, who beat time for us with a gold-headed cane. Both Freud and Jung would have had an explanation for this sudden fury of mental and physical activity. In my own way I was trying to make up for lack of love and affection at home. My timid attempts at tenderness were met by my husband with:

'You must be tired—why don't you see a doctor?' Or 'The spring is not good for you.'

My Aunt Cécile was seriously ill at this time, and when I went to see her, she said she could tell I was lonely. She told me to read Péguy's 'La Petite Porte de l'Esperance' for solace.

I wept away my twenty-first birthday, alone on my balcony, blurring the lights of Paris with my tears. I took out one of my school books and forced myself to study for two hours—that was one way to forgetfulness.

Part of that unhappy summer I spent at my mother-in-law's house at Meaux, swimming and boating, and in October I returned again to Paris.

I was walking up the Champs Elysées one day, coming from the Ecole de Louvre, when someone at a sidewalk table at Fouquet's caught my eye. I stopped—faint with the shock of recognition. It was Michel. Even as he rose I was brushing back my hair, tucking my blouse into my pleated tartan skirt, trying to smile. But I was trembling. Michel put his arms around me, and asked gently why I had not replied to his many letters.

'I have a husband and a child,' I said.

He insisted I have a coffee, and we sat there almost in silence. It is strange that we who had so much to say to each other should now have been lost for words. A German soldier passed, and Michel told me he and some of his friends had determined to make life difficult for the Germans. He did not go into details, and I did not question him. He was working at the time in the Boulevard Haussman. He had a boring job but it had the advantage of a canteen, which helped solve his food problems—and eventually mine. Through Michel I started to get some of the butter, eggs and jam and other items that Didier needed.

Now that we had met again, Michel and I saw each other from

time to time. We went to the theatre or took long walks or simply sat somewhere and chatted. It was not the old relaxed relationship, for always in my mind was my duty to try to understand Henri, although that was proving more and more difficult. for me.

Michel used food as an excuse to see me. He would arrive with a briefcase from which he would extract a Camembert cheese. Or he would telephone and say:

'May I bring you some jam?'

I frequently visited my Aunt Cécile, whose condition had deteriorated. On October 15, 1941, I went to see her, taking some raspberries with me. My cousin Marie-Thérèse, her daughter, was there.

We sat her up in bed to eat the fruit, but she could not. With infinite sadness she said:

'This is the last food I shall ever see.'

And with that she died in our arms.

We tried to call the doctor, but there was no-one there. We tried the nursing sisters, but they were all gone. I suddenly said to Marie-Thérèse:

'You know, if you leave dead people without dressing them, they go absolutely stiff. We must do it immediately.'

So we two poor naïve girls removed her night gown, washed her body, and dressed her in her best pink crepe-de-chine negligée. She kept slipping away from us, as she was six feet tall, and I was frightened she would fall off the bed. We closed her eyes, combed her hair, and I remember putting rouge on her cheeks. The whole episode was horribly gruesome. But that was the way things were during the war. Poor Marie-Thérèse was in an agony of despair.

Michel's campaign against the Germans, although I still knew very little about it, had inspired me to do what I could in my own small way. On November 21, the anniversary of the Allied victory in the First World War, I gathered a group of my girlfriends and we all dressed in the French national colours—red, white and blue—and sauntered along the Champs Elysées. One of the girls, Jacqueline Marceron, wore a blouse decorated with Scotsmen playing bagpipes, and walked ahead of the group while we whistled 'It's a long Way to Tipperary'.

We inspired many of the people who saw us to display some version of the tricolor. The Germans were furious, but we were not causing any obstruction and we were moving, so were not breaking any rules. Under their rigid system, they could do nothing.

But our behaviour was dangerous provocation, and we knew it.

One morning in December 1941—delighted by the news that the United States had entered the war after Pearl Harbor—I was playing with the baby while decorating a Christmas tree. Didier was two years old, charming and pretty, but very thin because of the lack of some of the essential baby foods. He himself wanted to put the star on the top of the tree, and I lifted him up, when suddenly I felt a pain and a feeling of nausea, and knew that I was pregnant again.

When I next saw Michel I told him about it, and said that we should stop seeing each other completely. We were crossing the bridge between Notre Dame and the beautiful Ile St. Louis, in the middle of Paris. I leaned against the embankment along the Seine, facing him. He was terribly upset by the news. He wanted to know why we could not still keep seeing each other.

'We are doing nothing wrong,' he said. 'We are not hurting anybody.'

'It's not that,' I said. 'You are so much in my thoughts, I cannot give myself as fully and completely to my marriage as I should.'

I said we ought to part for good. I could see in Michel's brown eyes that he was hurt, but he could see that I was determined. We walked and talked a little longer. He still tried to get me to change my mind. In front of Notre Dame I turned to him and finally said:

'Michel, we must not see each other again. Goodbye.'

We were not to meet again for many months.

I went to my mother-in-law's house at Meaux to prepare for the birth of my second child, and stayed there until September. My life there was uneventful except for a frightening incident with a new maid. She asked me for a night off, and when I refused because she had been out all the previous day, there was a scene during which she ran to the cradle, removed Didier and held him out of the window.

'If you don't say "yes", I'll let him drop,' she threatened.

I believed she meant it too. Of course, I told her she could have the night off, and she handed me the baby. And, of course, I dismissed her.

On my return to Paris, my maternal grandmother managed to assemble enough food for a dinner party in my honour. Henri took me home at midnight, but at 2 a.m. I awoke with unmistakable pains. I had a suitcase all ready, and I telephoned the hospital to send an ambulance. Whether you got one or not in occupied Paris was a matter of luck. You simply telephoned, waited and hoped. I dragged my suitcase downstairs and sat on the top of it in the soft night wind and looked over the sleeping city and the basilica of Sacré Coeur.

Henri was asleep upstairs, and I saw no point in waking him. What worried me was that the baby was kicking very hard and that I might give birth in the street. It was half an hour before the ambulance came, and when we arrived at the hospital, a nurse examined me and said:

'I must call the doctor immediately. Keep laughing.'

Laughing loudly is supposed to slow down the birth contractions. So I laughed and laughed. But Caterine was eager for life. She was born a few minutes later—a beautiful little girl with huge eyes like two cornflowers in her small pink face. She weighed nine pounds. The date was September 17, 1942.

I left the hospital for our apartment, which had the heavy handicap of being close to the Gare de Nord and the Gare de l'Est, one of the chief targets of the bombing attacks on Paris. There was a cellar which served as a bomb shelter, but the doctors had ordered me to remain in bed for a while because they feared a clot in my leg, and I held the babies tightly against me whenever bombs exploded nearby.

After one particular raid, Henri came up from the shelter, chuckling about our laundry woman Louisette who, he said, was so frightened that her toes spread out and she had to take off her shoes. I was so silent that he broke off the story to ask me what was the matter. I pointed silently to the shattered windows, beyond which rose the smoke of many fires, and to the devastation within our own apartment. The cupboards had blown open and bags of lentils, sugar and salt had spilled out of their paper packets onto the floor. Everything was mixed up.

That night I felt more alone than ever before.

12 *The spirit of France*

THE DOCTOR SOON gave me permission to leave my bed, and one of the first things I did was to go looking for shoes. In Paris in 1942 there was no leather, so shoes were made of carved wood or of cork, and covered with material—in fact exactly like the 1973 fashions.

I knew an Armenian in Belleville, behind Montmartre, who would make shoes in his spare time if you brought him the covering material. He was not actually a shoemaker but a baker, but that was the way things were on the Black Market. You bought sugar from your butcher, meat from your grocer, butter from the cleaners, and the concierge might have some jam.

I had some spare tartan material from a skirt, and the little man covered my shoes with it. I finally decided to learn to make shoes myself. I bought some cork platforms, fastened material to the cork with fish-glue, and soled them with a scrap rubber. The result was very chic—for the time.

To conserve material, which was so scarce, we wore our skirts at about knee level. We piled our hair up on top of our heads, and resembled Madame Pompadour above and an apache dancer below.

I remember, while pushing Caterine in her pram along the Champs Elysées, that an overwhelming feeling of oppression came over me. I was only twenty-two, and I felt that my youth, with the fun and joy that people of my own age were entitled to expect, was slipping away.

All over beautiful Paris there were barriers that closed off sections of pavement round the commercial buildings, apartment houses and hotels which had been taken over by the Germans. One day I came out of my building and saw in the garden a shepherd who was resting on the iron bench while his 200 or so sheep nibbled the grass and flowers as if they were in a peaceful meadow and not surrounded by the stone and steel of a great city.

It was a strange time.

It was possible to follow the course of the war by a close inspection of the walls of Paris, which told a changing story. First of all, before the fall of France, there were the 'Be Calm' notices put up by the police. Then came the 'love the Germans' type, with caricatures of Churchill and Roosevelt and the sunken American fleet after Pearl Harbor—put up of course by the Germans. Later the Resistance began to post its defiance.

From time to time the Germans would put up lists of names of hostages captured, tortured and executed. These always ended with the words 'Ils ont été fusilés aujourd'hui'—they were shot today. For many a brave man, this was his only epitaph.

I saw the first hand-lettered Resistance posters in 1942. I stood there spellbound, tingling with excitement, desperately proud of the men who risked their lives in the dead of night to spread their message through Paris. Later I was to learn that Michel was one of them. The spirit of France never burned more fiercely.

I could never get used to the enormous bus-loads of German tourists who came on sightseeing tours to gloat over us—the conquered. The German soldiers had orders not to interfere or fraternise with the population, but this rule did not apply to civilian Germans, who would tap you jovially on the shoulder to ask directions and then ask you to pose for a photograph with a member of the 'master race'. They could not understand why so few French people welcomed their approaches.

People developed the 'Paris look'—they looked through the occupying troops, not at them, pretending that they did not exist.

Travelling in occupied Paris was also a problem. We had bicycle taxis—a kind of cage on two wheels, hooked to a bicycle. There were only a few drivers, and one soon got to know their names and capabilities. They were all controlled by one firm, and one would telephone and say: 'Send me Jacques' or 'Don't give me Albert, he's so slow'. Some of the 'cyclo-taxis' were painted blue, some red and some green. One could telephone and say 'I'm wearing a blue dress, so do send me Jean'.

One stage star, renowned for her elegance, had her own cyclo-taxi in which she went to the theatre every night. It was a tandem bicycle pedalled by her 'chauffeur' and her 'footman', who became the talk of the town. This seems flippant now, but at the time it saved our sanity.

At the stations there were baggagemen who would carry your cases from the train to your apartment. They were big and tough and looked dangerous, and as they walked so fast, you had to run to keep an eye on your luggage.

There were curfews too. When the German authorities suspected trouble, they ordered the citizens off the streets by 9.30 p.m. Otherwise the deadline was midnight. If you were caught after the curfew, you would be taken to Police Headquarters by the 'Feldgrau'—the bicycle patrols who wore greenish-grey field uniforms. If your identity papers were in order, you might get nothing worse than a command to polish boots or clean windows or floors before being released at 5 a. m. I was stopped several times, but the Feldgrau were not generally oppressive, they were simply soldiers obeying orders.

Our major worry was that the Gestapo might intervene at any moment—with all its inhuman apparatus—so that even minor detentions could be alarming. Some Germans were easygoing, others miniature models of Hitler. It was a matter of luck which you encountered.

One evening Michel and I had gone to see Jean-Paul Sartre's 'Huis Clos' at the Vieux Colombier Theatre. We were sitting there, completely absorbed in Gaby Sylvia playing the mother who had killed her child, Michel Vitold as the anarchist and Arletty as the lesbian, when the usherette tapped Michel on the shoulder.

'Monsieur and Madame,' she whispered, 'will you please give up your seats?'

Standing by her was a German officer and a woman.

'I have paid for my seats and I shall keep them,' Michel retorted.

The whole theatre was tense. Suddenly a couple got up a few rows behind, and the man said 'We do not like the play. Have our seats.'

Michel's action was foolhardy, and he was obviously young and the German might have made allowance for that, but as we left the theatre we were arrested and questioned, and Michel was detained and beaten.

But we would not have been French if we did not squeeze some humour out of life.

One of my friends, Monique, was involved in an incident that seems funnier now than at the time. She had a lover, Pierre, whose underground courier work involved him in dangerous trips to the frontiers. Her husband, Raoul, was no more suspicious than most husbands of beautiful wives, but he was kept busy at his factory, and Monique was on her own most afternoons—or almost alone!

Pierre returned from one of his hazardous assignments with a rare bottle of Dubonnet. He danced into Monique's apartment and proposed that they drink it during the lulls in their love-making. But first, as he felt grubby after his trip, he asked Monique to run him a bath. The bathroom, like every other room in that lavish apartment, was the size of a parade ground, and it was natural for him to suggest that Monique take a bath with him.

They were both in the water when they heard a key at the front door. Raoul, on a sudden impulse, had decided to come home and quell the nagging suspicion of infidelity. Pierre leaped from the bath, seized his clothes, and hid in a cupboard. Monique grabbed the Dubonnet and sat on it in the bath. In her panic she switched out the light. Her husband wanted to know why she was bathing in the dark.

'My eyes hurt,' Monique quavered.

'But why take a bath at three in the afternoon?'

Monique was trying to think of an answer when Raoul switched on the light.

'You're bleeding', he gasped.

The Dubonnet was pouring out of the bottle into the bath.

'I do not feel well,' Monique said, playing for time, 'Quick, send for a doctor.'

But even a jealous husband, on close inspection knows the difference between Dubonnet and blood, and with a bedroom-comedy 'Ahah!', Raoul began to trace a trail of water to the cupboard. The only weapon to hand was his own small pocket penknife. Armed only with its ludicrous blade, he opened the door and shouted: 'I will kill you.'

Pierre sprinted past him, half-dressed, out of the apartment Raoul puffed after him, penknife at the ready. Monique, barely covered with a bath towel, followed shrieking behind them. She was a well-endowed young woman, and I doubt if her male neighbours noticed the two men.

One of my closest convent friends was Christiane Dusanter, whose father was the biggest shareholder in the Banque de France and whose older brother Guy introduced me to Zen Buddhism and the poems of Czeslaw Milosz and Rabindranath Tagore.

In the summer of 1943 I discovered I was pregnant again and Christiane invited me to spend a week or two at the beautiful Dusanter château, Tirlancourt. The invitation was welcome, not only because the Dusanter ménage was deliciously mad, but because it was a chance to have milk, cream, butter and good food again. I took the year-old Caterine, and Didier, now aged four, with me.

Papa Dusanter and his wife were gentle, lovable people who had always had too much money and who had raised their children in a state of affectionate anarchy. Everybody in the family engaged in practical jokes. Monsieur Dusanter met me at the station driving a gasogene—charcoal powered—automobile, and told me that his 17-year-old son Yves had a new tutor—a priest.

I thought the priest unusually young and handsome, and was shocked at dinner by his light-hearted attitude towards the Catholic hierarchy. After dinner Yves put on a jazz record, and the priest started jitterbugging! Of course, he was a friend of the family who had been persuaded to dress up to shock me.

Monsieur Dusanter had wired up his house so that he could,

from a secret hideout, make 'broadcasts' pretending to be Marshal Pétain or General de Gaulle. Like almost the entire population of France, the Dusanter household gathered each night at 9 p.m. to listen to the BBC news from London. Following this, Monsieur Dusanter would announce from his little studio such items as a request for all women to turn in their gold rings so that a statue could be erected to de Gaulle—or, mimicking Pétain, for French women to be nice to the Germans as they were 'only poor, lonely lads away from home'. Gradually, as these announcements became more and more extraordinary, everyone noticed that Monsieur Dusanter was never in the room at the time, and his secret was uncovered.

A genuine tutor did in fact arrive for Yves while I was there. He did not stay long. The first day, they put the gardener's six-month-old baby in his bed with the message 'You gave this to me, so I'm giving it back to you'. The second day, 12 alarm clocks were hidden in his room, set to go off at 15-minute intervals during the night. The third day, he put his shoes outside the door to be cleaned for the morning, and found them filled with toothpaste.

The fourth day, he left.

I felt partly responsible for his departure as some of the pranks were my idea.

During that time an old man we had befriended died and left us his house at St. Leu la Forêt in his will. It was an old-fashioned place, filled with bric-à-brac—one of the ugliest little buildings I had ever seen, inside or out. The old floral wallpaper was so hideous that I spent hours hosing it down to soften and peel it off. But the house had the advantage of being only 20 kilometres from Paris—much closer than Meaux—and a possible refuge from bombs. It also had a fruit and vegetable garden, which was very useful for the children.

It was impossible to find painters or plumbers since all the able-bodied men were in the factories or fighting, so I decided to re-decorate the house myself. The neighbours were fascinated, watching me and my two maids attack the building with water and green soap, but within a week we had everything gloriously clean. Sadly there was no paint available to obliterate the green and yellow striped exterior.

I bought myself a white bicycle and I used to carry Caterine in the basket in front and Didier on the back into the forest to pick flowers, or to nearby farms to get eggs, milk and butter. They looked adorable with their blond hair and blue eyes, Caterine's curls making her look like an angel.

I read a great deal. One book that gave me much to think about was Leconte de Nouy's 'Revolution of the Creation'. Its theme of respect for humanity seemed particularly apposite at that time.

In September 1943 I had a visitor. It was Michel. He had come to tell me that he had joined the Resistance.

13   *'Vous qui passez sans me voir'*

ALTHOUGH MICHEL HAD known me for years, he could not take chances with the lives of his friends—although he would have trusted me with his own. So his visit was really a test.

He told me he had started his Resistance activities in Lyons and that he had escaped the Germans by running into a house built on a hill which had entrances on two levels. He brought with him Pierre Guermot, the instigator of the group, and they spoke with the same carefree enthusiasm about their work as if they were talking of a game of cops and robbers.

Naturally I had heard a great deal about the Resistance, and was aware of patriots who had banded together to work against the Germans. Once Maurice, the nephew of my village baker, had hinted to me of secret meetings in their basement while the bread was in the oven.

I was happy to see Michel. It brought back memories of my youth at Neuilly, and of peace. He did not stay long, nor did he say when he might return.

It was at St. Leu, several months later, that I next saw him. I am certain he had waited deliberately to make sure I was a safe contact. He arrived unexpectedly and said he wanted to have a serious talk with me. He suggested that first we walk through the Forest of Montmorency because he had heard that this was where the Germans were building their secret-weapon installations—the V1 flying-bombs and the V2 rocket bombs which did such damage in London.

We walked casually along in the forest, apparently intent in conversation while we looked about as closely as we could. Not surprisingly, the entire area was too heavily guarded and we did not get into the restricted zones.

Then Michel told me what he really wanted of me:

'As you know,' he said, 'some of us are working for the Underground movement, and we need someone for courier assignments. Will you do it? All you have to do is carry parcels and packages. I won't tell you what's in them, so you will not know.'

He said his group consisted of young people of about 18 years of age whose aims were to hinder the Germans and help escaping prisoners. There was a certain amount of danger in their work, but the good it might do made that unimportant.

I said I would be glad to help. There was nothing heroic in my decision. I was young enough to feel as though I, too, were simply taking part in some new and more exciting game.

My biggest asset to the group, I think, was my innocent appearance—no makeup, a freckled face and long straight hair—and the obvious fact that I was slightly pregnant. I did not look to the Germans like a girl whose white bicycle was packed with gun-parts or banknotes or false identity papers.

Michel had said he would not tell me what my cargo was, but I learnt to distinguish by feel what was in the parcels. Michel soon realised I knew what I was carrying, and took me a step further into the group. I was taught for example how to remove the stamp from a genuine identity card issued by the Préfecture of Police by using half a fresh potato, and how to transfer it to a counterfeit card for Resistance use on behalf of people who wanted to escape.

We used to meet in the Triolet bar on the Rue Godot de Mauray. The street was notorious for its prostitutes, and ideal for a rendezvous because it was not unusual for women to spend a lot of time lingering over their drinks.

The Triolet had a pianist, Paul Durand, with whom I became friendly. He once played me a beautiful melody and asked 'What do you think of this?' It was the haunting, wistful song 'Vous qui passez sans me voir' which was to become one of the biggest

Maternal grandfather

Maternal grandmother—Mémé—she was petite but indomitable

Top—Marguerite, my sometimes mother

Left—Tante Cécile, beautiful and gentle

Right—Tante Lou, the redhead like me

Paul, Marguerite and a grand sacristan. . . .
They made it at last

Father was very handsome, his mother was beautiful

The family. How sad and ugly can you be

My favourite picture, aged 3

My cousin Marie-Thérèse, always immaculate, suffering because my vest is showing

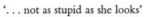
'. . . not as stupid as she looks'

17 years old and pensive

Michel—handsome, intelligent, gentle, what a waste of a life!

Proud mother with first-born son Didier

Didier, Caterine, Gilles—all good-looking, how lucky!

At Argentières, where I decided that my life was my own

A radiant couple!

Life is fun

hits of the war and was to take him from the Triolet to leader of the band at the Casino de Paris.

Years later when I was a television producer, I wanted someone to write music for a series. I had listened all day to recorded music, and I was tired. My secretary opened the door and announced Monsieur Durand. I did not look up from the letters I was signing, but suddenly the room became charged with some strange electric force. I raised my eyes and there—I could hardly believe it—was my pianist friend from the Triolet.

I stood up muttering 'Paul', and fell into his arms. We sat on the sofa, recalling old times. Needless to say, he wrote the music for my series.

There was another meeting-place at La Brasserie Viel in the Boulevard de la Madeleine, which was ideal because it had such a large and crowded pavement café. I used to slip in and take a table before the peak hour, holding a certain newspaper folded in a certain way. Then my contact, identifying himself similarly, would linger near me. As soon as I said: 'How much for my coffee?'—the recognition code—he would move swiftly over and ask: 'Is this table free?' I would say it was, pay my bill, and depart, leaving my paper behind. When in turn he left, he would pick up my newspaper instead of his own. Hidden inside my paper might have been claim tickets for the luggage room at the Gare St. Lazare or the Gare du Nord, or a message of some sort.

We had other methods of recognition. One was to strike a match from top to bottom of a box of matches rather than along the side. I kept this habit for some years after the war. Once in the Park Hotel in Copenhagen my telephone rang. It was a wartime friend.

'Robert,' I exclaimed. 'How did you know I was here?'

He said he was signing the register when he saw a box of matches with vertical strike marks. He thought it might be coincidence, but it might also have been that he had stumbled on a member of the French Resistance, so he had asked to look through the hotel register and had found my name.

We used also to meet in a place on the Rue Verneuil and, later on, in an attic in Neuilly above the studio of a friendly painter and decorator named Georges Pescadère. And we had hiding places everywhere for picking up packages. At La Brasserie Viel, for example, there was a hollow place under the washbasin in the lavatory. Men and women used the same washroom and it was a marvellous spot to hide things.

Only rarely did it occur to me that what I was doing might be dangerous. I was more concerned with my baby coming, and knew that I would soon have to halt temporarily the work in which I was now so completely absorbed.

One morning, pedalling along the Rue de Rivoli, with parts of machine-guns in my saddle-bag for delivery to an address at the top of Montmartre, I went through a red light near the famous golden statue of Joan of Arc. A German policeman ordered me to halt.

My throat was dry and my heart began racing madly as he approached. It seemed to me that he must know something, otherwise why was he looking at me so intently, running his eyes so carefully over the bicycle? I thought: this is it. He will examine my saddle-bags, and I will be in the hands of the Gestapo! The policeman gazed thoughtfully at me but evidently decided that a pregnant girl could not possibly be involved in anything illegal. He checked my identity, reprimanded me for crossing a red light, and fined me 100 francs. I had only two 20-franc notes on me, so I folded them tightly, hoping that he would not notice the slight difference in colour, thrust them into his hands, jumped on my bicycle, and peddled away.

As I passed Jeanne d'Arc, I looked at her and said 'Please help me'. I turned the first corner on the right, jumped off my bicycle, pressed the release-catch on the door of a building, and wheeled my bicycle into the hallway, where I stood trembling. The baby was jumping, and I decided that I must stop my activities there and then before they endangered the baby's nervous system.

In addition to gun-parts and other material, I also carried verbal messages in code. I would look up a contact and report 'I have the nail of my grandmother' or 'Bernard found the Milky Way'. To the right person, one of these phrases might be a specific instruction to go to a certain field at a certain hour to be picked up by a plane!

Those of us who had to go to the provinces would communicate by postcard with innocuous messages about the weather and their health. The real messages would be written invisibly between the lines, with lemon juice or urine, and the card would have to be held over a flame before the hidden writing could become visible.

Other messages were written on the underside of upside-down postage stamps which we then steamed off. In such ways we were told when and where to go somewhere.

We had another, more elaborate, method of making contact. Since Neuilly was our headquarters, I would go to the Sablons métro station and stand under the sign 'Directions Maillot'. My contact would stand on the other side under the sign 'Directions Vincennes'—the two opposite terminals. We would wait until two trains had passed in each direction, then we would go up to the street and walk towards the nearby Bois de Boulogne.

Once inside the forest, it was easy to see whether you were being followed. If the coast was clear, we would join up and walk through the trees, arm in arm like lovers. although most of the time we had never met before. The messages or packages would be exchanged, and we would part, waving a fond goodbye.

Sometimes things did not go exactly as planned. Once I was told to take a parcel to the Père Lachaise cemetery in Paris, where Chopin and Balzac and the immortal lovers Abélard and Héloise are buried. I was told to find a certain tomb, where I was to kneel and pray with the parcel in front of me.

Never have I been so devotional. I knelt on the hard ground for two and a half hours. A funeral procession came to a nearby grave. The coffin was lowered, prayers were said, and the mourners departed. Still I knelt—and prayed. As dusk was falling the warning-bell rang for visitors. I took my parcel and hurried away.

Michel did not tell me what had gone wrong, and I had learnt to ask few questions. The less one knew, the better. Once, when one of our friends had been arrested, I heard Michel and Pierre Guermot considering how to spread the news to the others. It was about the only time they discussed operations in front of me. Afterwards Michel confided that Pierre was the actual leader of our group.

On another assignment I had the scare of my life. I was sent to a house in a pretty square in Montmartre. The day was sunny, and I was humming. The door was opened by a man. I gave the password, and walked into a room which, when my startled eyes became accustomed to the darkness, seemed to be littered with bleeding corpses. I fell back with a frightened cry. The man raised his bloodstained hands and laughed: what I had thought were bodies were pieces of veal which he had brought from the country in suitcases and was cutting up for our friends.

My third child, Gilles, was born on April 6, 1944—slightly premature and underweight, not surprisingly after a year of privation, but he was a lovely baby with blond hair and blue eyes.

After I was released from the clinic I went back to St. Leu la Forêt. I used to travel up to Paris in the morning and return to take care of Gilles in the afternoon. On the train one day we were strafed by low-flying planes. A man sitting near me pulled me to the floor and pushed me half under the seat.

Whoever he was, he saved my life. When I crawled back after the attack was over, there was no-one in the car. The seat I had been sitting in had been slashed by machine-gun bullets and even the book I had been reading was chopped to pieces.

14   *Gilles*

GILLES DEVELOPED A cough at the end of the first week of July 1944 while at St. Leu. The country doctor thought the child had tracheitis. We fed him syrups and rubbed his little throat, but it did not seem to do any good. I was desperately worried as I cycled towards Neuilly where, on July 15, a rendezvous had been arranged in an empty attic.

We sat on the floor. The war news was good—the Allies had landed in Normandy on June 7 and were now rapidly fighting their way through France. But Michel and our friends were in despair. The night before, as they had cycled through the Place St. Augustin, one of the girls, Roselyne, had collided with a bollard in the middle of the road, and fallen, cutting her knee. She had bled too heavily to continue riding, and the others had been helping her walk when a German military patrol stopped and demanded to know why they were out after curfew.

Violation of the curfew was not a serious matter, but Michel and his friends were carrying six million francs—an enormous sum at that period—as well as a large number of forged identity cards and a list of Resistance sympathisers. The evidence was enough to have had them all executed, and fatal for the people on the list.

There were always plans for such an emergency, and Michel put one into operation. Two of the boys started a noisy political argument in German while the rest of the group dumped all the incriminating evidence inside the lobby of a nearby building.

They were all held at Military headquarters till 5 a.m. and released.

Now there was the possibility that the concierge of the building might find the material, and turn it over to the German authorities. The odds were that she would be patriotic and hide or destroy it, but Michel felt he could not take any chances.

When I came into Paris that morning, it was stiflingly hot. Michel and I took our bicycles and rode all over the city, warning our friends that the situation might be dangerous and they must move or hide for at least a month. We covered at least 20 kilometres under a blazing sun, then returned to my apartment in the Faubourg St. Honoré, where we discussed what else we must do. Michel thought it prudent to visit some friends in the south of France. I had the children, so I thought my best course was to return to St. Leu and hope for the best.

Michel paced the room deep in thought. 'Nicole', he said finally, 'I must go back to Neuilly. We haven't been able to warn everybody that the meeting there has been called off. I must be there to warn them.'

This loyalty was to cost him his life.

In the attic at Neuilly, there was a feeling of oppression, made heavier by the hot weather. Because there was nothing to eat or drink, and because I was the least important member of the group, I volunteered to go out and buy some fruit. If only we had dispersed immediately!

I was returning from the fruit-shop when I saw three black limousines screech up in front of the house. Black limousines meant only one thing in Paris—the Gestapo. I froze. I could hardly move or breathe. From the edge of the silent crowd that quickly gathered, I could see Michel and all my friends being dragged from the house and bundled roughly into the cars, which roared off at typical Gestapo speed.

The concierge, I learnt later, had taken the francs to the police. She was frightened that the money had been planted by the Gestapo who, if she did not turn it in, would accuse her of working against the régime. The police turned the money over to the Germans. The Gestapo took over from there, in their own direct style. They went to Michel's address, put a gun at the head of his 72-year-old grandmother and demanded his whereabouts. The old lady was so frightened that she blurted out the address in Neuilly.

I was carrying two kilos of redcurrants and cherries, which I dropped into the gutter, and I ran to the house of one of Michel's relatives—as his mother was away—who had only one panicky thought in mind—not to get involved—and told me to leave at once

Everyone else had gone to the country, as Parisians do after the end of June, so I decided to go straight to the German commander of the Neuilly district to tell him that some people I knew had been picked up, and to ask what would happen to them. The officer was pleasant enough. He said Michel and the others had been taken to Fresnes prison but that he would do everything to 'liberate these young people'.

I thought of Gilles and the hacking cough, which some instinct told me was more serious than it appeared. I got on my bicycle and pedalled at top speed the entire 20 kilometres (twelve miles) to St. Leu. At one point I looked back. There were two German cyclists. I was being shadowed. No wonder the German commandant had been so obliging: he thought I would lead him to the rest of the group.

Gilles was much worse when I got home. I called the doctor again but he was unable to come immediately. After several anxious hours, I telephoned the doctor in the next village and begged him to hurry over. It was an hour before he could manage it. After a brief examination he said: 'Madame, your child has an advanced stage of whooping cough.' He prescribed three kinds of injections and arranged for a nun to come each day from a nearby convent to give them. None of my children had ever been ill before and rarely went out of the garden. I was so distraught that I pleaded with the doctor to look at Didier and Caterine, too, but they were sleeping peacefully and were obviously healthy. How Gilles caught the whooping cough was never explained.

The days that followed were the worst I have ever known. Racing between St. Leu and Paris every day, I was fighting two battles—one for Michel and my friends, and the other for my son. The first time I returned to Paris after Michel's capture I was arrested and taken to the end of the Avenue de Blois near the Porte Dauphine, to a huge building that had been requisitioned for the Gestapo.

A Gestapo officer tried to make me sign a paper confessing that I was part of the Resistance movement. I refused. The questioning went on for hours, but in my anxiety over Michel and Gilles I did not have time to be afraid.

'You are being very stupid', he shouted at me at one point.

I replied that I was not being stupid—just honest.

'We know you belong to the Resistance,' he snapped.

I said he was quite wrong; I was only a housewife. Now he stopped shouting and walked about the room, never taking his eyes from me—or rather from my body.

'If these people are your friends,' he said, his eyes fixed on my bosom, 'and you really want to help them, I know a way.'

'What way?' I asked, and knew immediately that the question was unnecessary.

'Every Frenchwoman knows the way I mean,' he smirked.

I spat out the word 'swine', and immediately my interrogator was back in his Gestapo role. He lit a cigarette and held it near my cheek. But he did not burn me. He slapped me, then threw me heavily against the wall. Another slap knocked me down.

I was lucky. He was called out. I waited and waited in a corridor. At the end of the day I was freed, and I hurried to St. Leu and Gilles.

I was not out of German custody for long.

One afternoon soon afterwards, I was in the garden. Overhead, planes were engaged in a dogfight, and from time to time shrapnel actually fell into the garden. There was the smell of ripe tomatoes. Even today when I eat tomatoes, it brings back that scene. At one point a large plane caught fire just over our heads; we did not know if it was German or Allied, but we could see airmen parachuting from it.

Soon we heard that it was an Allied bomber. Two of the

crew landed in the cemetery and escaped; two others fell in the forest and got away. Two were captured. One landed on someone's lawn nearby, and one fell in my garden. He was a young Canadian, and very frightened. He was wearing distinctive khaki flying overalls. Almost as though the scene had been rehearsed, my neighbours rushed into my garden, stripped away his overalls and began peeling off their own clothes. One gave him a jacket, another trousers, another a shirt. I hurried him to the back of the garden, where another of my neighbours rushed him further on to the forest—and escape.

But we were not quick enough to protect ourselves. Two German motorcyclists roared up from local command head-quarters, and said 'Where is the parachutist?'

'I have not seen anyone,' I said.

The Germans simply pointed to the flying overalls that were still on the ground, and to the parachute caught on the spiked fence. I was arrested once more.

They went into the house, ordered my maid out with the children, and threatened them with machine-guns, swearing they would burn the house unless they found the parachutist by dawn. The maid broke down and wept, but I told her we were right in the centre of the village and I did not think the Germans would risk a fire. At this the soldiers rushed into the house again and started throwing furniture through the windows. They also tossed out clothes, sheets, towels and anything else movable. The children became frightened and began to cry.

As the soldiers pulled me away, I again shouted to the maid not to worry, that they would not destroy the house. I did not believe the Germans would go to such an extreme, and I was right.

In the morning I was released, but two Gestapo plain-clothes men followed me wherever I went. As a result, I made no effort to contact anyone except Michel's mother, Mamy.

I have often wondered what happened to the Canadian airman and whether we shall ever meet again. We have much to talk about, and I would like to see him.

I went to Paris as often as I could tear myself away from Gilles. But there was little I could do. Michel was taken from

Fresnes to Compiègne, packed tightly in an open truck with other prisoners.

Nevertheless he managed to tear a page from his Hermès diary and scribble a note to me, and although armed Gestapo guards were on duty, he dropped it unnoticed as they passed through a village market-place.

One day a woman called on me, wearing the typical black pleated satin apron of the French market vendor. She was short, stout and plain. She said she had seen a young man throw a note from a German truck, and since it bore my name and address, she had decided to deliver it in person. We both knew she had risked instant execution by concealing the note from the Germans. She explained:

'I know how you must feel. I, too, have someone in a German concentration camp—my son.'

Among my most treasured possessions is Michel's note. It reads:

'Ma Chérie. I wish you could feel how much I love you and how near I am to you. I think about you all the time. I think constantly of the great love within me and the solace you bring me. I would like it, if during our separation, all your thoughts were for me. But that is impossible. Your love, I know, will not change but there are so many other things you must think about. I wonder if you will always be so close to me and so full of that great love which is all my happiness? Be brave and be patient. Remember that I love you and that this little moment of separation is not for ever. It will permit us to find ourselves even closer to each other with a love more deep and more complete. Do kiss Gilles for me. Do think of me. I love you. I love you. And it is my only comfort. I will see you very soon, my love. I love you, my darling. I kiss you very tenderly. Be brave. I love you. Michel.'

I learned later that Michel was transferred to a concentration camp at Elrich in Germany where he was savaged by guards with the butt-end of their guns because they said he refused to obey orders.

The Allies were now beginning to threaten the German positions near Paris, and everyone knew that the day of liberation was not far off. They all wanted to be ready to fly flags on that day, and all the stores sold out of red, white and blue material. The only thing left to do was to go to the chemist and buy blue and red dyes. And in St. Leu, as in the whole of France, laundry-lines were brilliant with pieces of cloth waiting to be sewn into flags.

With the Allied approach, the Gestapo guards were withdrawn.

Gilles's condition became worse. The electricity and water were cut off. Luckily I had filled some containers with water and piled some cut wood in the garden.

To keep Gilles alive we had to give him a very hot bath every fifteen minutes and then a cold bath, and we had to rub him to help his circulation. He was three months old but he weighed less than he did at birth. He was a tiny frail skeleton and I had to carry him on a pillow. His body was blue and his eyes had turned inwards so that only the whites showed. I cried every time I looked at him.

Now the Allied bombings started in earnest, and the doctor stopped coming.

'Why should I risk my life for a baby who is going to die anyway?' he asked.

The nun also stopped coming. 'I'm frightened of the bombs' she said, simply.

I could understand that.

We had as many as seventeen bombing raids a day. The objective was the bridge at Pontoise, and since the Allies were bombing from high altitudes to escape anti-aircraft fire, their bombs often landed nearer St. Leu than the bridge.

I was running out of medicine for Gilles, and the chemist in the village could not get supplies. He suggested there might be some in another village some seven kilometres away. I did not dare reassemble the bicycle, which I took apart and hid when the Germans began seizing anything on wheels to aid their retreat. So I started walking there.

A few minutes along the road I was spotted by the very Gestapo man who had been guarding my house. I was taken into custody and brought before a lieutenant in charge of the troops at a railway crossing—an Austrian who spoke quite good French.

I told him that my baby was sick and would die if I could not get to the next village. He listened to my story with some sympathy. Then he said:

'The trouble is, madame, that you are walking towards the enemy, and we know you are working with them. I will send two soldiers along with you. If you take a single step out of line, they have orders to shoot you.'

I said I did not care if he sent the entire German army to guard me, as long as I got my baby's medicine.

So with two Germans carrying sub-machine guns behind me, we set out along the road. As we crossed the village, the shutters of the houses banged closed. The people thought I was being taken away for execution, and this was their way of protesting.

The chemist at the next village also slammed his shutters, but in his case it was out of fear of the Germans' intentions. I knocked on his door and rang his bell but could get no answer. I hammered and pounded my fist against the iron shutters, and screamed for attention. Finally a window on the first floor opened and the worried face of the chemist appeared.

'What is it?' he quavered.

I said: 'Please open up. My baby is dying and I must have some medicine.'

He said: 'What do you need?'

I was nearly hysterical with anxiety now and I screamed up at him: 'Sea-water serum and Glucose serum and eucalyptus baby suppositories.' I gave him all the dosages and other details mentioned by the doctor. He said:

'Stay there and I will go downstairs and get it for you.'

I thought he meant he was going to open up the shop. But instead after a few minutes his head appeared at the upstairs window again.

'This is all I've got,' he said.

And with that he suddenly began to toss bundles out of the **window** at me. I have never lived through a more terrible moment. The serum came in a glass tube ten inches long. If it had broken, if I had failed to catch it, my baby might have died. I managed to catch the items one by one.

Through the blazing heat of that day I walked back the seven kilometres with my faithful Wehrmacht escort, who looked to me at that moment like so many war-weary angels, machine-gun and all.

By the time I got back home the baby was in a coma. I could hardly detect any breathing. I had never given an injection in my life. Could I do it? Gilles was so frail and tiny. I was frightened as I pinched the skin at the shoulder to insert the needle. The sea-water serum made an enormous bulge and I had to rush out into the garden where I was violently sick. I thought I had killed my baby.

Now came the more dangerous injection. The Glucose serum had to drip slowly into the body through a long, thin flexible needle. Every prayer I had ever learnt was on my lips as I pushed the needle into the skin above the little stomach. What if I should penetrate something vital? On my knees beside him, I waited and hoped. Then the drops of life-giving serum flowed through the needle, and the fragile body stirred.

Gilles was going to live.

15   *He was 24 years old*

FRANCE WAS NOW engaged in the drama of liberation. Allied troops were approaching, and Red Cross vans toured the streets of St. Leu with loudspeakers, urging everyone to go into the cellars, as the Germans were expected to defend the area street by street.

For three days the fighting raged—a cannon sited just at the end of our street boomed a constant, deafening staccato. I could not go to the cellar: Gilles had to have hot and cold baths every few minutes night and day. I had run out of water and was using the same water again and again. We had run out of wood, and I had chopped the branches of a tree for fuel, and choking smoke from the green wood filled the house.

At six o'clock in the morning of my fourth sleepless night, I heard cheers and cries of 'Long live the Allies' and 'Long live France', and the first Allied tank moved through the village towards Paris. I gathered some apples and gave them, with a bottle of brandy specially hidden for the occasion, to the Canadian troops who had freed us.

My first thought was to reassemble the bicycle and get to Paris to find medical help for Gilles and to see what could be done about Michel. From under my bed I recovered one wheel, from the top of the wardrobe another. The gear-wheel was hidden in the cherry tree and the chain somewhere else. The handlebars were in the branches of another tree. The German need for transport in the final hours was such that I saw them shoot at the daughter of the baker and take away her bicycle, simply because they had not time to struggle with her for it.

I rode furiously towards Paris, and as I was passing under the railway bridge at St. Denis, three helmets of a type I had not seen before rolled into the road in front of me. I braked hard to avoid hitting them. As I came to a stop, some 30 American soldiers swarmed out from both sides of the road and surrounded me. These were the first Americans I had ever seen, and they looked like the European idea of Texas Rangers—tall, tanned and tough. They were picked fighting men and were leading the American advance.

But they were wild—so wild that a special curfew was later imposed on them in Paris.

Two of them took my bicycle and began skylarking on it. The others dragged me into the grass and began to strip me. I fought with my teeth and my nails. I punched, kicked and screamed. But I was nearly naked before a group of French peasants arrived, carrying 'gourdins'—big wooden canes for beating grain. They hammered away at the Americans, who gave up the attempted rape in high humour and laughingly went away to resume the battle for Paris.

The peasants covered me with an overall, and took me to a farmhouse, where I was revived with Calvados. They found my bicycle in the field, minus the chain, but finally they produced another chain, and I resumed my journey to the capital, wondering about these extraordinary people who could interrupt a battle for a girl.

I did not, of course, know Americans then as I do now.

In Paris I went straight to a hospital and told them about Gilles. They immediately sent an ambulance with an incubator. A few hours later they told me that my treatment had saved his life and that he would recover.

My relief and exhilaration that Gilles was safe were soon overtaken by the bruising treatment I had received from the advance troop of American soldiers. I could not face the thought of the long cycle ride back to St. Leu, and I headed instead towards my home at the Rond Point des Champs Elysées. On the way Michel was in my thoughts. Where was he? What could I do for him. Why was he not here to share in the joy and excitement of the day? My dream was broken by Michel's voice shouting at me—or so it seemed.

On that day of magic even an amazing coincidence seemed right and natural. The voice was that of Michel's brother, Antoine, who was with another of my childhood friends, Gérard de Royer. As aides-de-camp to French generals, both were among the first to enter Paris. They jumped from their jeep, and we embraced and laughed and cried and spoke of Michel.

'I will be in Elrich in four days and I'll liberate him myself,' Antoine promised.

It was also a day for believing, and I wanted to believe. We put my bicycle in the courtyard, piled into the jeep and headed for the Champs Elysées to join the rest of Paris in celebrating victory.

Everybody who could get there poured into the great boulevard. Lines of people 12 or 15 abreast, with arms linked, marched up and down, singing the Marseillaise. Others waved flags. Strangers kissed and hugged one another. Everyone chanted the word 'Victory'. All the cafés and bistros were open, but nobody paid for drinks. The city was delirious. Both Antoine and Gérard were very handsome, and girls fought to get into the jeep to kiss them.

Sporadic fighting still continued, with sharpshooters stationed on the tops of buildings. There was a sudden burst of machine-gun fire, and everybody within earshot fell flat in the street. Soldiers were chasing people—I assumed they were Gestapo or German spies—over the rooftops, as fast as if they were running in the streets. Antoine drew his pistol and fired at the fugitives. When the shooting stopped, everyone stood up and began embracing again.

Antoine could hardly see to drive because of all the girls on the bonnet; he whispered to us to hold tight, and then circled at high speed until all the extra passengers were catapulted off.

It was mad. It was crazy. It was liberation day.

We parked the jeep in the Place de la Concorde and walked towards the Crillon. On the way machine-gun fire broke out again. A little boy standing near me in the crowd was killed by a bullet.

His grandmother became hysterical. One tragedy in a day of joy.

One of the drunks at the Rue de Provence confronted Antoine and, pounding Antoine's chest with his fist, sneered:

'Why have you so many decorations? Are they fakes?'

Antoine, who is tall and strong, objected.

'You are a drunken lout—but you won't be drunk any more,' he said, and dragged the man into the gutter, holding his head under a hydrant while Gérard turned on the water. Antoine dragged the half-drowned man clear, pointed to his medal ribbons, and said: 'Are they still fake?'

'No,' the man gasped. 'They are real.'

From the Rue de Provence we went on to a popular ballroom where everybody changed partners as they danced, and I was afraid I might lose my companions. And so the night disappeared hysterically, incredibly.

Towards dawn the boys remembered they had to report back, and we took the jeep to the rendezvous—a funeral parlour with an adjoining garage where the hearses were stored.

'Let's have an hour or two's sleep somewhere,' Antoine proposed. He climbed into a hearse, and said: 'Let's sleep here.' We all curled up but I had trouble sleeping because the woollen funeral robes scratched the skin of my cheek.

The next day, anxious about the children, I returned to St. Leu. It was a lovely warm August day. Didier was making sandcastles which Caterine smashed with her little fists. She was a pretty child with heavy blond curls and blue eyes, a miniature of the beautiful girl she is today. Didier was furious at the destruction of his sand-castles, so I sat on the sand with them and showed Caterine how, by fetching her brother little stones, twigs and leaves, she could be constructive. The peace and quiet of being with my children in the garden was a joy after the hysteria of the liberation.

Gilles was breathing normally and I knew he would soon recover.

One of my first calls was on the village chemist—a flamboyant character whose name, Jeanbel de la Hussaire, would have been more appropriate for one of the Three Musketeers.

His clothes were elegantly outlandish, like an old and degenerate Marquis who had seen better days. He wore very natty beige wool trousers with black piping down the sides, white silk waistcoats, black jackets and an extraordinary affair of several ribbons tied in fluffy bows and fastened at his neck with a horseshoe-shaped gold pin. He was also deaf and shortsighted, and whispered all his conversations into my hair.

The reason for my visit was to get medicine for Gilles. The shop was an old-fashioned dispensary with a large glass bowl of green fluid in one window and a similar bowl of red fluid in the other. The dark-green shop-front faced the market square, on either side of which were ranged the town hall, the school and several other small buildings.

A piercing scream, which even the chemist heard, brought me running to the shop entrance. The square, in which a big crowd might normally have numbered 150 people, was now tightly jammed with at least a thousand. On tiptoe we could see that on the steps of the town hall someone was shaving the head of a woman. Other women were being shoved through the crowd, and the man on the town hall steps was waving a pair of sheep shears. I had never before seen women so roughly handled.

The crowd cursed the women as collaborators with the Germans. At the same time, several villagers ran up the steps and tore at the women's clothing until they were completely naked. A man with a brush dipped in tar painted swastikas on them, back and front, and the victims were spat upon and struck by stones.

I saw a young girl holding a baby in her arms, whom I recognised as one of my neighbours. She was hauled up the steps, with her husband struggling to free her. He was also a young man, but he wore in his lapel the ribbon of the Légion d'Honneur and also the Croix de Guerre for distinguished services to France. How the girl maintained her dignity in that situation I do not know. But she stood there, cradling her baby and weeping softly, while her husband pleaded with the crowd.

'I have been decorated for fighting Germans,' he said. 'Have respect for these medals won in defence of French soil. This is my wife. This is my child.'

But the mob drowned out his voice. A couple of men pinned his arms while another man shaved his wife's long hair, which he threw into the baby's face. The infant awoke and began to cry. It was more than I could stand. I fought my way across the town square, mounted the steps, and shouted.

'You simply cannot do that. What has the baby done that you want him to live with shame all his life?'

Then the people, the same ones who had closed their shutters a week earlier because they thought I was going to be executed, turned on me, jeering: 'Why don't you have your head shaved in her place?'

'I will,' I said, 'if that is what you think you want to do.'

There was a pause, and I could feel the anger of the crowd beginning to ebb. The mayor ordered all the women to be released. The young girl and her husband thanked me. She had been a student in Germany before the war, and one of the boys she had studied with had visited her in his German uniform.

Depressed by the savagery and stupidity of the mob, I returned to Paris. I spent most of my time at the Hotel Lutétia on the Left Bank which had become a clearing-house for information on concentration camps, and a reception centre for returning Frenchmen. The news from the front was so vague and contradictory that people waited all day to question the returning men themselves.

The returning prisoners wore grey and blue pyjamas with numbers on the pockets and numbers tattooed on their arms. From time to time someone would identify a group of men as from a particular camp, and crowds of anxious relatives and friends would jostle about them, begging for news of a father or brother or son.

Only too often one of the prisoners would reply: 'Yes, I knew him. He's dead.'

I saw people faint, fall into a frenzy of despair, literally tear at their hair in grief.

All the time I was at the Lutétia I was obsessed by a premonition I had in a dream. I was once again at the church of St. Pierre at the wedding of Michel's sister, Françoise. I saw the whole marriage ceremony again—flowers, smiling people, pretty dresses. Then the organ played Mendelssohn's wedding march, and I turned to watch the bride and bridegroom coming down the aisle. Instead I saw Michel. He looked ill. Terribly ill. He was coughing. Grouped around him were his friends of the Resistance. He was so weak they had to help him along, and suddenly he stopped moving and lay down. I knew then—months before we got the official word—that Michel was dead.

One night I arranged to go to the Comédie Française with Mamy and two of her sons, Antoine and Christian, to see 'Antony and Cleopatra'. The young men arrived ahead of their mother at my apartment on the Faubourg St. Honoré, and I knew from the restless way they paced the room that something was wrong. They would not talk about it but I became so insistent they said they would tell me all they knew.

At that moment the maid announced Mamy, and the boys signalled me to be quiet. I sat through the entire play digging my nails into my palms without seeing or hearing. Mamy spoke to me two or three times, and I tried to smile for her sake.

After the play the boys took their mother home and then went back with me to my apartment. And there Antoine revealed what was worrying them. He said he had spoken to a returned prisoner who had seen someone wearing Michel's cashmere sweater.

This almost certainly meant that Michel was dead, although as we had heard earlier that he was in the infirmary, it was just possible that the sweater had been taken from him while he was ill and that he had recovered.

We desperately wanted to believe in this possibility; none of us really did. I could not keep myself from crying and Antoine told Christian to stay with me while he returned home so that Mamy would not become suspicious. Christian said it was a time to believe in God. And I wept and said I could not believe in a God who let things happen that way.

I went back to St. Leu next morning, and a few days later Antoine and Christian came out to tell me they had received official confirmation that Michel had died on January 22, 1945. He was 24 years old. They had to go back to Paris to take care of Mamy, who was ill with grief.

When they went, I started to cry. I cried for four days. I could not sleep. I could not stop the tears. I lay awake all night, listening to the leaves of the poplar trees in the garden sighing as they wept with me.

For weeks I resented everything. The sun had no right to shine, nor the birds to sing. It was May and beautiful, but I felt it should be winter—cold, rainy and miserable.

I belonged to Michel and I, too, felt dead.

I did not want to live.

16   *Anyes*

GENTLE, SENSITIVE MAURICE, the baker's nephew, came to speak to me when he was not helping his uncle to bake the bread. He had come from somewhere in the north to escape the S.T.O. (Service du Travail Obligatoire—forced labour as instigated by the Germans). He was educated and perceptive.

After he had not seen me for a few days and heard of Michel's death, he sent a touching, beautiful letter about living. It was exactly what I needed, and now I felt it my duty to put my head under the cold water and face reality.

I sat in the garden with the children. They were jumping with joy because the black cherries were ripe. I took a basket and a double ladder, and soon they were transformed into cherry-stained golliwogs.

The positive side of my nature took over, and I occupied myself by collecting 14 kilos of cherries and reducing them to a sugarless jam.

Without even being noticed, Maurice had entered the garden and begun helping us to remove the stones. He sat beside me and spoke of hope, the beauty of nature and the God-given fruit. In his simple honest way, he took me out of my utter despair.

Michel's brothers and Mamy, that wonderful human being, did their best to relieve my agony through the months and years after Michel's death.

Mamy put Michel's room aside for me in their apartment, so that I would always have a place whenever I wanted to stay with them.

[108]

I loved to be in that room. It comforted me and I felt near Michel.

I knew I had to survive mentally and physically. Now I had three children who needed me. Didier was then five and a bright little boy. Caterine was nearly three, a mass of golden curls framing her blue eyes. I bought her a tiny white fur coat, and my grandmother exclaimed that she looked like one of the angels carved on the Cathedral of Strasbourg.

Gilles was still too thin but his smiling good nature made him an attractive child. Anyes, my fourth child, was to be born on December 7, 1945, a lovely baby with huge blue eyes and long dark lashes—smiling and tranquil.

By the time Anyes was born, I had become thoroughly used to having children. It was during the afternoon when I suddenly felt a little strange, and I thought to myself: 'Oh the baby is coming.'

And once again I packed my bag and went to the clinic. The doctors said that the baby would arrive in three days. I insisted that it was going to be born sooner, and they could not be bothered to argue.

'They all say that,' the tired nurse commented. 'Now please get into bed.'

A tray with my dinner of veal and endives arrived. I knew that the baby was coming closer and closer. I was about to have my first mouthful when I told the nurse that she had better call the midwife, who was just like the nurse in insisting, slightly angrily, that I was imagining things.

But as she swept away my tray to prove how wrong I was, she screamed:

'The baby *is* coming. You must cough or laugh to stop the labour.'

And of course I laughed, because the way she rushed about, demanding that the nurse fetch her sterile hat and her white blouse, made me hysterical, as did the fact that, because she was in a hurry, she pulled everything on the wrong way.

I was still laughing when Anyes was born. I remember asking them not to take away my veal and endives, as I would finish them. And I did!

I had a marvellous nanny so I was able to spend a great deal of time thinking of my future and what I would do with it.

The building in the Faubourg St. Honoré, where we had moved in 1942 after Caterine's birth, had a strange atmosphere. It was like a castle, with various members of my husband's family occupying each floor, except for the top where all the maids were dumped in the cold.

When I married, my mother gave me a cook. I had learnt a great deal in the convent about algebra, Latin and Greek, making tapestries and the lives of the saints, but I was not taught to boil an egg.

In those days a girl of good family simply did not enter the kitchen. It was not done. So it was a double tragedy a few months later when Louise fell downstairs, broke her hip and had to go to hospital shortly before lunch.

I will never forget the first meal I ever prepared by myself. It was a catastrophe. Looking in the cupboard, I found some lentils, which are so good prepared with smoked sausages and ham or pheasant. I washed them, put a lot of butter into the frying-pan, and put the lentils into the butter. Henri arrived to find me wondering what had gone wrong.

The next morning I went shopping and told the dairywoman of my misfortune. She said one of her customers had a 16-year-old niece up from the country for three weeks or so, and the girl would be able to help me with the washing up and the peeling of vegetables and other kitchen chores.

I liked the girl immediately—a redhead with glowing white skin, named Geneviève. She did not know much more about cooking than I, but we decided to learn together, and with the help of Tante Marie's cookery book and patience, she became fabulous. Thus began the interest I have in cooking today.

An American who once lunched on cold bison pie at Woburn Abbey said that what impressed him most on a return visit some years later, after my marriage to Ian, was that the food had become so superb.

Geneviève matured into a young woman who was almost a second mother to the children. They adored her. She was also the only one who was able to come to terms with Henri, whose un-intentionally brusque manner cost me one governess after another. As time went by Geneviève adopted my hair-do, my reading habits, my clothing styles, and even spoke like me on the tele-phone. Her puppy fat melted away, revealing a most attractive figure, and I discovered one day that my friends—the male ones—were taking her out!

One night I was having dinner with a friend at the Tour d'Argent, when he said:

'Don't look around. Your cook is at the table behind you.

Later I glanced back and there was Geneviève, chic in a black dress, with one of the Italian delegates to UNESCO.

It was a pleasant shock for visitors to find in my house an intelligent young woman reading Schopenhauer, and to discover she was the cook.

I lost Geneviève when I went to live in England. After three months in Britain she found she could not adjust to the climate, which she considered only slightly less chilly than the British themselves. I must say that at first I agreed with her.

The British take a long time to accept foreigners. First there is a period of suspicion and study, which in my case lasted about two years. I had the feeling people were anxiously examining me, wondering what I might do. After all, I was French! Perhaps they thought I might break into a can-can.

After my two years' probation they must have thought I was all right, because they started to invite me to dinners and parties at their homes. And now I have many, many friends.

Only the width of the Channel divides my native land and my adopted country, yet there are great differences in outlook. In France people are always extremely friendly and they are always happy to see you. They may not take you into their homes, but this is only because they consider they are doing you a greater honour to entertain you in some magic bistro they may have dis-covered. Home is the kind of place you take an aunt from the provinces or the godmother of the children. This sometimes con-fuses the English and the Americans who entertain at home be-cause they do not have family bistros as in France, and whose restaurants are used mainly by businessmen or rich people. The French are often misunderstood on this account.

The apartment in the Faubourg St. Honoré was huge, with 27 windows and many rooms overlooking three different streets. I furnished and decorated it with love and care, mainly from the very generous allowance my father had given me from the time of my marriage. For the children I wanted comfort and cupboards, and I decorated their rooms to suit their personalities.

I chose blue toile de jouy, modelled after the Trianon of Marie Antoinette, for the girls. My grandmother sent from her country house my two eighteenth-century mahogany beds, which I placed in an alcove, from the top of which fell curtains and ruffles. For the boys I designed one room like a cabin of a boat, and the other in Scottish style with tartan curtains and furniture.

I decided to do a room for myself, and I had French craftsmen instal an eighteenth-century boiserie bibliothèque for my collection of books. An artist spent weeks painting the entire story of Paul and Virginie on the walls around my bed. I also brought back tiles from Pompeii for the bathroom. I never actually lived in the room, because I left the house before it was finished. It was a lovely place and it was a great pity I was never to be happy there.

Adapting myself to peace was not easy. There were still echoes of the war—some sad, some amusing. Just after liberation day, when I commuted between Paris and St. Leu every day, I was cycling to the Gare du Nord to catch a train. I turned right at a red light. A few hundred yards further on, two policemen on motor cycles stopped me and said I had gone through the light. I asked them please to let me go as I had a train to catch and, in any event, I had made a perfectly proper right turn.

They demanded my identity papers and, furious that I would now miss my train, I stormed:

'What's the matter with you? There are still spies with machine-guns shooting at people from rooftops, and all you can do is run after a girl in a summer dress in the street. Why don't you chase Germans?'

'So you don't like the police, eh?' said one of them.

'Let's go to the commissariat.'

At the district headquarters of the police, I was accused of refusing to produce my identity papers, and put into an enclosure made of chicken-coop wire to await my turn while they called the station roll.

I was still seething, and I shouted that the police might also better spend their time cleaning the dirty windows of their headquarters than arresting honest citizens with trains to catch. The commissaire threatened to keep me overnight, and I replied that I could not get another train until morning anyway, so I might as well spend the night there.

Then I noticed I was not alone. Also in the cell was a man arrested for stealing from his boss, and two 'ladies of the night', picked up for operating in broad daylight. At first they abused me in rich, coarse language because I was not a member of their profession.

There were also four motorbikes parked in the cell, each with a horn. I suggested to my cell-mates that every time the commissaire called a name on the roll, we should toot the horns so that he could not hear whether the policeman was present. The male prisoner was too frightened and instead pushed a bit of paper into my pocket. I left it there.

The girls were bolder and thought it a great idea, and we sounded the horns until, by the tenth name, the chief gendarme was purple and exploding with rage.

He stopped the roll-call, came to the cell, and snarled at me:
'Get out of here.'
I said:
'No, I am quite happy. I will stay.'
He turned to two of his biggest policemen and said:
'Throw her out into the street.'
So I went.
On the piece of paper was written a message:
'Go and see my mother and tell her to bring me some blankets, biscuits and some red wine.' The address was indicated.
I went to see the woman.
'I am a friend, and I have some bad news for you,' I said.
I looked at that wretched, desperate face. She was so obviously

expecting bad news. Her son must have been habitually in and out of jail. I spent an hour trying to comfort the old woman.

Naturally after my prison scene, the commissaire de police was not likely to forget my face—nor I his. Not even after a considerable passage of time, as I discovered when Henri took me with a party of friends to the horse-racing classic, the Grand Prix, a year later. When we arrived at the enclosure, a policeman on duty there stiffened. There was an awful moment of mutual recognition.

It was my commissaire!

'Aha,' he said, ignoring the rest of my party, 'you're much quieter than when you were in jail.'

Our friends were excited at the news that I was a jailbird, for I had not told the story of the arrest to anyone. Now I was standing there, in my big white hat and garden party dress, blushing in my effort to explain. My friends thought the incident very amusing indeed, but Henri was stern, even when the commissaire de police, laughing even louder than they, gasped:

'Well, I've had my revenge on you at last for the day you made my life so impossible.'

At this time I had word that one of my friends—I will call him Paul—who had left France at the beginning of the war to enrol in the Royal Air Force, was now returning. During the war I learnt that his entire family—his father who was a rabbi, his mother, two sisters, an aunt, an uncle, a cousin and his grandparents—had been taken from where they lived in the eighteenth arrondissement and sent to Ravensbruck. I had made enquiries about their fate, and discovered that the entire family had been killed in the mass slaughter of the Jews.

Now Paul was returning. He did not know of the tragedy, and I felt that at least one friend should be there to meet him and break the news. He embraced me at the airport and looked eagerly around. He asked: 'Where is the family?'

I said: 'Let's go to my place. I want to talk to you.'

'Where is my family?' Paul insisted, his eyes still searching the reception building.

He allowed me, perhaps half-suspecting that something was

wrong, to lead him to my car. As we drove through the Faubourg
St. Honoré, I held his hands and said: 'Paul, you know why I have
come to meet you in place of your family?'

I will never forget his eyes, tormented by a fear he did not dare
express. We drove in silence for a while. He almost whispered the
word: 'Dead.' It was not a question.

I said: 'Ravensbrück.'

'Everybody?'

I nodded.

For long minutes the car wove through the heavy traffic, and
then Paul began to sob. A sob. A pause. Another sob. And then
this man, his chest ablaze with ribbons for his bravery, bent over
almost in two, his head in his lap, and wept with all the heart-
break of a little child. There was nothing anyone could do about
it. Nothing.

I sat silent at his side until I stopped the car in front of my house.
Paul raised his head.

'I do not want to go in,' he said.

I directed the driver to go to the Bois, and for two hours we
circled through the woods and beside the lake. And all the time
Paul sobbed. I could not find any words that would help.

Paul raised his head again.

'Can I go to my own place?' he asked.

I drove him to his apartment and he turned to me and said:

'I would like to be alone.'

For a terrible moment I wondered whether it would be safe to
leave him alone. I asked him to come to my place. He shook his
head.

'I would rather be alone.'

I had to let him go, but that night I drove over to his apartment
and I rang the bell and went in. He was sitting there, a beautiful
bowl of crystal glass in his hands, and he said:

'This is the first time it has been empty. My mother always kept
apples there for me.'

Again, what could I say? I suggested we ought to eat somewhere.

'Yes,' he said, 'I must take you to dinner.'

Afterwards I begged him to go to my country house for a rest. I tried to speak—but only clichés occurred to me.

'War is a linking of countless personal tragedies. There is nothing to be gained by brooding yourself into a breakdown.'

A week later he was still a man bent with grief. I was almost running out of ideas to help him when I had to look up a number in the telephone book. As I riffled the pages I had a thought. There must be other people with his surname in Paris. Perhaps I could find him a new family to replace the one he had lost.

I found one listing for his surname in the suburbs of Paris.

'Let's take the car and visit them,' I said.

The address was that of a factory. Paul was shy about making an approach, but I went into the office, introduced myself and began a story that must have seemed astonishing to the factory owner. But he listened.

'I have a friend,' I said, 'who is very distressed because his whole family was taken away by the Germans and killed. You both have the same surname. Could you help him? Could your family be his family? He needs to find someone to whom he can belong.'

Paul and the factory owner had nothing in common except their name, but after a moment or two of embarrassment, their meeting became emotional, and I quietly left the office while they talked.

The man was also Jewish, with a strong sense of family and tradition. He insisted on taking Paul home, and invited him to stay with his family whenever he wished. After a while Paul even used to go on holidays with them. He had found a new family and his pain had eased.

17 *Desperate gaiety*

THE WAR YEARS not only left their holocaust of human débris but a generation of young people whom peace would disappoint. They had extended themselves, often far beyond their normal reach, and now what was left for them? For my part, there is one sense in which I have always said, 'Thank God there was a war', for without it I would never have grown up and broken away from bourgeois traditions.

I spent many hours on the Left Bank, then becoming the capital of the cult of Existentialism. Like many others I was in search of myself as a person, and whenever this happens, in whatever era of history, much goes on that is best forgotten.

In my case I was more often an observer than a participant in the desperate gaiety. Life was cheap and nothing was important.

We were young, France was free again. Morals were strange. I remember sitting with a girlfriend at the Deux Magots, where Jean-Paul Sartre, Simone de Beauvoir (who went to the same convent as I) and others were trying to work out a philosophy for a nation struggling to regain its self-respect. A man paused at our table, smiled with delight, wrapped his arms around my friend and cried:

'Darling, how wonderful to see you again.'

She looked puzzled, but replied:

'Oh yes, it's been a long time, hasn't it?'

When he left she said:

'Now who on earth was he?'

It was not until later that she remembered she had lived with him for a week only a few months earlier!

I was very interested in Sartre and his followers, and the bright and attractive Jean Cau, his secretary. I had read all Sartre's books and the bible of Existentialism, 'Le Chemin de Liberté'. We sat around him at the Deux Magots like disciples at the feet of Plato or Socrates.

I always thought that Sartre made a lot of sense. Then the group became too big, and we moved to the Café de Flore. When the Existentialists grew out of the Café de Flore and transferred to the Boulevard de St. Germain, my friends did not follow. We continued to use the Deux Magots and the Café de Flore, and usually wound up the night reorganising the world at a little bar called the Montana or at the Club St. Germain, where Jean-Claude was in charge. Another place we frequented was La Librairie, which had a jazz group downstairs. The guitarist was Sacha Distel—later to become a name on everyone's lips. One of the jitterbug dancers was Jean-Pierre Castel, now a big star in his own right. I used to say to him 'Come on, Jean-Pierre, teach me a new step.' And we would bounce around the floor.

Nowadays I watch my daughters practising the latest dance-craze. As we French say: 'The more it changes, the more it is the same thing'. And anyone who says that Paul Getty is stuffy or sad should see him learning a new dance with Caterine or Anyes!

One of our favourite restaurants was the Brasserie Lipp, which was yet to become the gathering-place for statesmen and politicians. The velvet-eyed Monsieur Cazés used to give prizes for the best prose and poetry of the month, and although he ran a public eating-house—with the best beer and sauerkraut I know—it was more like a club, and still is.

Some of my friends referred to that post-war period as 'the wild time'. It was not completely that for me, but I must admit that the most extraordinary things seemed to happen to all of us.

There was my friend the Marquis who invited me to dinner. I arrived at his house, and he called out to me from another room to wait a few moments in the library, saying that dinner would soon be ready. The minutes went by and my healthy appetite

began to clamour for food. I asked what was holding up dinner—
my one and only absorbing interest of the evening.

'Go and sit down at the table,' said the Marquis from the other
room, his voice oddly muffled. 'I will be there in a moment.'

I finally found the dining-room, with its beautifully laid table,
and sat down. I nibbled at the caviar and the foie gras, but there
was still no sign of my host. Suddenly I heard a dog barking from
under the table. I looked, and there was the Marquis, his face made
up like a dog, a dog-collar around his neck with a leash attached
to the table leg. He barked. I was horrified.

From under the table came a piteous whining.

'I am hungry . . . throw me some food.'

'Come and sit at the table like a man', I said. 'You should be
ashamed of yourself.'

I fled home, dismissing the incident from my mind. It was no
more than that.

I had begun to find deeper meanings in such things as music and
art where once I had accepted them merely as among the lighter
pleasures of life—to be enjoyed but not dissected. Where I used
simply to listen to a concert, now I also read the life of the composer and why this particular work was written.

Once I used to go to museums only to admire the beauty of
works of art. Now, if I found a painting I liked, I would go to the
the Bibliothèque Nationale, read about the painter, and try to
understand why he painted that way and what he was trying to
express.

I spent as much time as possible with the children, and they
shared in my own education, my own growing-up. I took them
to the exhibitions, and explained what I had discovered about the
artists. Didier was nearly seven, a slender quiet boy. Caterine, a
bright child, was five, and had just started school at the Convent
des Oiseaux. Gilles was two and still very thin, and Anyes a joyful
baby.

Christian Dusanter, who is Gilles's godmother, was to be
married in July, and Caterine was asked to be a bridesmaid. I
worked all night to finish a long white taffeta dress for her, in
Empire style, and I spent so much time on it that my own dress

was little more than pieces of material. Somehow I finished it, simply because I was determined to wear it. It was my first dress since the war and made of good material and not the shoddy stuff we had become used to.

I sewed in a zipper and then looked at the formidable hem of the long bouffant skirt. It was late and I was tired. I had to be up early to take Caterine over for the pre-wedding photographs. So I improvised a hem, and I wonder how many of those who complimented me on the dress realised that 200 safety-pins were holding it together!

Suddenly my whole life was to change.

Since my marriage, whenever my father wanted to see me, he would telephone and instruct me to meet him for lunch at a certain hour and at a certain place. It was not an invitation—it was a command; and no matter what I was doing, I always arranged to be there, and on time.

He summoned me always to one of the finest restaurants in Paris. He would order the food and wine in advance, and some time towards the end of a perfect meal, he would say whatever was on his mind. His purpose usually was either to tell me to do something or not to do something.

This day it was different. He went straight to the point.

'As you know, the factories have all been destroyed, and so I am short of money and will have to wait until the Government pays me war damages. This may take years. In the meantime I will have to cut your allowance, but I intend to give you the accumulation in a lump sum when my finances are sorted out.'

I had never been close enough to my father to discuss my marital finances, and he did not know how important his allowance was to me, since I liked to be independent to buy whatever I thought necessary or appealing. Now I would no longer have the extra money to do so. However, I told my father of course that whatever he wanted was all right with me. This was the kind of response that had been expected of me all my life.

My brain was already at work on how to solve this new problem. I had to consider the children's education. Henri thought there was great merit in sending them to one of the neighbouring grammar schools, but I was determined they should have the same education that I had had, in the best possible private schools. Apart from all else, I am a firm believer in strict control of young children and in the teaching of self-discipline, and in France this is best done in religious schools or convents. Private education in France is, however, very expensive.

Henri's idea of a holiday was to stay at his mother's house at Meaux, whereas I preferred to take the children skiing or to the seaside. I also liked to dress them well and expensively. I realised therefore that if I wanted to bring them up in accordance with my plans, I could not necessarily expect Henri to indulge my every whim. Some degree of financial independence was vital to me.

By the time the coffee was being served, I had reached a decision. I would go to work.

18 'The women of our family do not work'

WHAT JOB COULD I possibly do? I had learnt a great many things in school, and even from life, but nothing that could be readily turned into cash. I had no special talents that I could see.

Just before we married, my parents-in-law had bought for Henri, from an aged friend, a firm that produced designs for fine textiles and wallpaper. This firm seemed the most obvious possibility, if I could think of something that I could do to help it—and myself. One day I asked Henri if he had ever given any thought to an export branch, and would he object if I could organise one? Henri was highly amused but said he would not stand in my way if I wanted to try.

I dreaded breaking the news to my father. Although I had been married seven years and had four children, my father still considered himself master of my fate, as he had always been of my mother's.

'The whole idea is ridiculous,' he said, impatiently. 'The women of our family do not work—and that is that!'

He went on to say that my mother had remained at home all her life and that I, too, could play bridge and drink tea and gossip with my friends, as was expected of ladies of my station.

I tried to explain that I had a horror of bridge—which I had seen my mother relentlessly playing all through my youth. (I have changed my mind since then, by the way.)

I had never mentioned my part in the Resistance, and none of the members of my family had been aware of it. I could not bring myself to speak of it now. It seemed like boasting, although it might have convinced my father immediately that I had grown into a person and was not simply a female. Also I was too shy to explain that I wanted a measure of financial independence from Henri. It was true of course that my husband provided for me and that I was never cold or hungry, but I wanted a great deal more from life than a square meal and a roof over my head—more, I admit, than would have satisfied most women.

When father recognised I was determined, he said that though mine was a foolish whim, he would let me work for a trial period.

I am sure he thought that I would quickly become bored with the whole idea and be delighted to be Madame Milinaire again, watching the price of carrots rise.

My big test was a trip to Lyons to try to sell some of our designs. There were still no trains to that part of France because some of the bombed bridges had not been repaired, but a family friend, whom we thought completely trustworthy, was going to Lyons, and had a petrol permit to boot. He called for me in his car one morning, and off I set on what I felt was the highroad to business adventure.

My companion's mind was on a completely different sort of business. We drove pleasantly along until we reached the Forest of Fontainebleau, when the man, whom I will call Monsieur Jean, turned off the Route Nationale and headed through the forest. I asked him where he was going and he replied quite amiably that we were going to have lunch with friends of his who lived in the forest. It all seemed perfectly normal, and we chatted until we pulled up at a house. He rang the bell, and the door was opened by a grey-haired woman who said:

'Bonjour, Monsieur Jacques.'

Jacques! But his name was Jean! I became suspicious. In the dining-room a table was set for two.

'Where are your friends?' I asked.

The 'friend-of-the-family' mask dissolved, and Monsieur Jean, who was old enough to be my father, began to blurt out a breathless confession that he was madly in love with me, that he thought

I was ravishingly beautiful, that he must possess me, and why should we not spend a few blissful days together? I was, despite my appearance, still very much a child. I had never been a flirt, and I was shocked by his suggestion. I reminded him that I was married, and I added coldly that neither he nor his proposition appealed to me. Finally he said:

'Well, let's lunch anyway, and maybe you will change your mind afterwards.'

I think he felt he could get me drunk during lunch by mixing red and white wine. But in France children begin drinking at the age of six, and when I was 13, I could, blindfolded, name the wine I was drinking and almost the side of the hill from which the grapes were picked.

The wine had absolutely no effect, and Monsieur Jean did not even try to hide his disappointment. We had a very good lunch, and I went to wash my hands afterwards in an adjoining cloakroom, while he telephoned his office. When I returned, he was not there. I decided to go out to the car, but the dining-room door was locked. I looked around.

There was only one window in the room. It was open, but like many windows in French country houses—particularly on the ground floor—it was barred. Then I saw a little note that Monsieur Jean, or Monsieur Jacques, had slipped under the door. It announced that he had to hurry back to Paris as his secretary had told him that his wife had been rushed to hospital for an emergency operation. I banged on the door and I called out, but no one came, and I sat there trying to think what to do.

I was a prisoner for two days. The grey-haired woman fed me once a day—always eggs, which she pushed into my room on a tray when she thought I might be sleeping. I beat on the door with my fists, kicked at it and shouted to be released. But my woman jailer paid no attention. I screamed through the window, but we were in the middle of the forest and no one heard me.

On the third day Monsieur Jean returned and opened the door. And there began the most extraordinary chase—like one of those incredible scenes in the old silent-film comedies. I jumped over chaises-longues, sofas and tables, with Monsieur Jean leaping heavily behind me. He poured out his protestations of a passion undiminished by the illness of his wife. Behind the divan was a huge brown velvet wall-covering that hung loosely from the ceiling.

The back of the divan was built into a bookcase and I climbed on top of it, gathered the velvet into my arms, and said:

'If you come any closer I will rip down the curtain, and wreck your friend's house.'

'I couldn't care less what you do,' said Monsieur Jean, thickly, 'I am going to have you and that's that.'

He moved forward, and I jerked with all my strength on the velvet. It pulled loose from the ceiling, carrying down with it the wooden pelmet from which it hung. The wood hit him on the head, knocking him half unconscious, and the yards of velvet covered him like a winding-sheet. He was feebly struggling, but so tangled in the material that he did not even feel me reach into his coat pocket and take out his keys. I opened the door, and raced out into the forest. I was just starting up his automobile when he staggered through the doorway.

'All right, all right,' he said. 'I give up. I'm sorry. I shouldn't have done it. Let's go to Lyons. I promise there won't be any more nonsense.'

At that point I felt that returning to Paris, whatever the reason, would confirm my family's belief that I could not possibly succeed in business. But could I trust Monsieur Jean? I glanced at him He looked so crushed that I decided I could.

We drove to Lyons without exchanging a word, but I did a lot of thinking. I was astonished at Monsieur Jean's behaviour. It was the first time I had ever considered that I might be attractive to men. My relations with them had always been on a friendly, almost tomboy, level and I knew that my nickname among my friends was 'The Refrigerator'.

I had a sudden feeling of femininity, which faded when we reached Lyons and drew up at a rooming-house where Monsieur Jean had reserved adjoining rooms. I barely thanked him for the ride, and set off to find my own room. With that accomplished, I went to make my first business call.

My first appointment, at 8 a.m., was with Monsieur Chatillon, who has a silk business in Paris and a factory in Lyons. I arrived at 7.45 Monsieur Chatillon was young, elegant and sympathetic. I was terrified, but I need not have been. My meeting with him set the tone for the whole of my stay. I found the businessmen of Lyons hard-headed but pleasant and fair, and my trip was a commercial success.

It was not easy for me. I was desperately nervous at first. I was not used to going to restaurants by myself or being alone in a strange city. I used to walk down by the Rhône and plan for the years ahead—a good education for my children, and an interesting and attractive life for myself. I included Henri in all of these dreams. He was welcome to be part of my future. I wondered, however, how I could reach closer to him.

I returned to Paris with my orders and, to celebrate, arranged to take the children for a holiday by the sea at Guéthary on the French Basque coast.

My hair was still long—to below my waist—and just before we were due to return to Paris, I was combing it on the beach when suddenly it appeared to me to be a link with the past. I must cut it off to mark the new career on which I was embarking. One of my friends was doing some embroidery near me. I took her tiny scissors and, right there on the beach, I cut off my hair. It fell into the sea at my feet and floated away with the waves.

When I raised my head, my friends screamed. I looked like the women whose heads I had seen shaved after the liberation.

In a way it was my own personal liberation. I was going to fight with men in the man's world of business. It was appropriate that I should try to look like one.

19   *A poor little lost thing*

TRAVEL WAS STILL difficult, but Antoine Bompard had managed to get me a sleeper that was supposed to be reserved for French officers. Switzerland was the first neutral country I visited, and I was met at the station by two representatives of the travel bureau. Out of the corner of my eye I noticed something I had not seen for four years—a patisserie.

I left the astonished travel officials and went into the shop. In complete silence I began eating pastries—baba-au-rhum, cream cakes, éclairs, meringues, chocolate cakes and Napoléons—until I was exhausted, thirsty and slightly sick.

The shopkeeper was startled but practical. She counted every cake and charged me for 28. I mention this incident not as an example of gluttony—which it was—but because it was the first time since the war that I had seen pastries that were not made of noodles or grated carrots. I brought back some for the children, but they disliked the new taste!

My first overseas trip was to Manchester in England in September 1946. I caught a plane direct from Paris and landed in Britain, without knowing a single word of English—not even 'goodbye' or 'thank you'. I managed to struggle through the process of registering at the huge Midland Hotel, and then I set out to call on the first of my customers.

The staid businessmen of Manchester were the most wonderful and chivalrous people I have ever met in my life. They laughed because I did not speak any English, and suddenly competitors were telephoning one another to make appointments for me, and carrying my collection from one place to another. Life became wonderfully simple.

They thought I was a poor, little lost thing, and in those days I still looked a young girl. They did everything to help me. To this day, whenever I go to Manchester, I think of them. I shall remain eternally grateful to those marvellous Northerners.

I was living a very secluded life, and one of my few friends was Brenda Schofield, who worked in the reception section of the hotel and whose brother, Eric, was the editor of Kemsley Newspapers in Manchester. One day she took pity on the little French girl, to whom nobody spoke, who spent her hours after work alone in her room. She telephoned and asked if I would like to go with her to her brother's house. I was delighted to accept. Anything was better than a hotel room.

We went down to Hale in Cheshire, to a marvellous house, typically chintzy, full of gaiety and happiness. There was a daughter, Peggy, a little younger than I. Vera, who was head of the household, was a dream of a person—good, kind and warm. Although I could scarcely speak English, and she hardly any French, she made my stay comfortable and welcoming. At that time she had a broken arm, and when tea arrived she asked me to pour it for her. I turned to her husband and said:

'How many lumps of sugar do you take, Eric?'

'Two, please,' he replied.

Vera intervened: 'But you never take sugar in your tea.'

Eric replied, smiling: 'But, my dear, you have never asked me.

I was enchanted. I had always heard about the cool Englishman.

They knew about the scarcity of food in France during the war, and one day Vera said she wanted to cook something special for me. What would I like? One of my favourite dishes was gigot of lamb, and she said she would order it for me. Meat was still rationed in England, but the butcher managed to supply it. We were going to have gigot, my first gigot since the war, and I was elated at the prospect.

I went downstairs that Sunday morning and poked my head through the kitchen door to remind the cook to put a little garlic in with the leg of lamb. She was a large, happy woman from the Midlands, who used to call me 'Luv'.

Disbelieving her ears, she said: 'Garlic?'

I replied: 'Yes, for the leg of lamb.'

She shrugged: 'Well, all right, if you want it.'

She went to a huge stewpot and took out of it my beautiful leg of lamb which had been boiling for three hours and by now looked to my French eyes like part of a corpse, all white and lifeless, instead of being nice and crusty and juicy as it would have been had it been roasted in the oven, as we do in France.

I used to lunch in my room at the Midland every day because I was too frightened to venture into the dining-room, which was filled with strangers. I also had tea in my room. Generally I spent the morning and afternoon visiting customers, and the early evening checking my orders and entering the day's activities neatly in my logbook. I would dine in my room, listen to the radio, read a little and go to bed.

One night I was in my room after dinner. I had taken a bath and was in my towel robe, when I heard a knock on the door. I called: 'Entrez', but no-one came in, which I thought strange, since the waiter and the maid both had keys. So I again said: 'Entrez', and still no-one entered. Perhaps it was a pageboy with a cable. Clutching the front of my bath robe with one hand, I opened the door with the other.

I was face to face with a man, a complete stranger. I had never seen him before, even in the corridor of the hotel. He was very tall, and smiling. I looked at him and, in French, I said:

'What do you want?'

He did not reply.

I looked anxiously along the endless corridors. There was not a sign of life. I tried to push the door shut but it was blocked by an enormous shoe. I said:

'Go away.'

The man did not say a word. He just kept smiling. I called for the maid. She did not hear me. I shouted for the maid. Still no-one came, and now the man was smiling more broadly. I thought to myself that it was dinner time, that nobody was around, and that the beds having been turned down, the maids must have gone off duty.

What was I to do? I thought the man was a burglar, although he looked perfectly respectable and would not normally have attracted the attention of the hotel security service.

I tried to push him with my hand. Still smiling, he forced the door slowly open. I screamed again. The corridor remained empty. Then, in my panic, I did a very foolish thing. I ran for the telephone. By the time I reached it, the man was inside the room. I was very frightened. He locked the door and put the key in his pocket. I was frantically jangling the telephone, when he jerked it away from me, put the receiver back on its cradle, and placed the telephone on the floor behind the table. I fought to reach it but the man was strong, and shoved me across the room. I showed him that my bag with my money was on the table. He just smiled.

My room was on the third floor of the hotel, and even had I been able to get to the window, there would have been no escape that way. I was paralysed with fear, like a rabbit before the ferret that is to kill and devour it. And thus began the strangest of imprisonments. I cowered in a corner of the room, and the tall stranger loomed over me, saying not a word—just smiling, a gentle-giant smile.

Very deliberately he took off his jacket.

I tried to scream again but I was so horrified by now that the cry died in my throat.

Still smiling, he unbuttoned his waistcoat.

I made a last frantic attempt to get around him, in a panicky attempt to hammer on the door.

Not once did the smile leave his face—even when he pushed me gently onto the bed. And that is the last thing I can remember about that particular evening.

We stayed together for three days. He was a superb lover. I was introduced to a kind of sensuous animal loving that I did not know existed. I am not ashamed. It was an awakening that every woman should experience.

One result of this happening was that I became aware that I was attractive to men. Back in Paris, I suddenly discovered that my friends considered me a pretty girl with a good figure. All my swimming and athletics had not been in vain.

The Manchester experience had taught me one thing. I must know how to protect myself if necessary. I enrolled for a course of Judo at the Salle Pleyel. Policemen went there to practise self-defence. I used to train with them. As I grew proficient, it amused spectators to see a small, slender woman throwing the tall and broadly built guardians of the law over her shoulder.

Later, after I became expert in Judo, I found occasion to use it. I was at a party in Berkeley Square in London at the home of one of the directors of Marks and Spencer, and being tired, I left at 3 a.m. and started to walk back alone to the Berkeley Hotel. As I passed the shops near the Colony Restaurant, I saw reflected in the window-glass a man, apparently following me. I was a little worried. I was wearing a fragile pair of silk high-heeled shoes. I slipped these off and put them into the pockets of my fur coat. I thought I would be able to run faster without my shoes, and if it came to a struggle I would have better balance without heels.

Suddenly the man darted forward and lunged at my handbag. As I had been trained to do, I grabbed his arm in a hold the Japanese call 'Taiotoshi', which means 'Body drop', and spun around, throwing him heavily flat on his back. His face registered such surprise that, instead of being frightened, I burst out laughing, and left him lying there stunned.

On my first trip to America, too, I was thankful for those hours spent at the Salle Pleyel.

I had been to a party on Park Avenue at the home of Matty Fox, who was head of United Artists. At 3 a.m. I decided that it was time to go back to my hotel, the St. Regis on 55th and 5th.

I was just crossing Park Avenue and going up 55th Street when I noticed a car coming towards me. The driver, a man, was furiously banging a woman on the head in the seat next to him. Then he opened the door and pushed her out onto the sidewalk. I ran to the woman, who was terribly bruised and bleeding from the mouth.

'My husband is drunk ... it is terrible ... it is terrible,' she cried.

'Come with me to my hotel,' I said, 'and have a cup of coffee to steady you.'

As we limped along—she was completely stunned—a man walked towards us.

'Please help me,' I said. 'Her husband has thrown her out of the car.'

He was a lawyer from Cincinnati and, as it turned out was in New York for the first time. He was very nervous of the whole affair. As we were talking, the drunken husband returned in the car.

'Take her into the hotel immediately,' I ordered the lawyer. 'Leave this to me. I will deal with the man.'

He looked at me in utter bewilderment, but did as I said.

When the husband got out of the car and approached me, I simply threw him over my shoulders, and he lay flat on his back in the street. I then folded him up with my knees behind him and put my hand round his neck. You press with one hand while you push with the other, and it completely paralyses the neck muscles, as well as being very painful.

All the time I was saying, as I pressed on his jugular vein:

'Now you go back to your car . . . you go back to your car . . . and never touch that woman again because I am taking your name and address and I will go to the police and report you.'

I then released him, and he went back meekly to his car and disappeared. I sent the woman home in a taxi in the pious hope that she would be all right.

Every woman should learn how to defend herself. It is as sound a principle as the law of the jungle, for that is exactly what life is for many women.

20 *A gossamer thread*

BETWEEN 1946 AND 1950 my life developed a set pattern. I would travel three or four times a year to the textile cities of Belgium, Holland, Norway, Sweden, Denmark, Germany, Italy, England and Switzerland, spending as much time in each city as its commercial importance demanded. I might spend three weeks in Manchester, or three days in Brussels. I liked the idea of creating fashions and adored the jargon of the trade. 'Chinchilla' is so much more glamorous a description than 'grey'.

When I was not on the road, I led a normal—if somewhat stultified—family life. Perhaps not surprisingly, in view of my work, I found myself having less and less interests in common with my husband.

On a balmy spring evening I suggested we went for a walk, but he said he was tired. This trivial event brought matters to a head.

'But Henri, we are married . . .. we are parents. Why is it we are such strangers to each other?' I asked.

I had friends he did not want to meet, so I went out with them alone to the theatre or to concerts. He did not object. He used to say 'Pas d'amis, pas d'ennui' so often that I could have screamed. I told him I could not accept such philosophy.

Outwardly he appeared upset, but inwardly it seemed to make no difference. He preferred his quieter life to the fun and activity that I enjoyed.

Still groping for a solution, I said:

'I am sorry if I have hurt you. I will never bring the subject up again.'

This conversation marked the beginning of the end of our marriage. I was 27, too young to withdraw voluntarily from the outside world.

My marriage reached another crisis point in the summer of 1947. I had been working for nearly two years and at times I had felt very lonely. My only interests were my children and my job.

In the past few months there had been few occasions when my natural good humour had had a chance to surface. One of these was a dinner I gave in March for an elderly woman cousin of Henri's, Tante Emilie, who was a wealthy art-collector. She had bought all the Utrillos she could find, while the painter was still unknown, and shrewdly gathered many other artists who were later to become famous. I adored her—she was gay and witty.

We were having coffee after dinner when she left the room and did not return. Half an hour later, Geneviève summoned me urgently. Tante Emilie had dropped her wig in the lavatory pan and was drying it out with the hair-dryer and the help of the nannie!

In July I decided not to join my friends at the seaside but to go instead to the mountains, to Argentières, near Chamonix, to think things out. It would be quieter there, and I had too much to settle in my own mind to want to be around friends—especially friends in a holiday mood.

I was now a woman with a career, making a great deal of money, and I wanted to give my life some direction. Henri was my main problem. I hoped that by walking in the clean mountain air, and sitting on the grass while the children made daisy chains and picked flowers, I might arrive at some constructive solution as to how to save our marriage.

Life was difficult at that moment. The world of business was making me hard, cold and unapproachable. I had earned my nickname 'The Refrigerator'. I always wore straight suits with a blouse or pullover and flat, businesslike shoes. One of the street photographers on the Champs Elysées sent me a snapshot he had taken. I was appalled at my lack of femininity.

When Henri came to join us, I told him that I was worried about myself. His visit followed an exchange of letters in which we had opened our hearts to each other. He had apologised if, during the past nine years, I had felt he had been indifferent, saying that he realised he might have been selfish but that he had never wavered in his regard for me. I had replied that I was moved by his admission, but that our outlooks on life had grown too far apart. I wrote:

'You say you do not care any more about life, but I do. I care. I think life can be marvellous. I want to hold it and bite it. You are going to tell me, as usual, that I will break my teeth. It does not matter. I shall enjoy the taste. When I am old, I want to be able to look back and say my life was worth living.'

As women will, I brought up all the incidents of my life—the suitcase of letters and photographs and all the other episodes of our married life which had helped bring us to this point. But mostly I dwelt on Henri's seeming desire to withdraw from the mainstream of life while I was bursting to plunge into it.

'I feel myself becoming hard, and I don't like it,' I wrote. 'I respect your conscience and your way of looking at life. I do not want you to suffer, and I am crying as I write this because it is our marriage, and our life together. Try to understand!'

After this our marriage of course hung by a gossamer thread. I was desperately depressed.

The following winter I took the children for a long holiday to Home Mont Joie in Megèves, a children's resort run by Dr. Jean Séjourne, an uncle of my cousin Marie-Thérèse.

I registered at a nearby hotel and spent all day long skiing or playing in the snow with the children. It was a pattern I was to follow for some winters to come. I made many good friends at Mégèves, notably one of the most extraordinary people I have ever met—Philippe de Conninck.

Philippe was only 26 at the time, but he had already been a captain in the Resistance army and an adviser to the Pasha of Marrakesh. He had been married three times and had three or four children. When we met he was between marriages, and kept proposing that I become the fourth Marquise de Conninck, which amused me. I thought of him far more as a brother.

Philippe could paint, he could sculpt, he could play the piano like a professional, and he had written several books. He was one of those men, close to genius, who brighten their times. He inherited a large newspaper fortune at the age of 16, and went on a world tour on his own, leaving his money with a lawyer who was supposed to deposit large sums for him in various countries. Assuming that this had been done, he gaily handed out his cheques in Japan, India, America, Timbuctoo and everywhere else.

When he returned to France, he was arrested and charged with frauds amounting to thirteen million old francs!

He was able of course to sort out the misunderstanding and recover his money, but not before he had been clapped into gaol for 14 weeks.

After our first meeting at Megèves, Philippe went to Belgium and started an insurance business that was so successful that he was soon even richer than before.

Looking around for new worlds to conquer, he decided he would try for a medical degree, since he had studied at medical school for a few months some years before. But well before examination time, he had already concluded that he knew all he needed to know to practise, and he took up a medical post at a mental hospital. His confidence was such that the authorities appear not to have questioned his qualifications. He actually operated on some patients and even made improvements in treatment which he described in a book.

After that he went to a tuberculosis hospital in the south of France, and developed a drug of value in the treatment of a certain form of TB. But one of the doctors checked the records and discovered that he was not qualified and Philippe was in gaol again. He achieved his freedom with honour, and went off to Algeria, where he became prominent in the highest circles.

All this time our friendship remained close, despite the long periods when we were far apart. He would appear out of nowhere or he would telephone or cable to say that he was coming for a weekend. We just picked up where we had left off. He was the best brother I ever had.

When later I became a television producer, I received from him a typical cable, demanding a date, and I cancelled everything I had planned. He arrived on schedule in a white Jaguar, and off we drove to the country. With him, I never asked questions; the surprise was always worth waiting for. We drove to the beautiful Clos St. Antoine, near St. Germain, a twelfth-century abbey transformed into a hotel and restaurant.

Philippe had rented the whole restaurant, a magnificent beamed dining-room with a huge chimney covering an entire wall. Enormous logs were burning with scented flames, and white flowers were banked everywhere. Our table was in the middle of the room, set for two, champagne already in the bucket. The dinner was delicious, ordered by a master. We ate and drank and, as usual, discussed and solved the affairs of the world. As the bells of midnight sounded from a nearby church, Philippe stood up, raised his glass and said:

'Nicole, I am going to miss you.'

'Why?' I asked. 'And what are we celebrating?'

'I got married this morning.'

I gasped. 'But your wife—where is she?'

'At home,' he said. 'She must get used to my behaviour right away. Now let's go to a nightclub.'

Despite my pleas that he should go home, we danced at the Eléphant Blanc until 5 a.m. He finally raced away at high speed. He always drove so fast that I warned him he would kill himself. In fact he died in an automobile crash in the Place de la Concorde in April 1961. Ironically, he was not driving. He was a passenger.

These post-war years were neon-lit. Everyone seemed to become larger than life. We were the butterflies emerging from our chrysalises after years of darkness.

Another friend of our group, and another character in his own right, was Alain. His feet had been frostbitten during the war, and a doctor told him he would always have pain unless one of his little toes was amputated.

Alain found skiing so uncomfortable when we were at Wangenbourg that he finally agreed to the operation, and gave a party to celebrate it. He was operated on in the morning, and later that day we went to his beautiful house in Neuilly, and found him lying on a chaise-longue with his feet propped up on a pillow, like La Dame aux Camélias.

The operated foot was in bandages decorated with blue taffeta ribbon. On a table, on a gold plate, surrounded by flowers, lay the little toe. We toasted it in champagne, then went into the garden for lunch.

Alain was watching us through the open doors when suddenly he began to scream for help. We rushed in to find that the little toe had gone. The cat had discovered it and was bounding away with it—as with any other edible morsel. We tried in vain to catch it. Alain had to be content with the philosophical observation, 'It is not every pet that finds its master good enough to eat.'

My years as a travelling executive were eventful ones, particularly in a Europe just recovering from war; not really the place for a convent-bred girl to be tangling with the commercial brains of the Continent.

Constant travelling became part of my life, and I doubt whether, since that time, I have ever stayed in one place longer than two months. Even now I spend most of the year travelling, and imagine I will go on doing so until I die.

I was in Switzerland during the carnival at Basle, when the staid Swiss, wearing masks and gloves, pinch passing bottoms, dance with their secretaries and kiss strangers on the lips. The gloves were to hide the hands that might betray their owners' social position—a nicety that may be less valid today. I remember having to pick my way upstairs to my room over couples in deep embrace—an astonishing scene in a place as respectable as my hotel. In Zurich it became front-page news when a group of us after an all-night party, daubed red paint on the famous lions.

I combined a business trip with a sentimental pilgrimage to Ireland, where my ancestors came from. I am descended from an O'Brien who was librarian to Mary Tudor and who accompanied her to France in the sixteenth century and settled in Lorraine. My brother, Pierre, has blue eyes, dark hair and freckles and could easily pass for an Irishman.

One weekend I left Belfast by train for Dublin. Not knowing any hotel in Dublin, I had chosen one by its name, because I thought it sounded very Irish. In my usual way I preferred to mix with the people of the country rather than with an international crowd. I did not know what I was letting myself in for. I pushed my weekend case into a taxi and shouted the name of the hotel. The driver looked bewildered. I checked the name in my diary. He looked at it also, shook his head several times, and called to another taxi driver. They were soon joined by two more drivers, all conversing animatedly. Eventually they located my hotel on a map—and off we went.

We drove for what seemed an eternity, and I was becoming very worried when finally we came to a halt in the harbour. I stupidly paid the taxi driver, who went away. I should have known by the appearance that this was not an hotel for me. I suppose I was very young.

I entered. Sitting in a dingy little office was a very short fat lady, none too clean, with a red wig over her protruding white hair. I gave her my name. She traced a list of names with her finger in a black ledger. She was still shaking her head when she came to the fifth page.

I said: 'If you cannot find my name, either you have a room or not.'

'Oh yes', she replied, 'the hotel is empty, we have a room.'

She then shouted down the corridor, 'Ernest . . . Ernest', and an unshaven, middle-aged porter appeared, with no tie, waistcoat unbuttoned, cigarette tucked in the corner of his mouth, and wearing plaid woolly slippers full of grease marks.

We climbed five steps, went along a corridor, down three steps, along another corridor—turning and twisting up and down until I began to wonder if I was going to be thrown into the dungeon!

At last I was shown to my room. The floorboards were so old and full of holes that I had to be careful where I walked, but amazingly, the room was spotlessly clean, so I decided to stay— particularly as it was already 11 p.m.

There was no lock on the door, so I put the chest of drawers, which had a wash-bowl and jug on it, in front of the door.

I went to bed under an enormous eiderdown covered in red

material full of holes, through which feathers poked. The sheets were very rough.

Mercifully I fell asleep. Indeed I slept very well, but in the morning I looked like a chicken, for most of the feathers had escaped and found their way to my hair.

The following day I moved to the Gresham, and found 300 recently ordained priests jostling for positions like schoolboys to have their photograph taken. 'Now,' said the photographer, when everyone was arranged to his satisfaction, 'one, two, three, Cheese.'

And 300 priests shouted 'Cheese' in unison. The effect was hilarious.

I loved Copenhagen, with its beautiful copper roofs. One night a couple who had invited me to dinner started a violent domestic quarrel, a little the worse for drink. Because I did not understand Danish, and they thought it would be impolite to call each other names in a language I did not know, they translated the dispute, epithet by epithet, into French!

My life was once saved by a Danish customer, Mr. Dahl. We could not agree on a price for my wallpaper designs, so I booked a seat on a plane and packed my bags. While waiting for a car to take me to the airport, Mr. Dahl telephoned to say he had changed his mind. I cancelled my reservation. The plane crashed, killing everyone, including the opera singer Grace Moore and the Pretender to the throne of Sweden.

The hospitality of the Danes is as overwhelming as the formality of the Norwegians. I went to a dinner party in Oslo which was conducted as strictly as though we were dining at the court of Louis XIV.

Despite this formality, and their wry sense of humour, I liked the Norwegians. I had mentioned that I skiied, so some friends took me to Holmenkollen and urged me to try the 'gentle' jumping slope. It did not look gentle. I began to worry as I gathered speed, but I was really stiff with fright when I soared off the end of the run into the air for what seemed like five minutes.

I do not remember whether I landed on my skis or my bottom— I was so delighted to be back on land and alive. Then my friends explained that I had just tried the highest ski jump in Europe, the one used for the Winter Olympic Games of 1952.

In Germany I admired the soft rugs in the home of a business contact. I bent down to look at them and found that a number of rugs, as many as six, were fitted one on top of the other. 'Wartime loot from France,' he said. You can imagine my reaction.

In Hamburg some friends took me to see one of the sights of the city, the Red Light district. This is a long street walled at both ends against motor traffic, and lined with shops in whose windows the ladies of the evening display the merchandise for sale—themselves.

I remember one Amazon with a mane of thick, black, oily hair who wore high, black-laced boots and a broad black leather belt with two guns, like a cowboy. She was naked above the waist, and continually cracked a bull-whip. All around her were animal skins. When a man entered she lowered a kind of shutter. It was a decadent, kinky world I did not know existed.

One of the most degrading sights of this ineffable district was the all-in wrestling between women, naked to the waist, in an arena inches thick in mud. It was fashionable to sit on the balcony while two women scratched and bit and punched and tore at each other, wallowing like hogs in the filth.

In Sweden I asked someone to recommend a good sunny swimming resort for the weekend. I went down to a beach, wondering whether the Swedes might not think my French bikini too brief. I need not have worried. Everybody was nude!

In the summer of 1949, during the three-day August holiday of the Ascension of the Virgin, when Paris is as sleepy and deserted as a country town, I met one of the men who has had the greatest influence on my life.

The children had suffered with ear trouble and I had taken them to the mountains. Then I took them to St. Cast, which has a large sandy beach specially for children, and I returned to Paris without them. I began to redecorate their rooms, and to combine another flat with mine to make one large apartment. My mother-in-law complained bitterly when I installed plumbing and electricity in my maid's room, saying 'It is not necessary to make servants comfortable.'

Every day at lunchtime I went to my club in the Bois de Boulogne to swim and sunbathe beside the pool. I had taken with me a copy of Simone de Beauvoir's 'Deuxième Sexe', and was reading it between sessions of swimming. Madame de Beauvoir's writings have had a great influence in making me the person I am.

I came out of the pool after a long swim to find the book had gone. I was looking around for it when a man approached with it in his hand.

'I am sorry,' he said. 'I was curious about this book. I haven't read it yet and I saw that you were swimming.'

We sat together and talked, and I learned that he was Guy de Lacharrière, director of a UNESCO agency. It was the start of a treasured friendship.

I later met Guy in many places in Europe as his job with UNESCO required much travelling. To go anywhere with him was a revelation. He taught me to study people, and to appreciate architecture. As a connoisseur of bistros, he convinced me that the most enjoyable food need not always be found in the most elaborate restaurants.

He spoke many languages and had a fabulous memory. In Italy he might point out where Dante was born and quote long stretches of the 'Divine Comedy', or show me the patio of Romeo and Juliet in Verona and recite their death scene from Shakespeare.

He had two favourite themes—that people went through life wearing blinkers and did not realise how wonderful the world around them was, and that UNESCO could be the salvation of underdeveloped countries.

I owe a lot to that chance meeting at the Racing Club.

As a result of his early attack of whooping cough, Gilles was still unable to speak coherently, although he was nearly five years old. My own doctor said it was simply a matter of time, but I was becoming more and more worried. It was a worry that I had never confided to anyone outside my family, but I found myself confiding in Guy.

He recommended that I talk to a woman specialist, Dr. Aubry, who had done remarkable work with children. Under her care

Gilles began to speak, and, much sooner than I had hoped, he was completely fluent.

Dr. Aubry suggested also that Gilles should have his tonsils removed which were badly enlarged, so I decided to have all the children done at the same time. They had spent the entire winter with colds. It seems to be a family failing.

They were operated on at home by Dr. Jean Mousette, my brother-in-law, who is an ear, nose and throat specialist. Didier was operated on first, and his tonsils were put on a plate and left on the kitchen table. Next came Caterine, and the doctor looked in vain for the plate to add her tonsils:

'Where are Didier's tonsils?' he asked.

Gilles, awaiting his turn, said in a sweet voice: 'If you are looking for the strawberries, I ate them.'

He was the first, and I am sure the last, cannibal in my family!

Like Didier, whose health also worried me in his childhood, Gilles has grown up to be a handsome, athletic young man. Today he has a superb speaking voice and is an actor by profession.

Although I was spending as much time as I could decorating the apartment, I had a feeling it would never really be mine. I have redecorated so many places that I have not quite managed to live in that I could probably qualify as a builder or a plumber or painter. The knowledge of these trades was to be useful when I came to Woburn.

In 1950 we were again swimming at the club when Guy said:

'I have been invited to dinner by a South American member of UNESCO. Would you like to come?'

I said, 'No, not really, thank you.'

Guy insisted: 'It might be fun. It's in the country, only thirty kilometres from Paris.'

I replied: 'I don't feel like driving in the evening traffic. I think I shall go to bed early.'

Guy left earlier than I to return to his office. He came to say goodbye and, completely ignoring our previous conversation, announced:

'I shall pick you up at the corner of the Faubourg St. Honoré at seven.' Smiling, he added: 'You know I don't like to drive alone.'

I could not know that I was about to begin a great romance with a house. It was night when we arrived and I could not see much, but the English word 'rambling' describes it.

Houses have souls like people. There are happy houses and sad houses, and I know immediately when I enter. I cannot explain it. Either I am totally fidgety and want to leave, or I want to stay for ever.

During dinner our host told us that he was returning to Rio de Janeiro, and on the spur of the moment, for no logical reason, I said:

'I shall take over this house from you.'

Guy looked at me totally bewildered.

The house itself had little to recommend it. The paper was peeling from the walls, the curtains were tatty, the kitchen was a mess, the gas-stove was broken. The UNESCO man used it as a weekend retreat because it had a huge walled park full of trees, an apple orchard, and a wood in which one could ride.

Soon I was engaged in fixing up yet another house. I painted it from top to bottom, changed all the wallpaper, put in a telephone and a play-room for the children, revived the whole place, and arranged a new water supply.

Ronquerolles, with its charming shuttered windows, became my home and my refuge. No matter what problems faced me from then on, I knew I could find peace in the big house on top of the hill.

I began the custom of holding open house every Sunday with a huge buffet and everybody welcome—a warm, friendly, stimulating mixture of Frenchmen, Americans, Englishmen, and others. We were so noisy that the people in the village called it 'La Maison des Fous'—the Madhouse.

21   *Shelly*

IN 1951 I had another narrow escape involving a plane, and this time it led to a major change in my life.

I was flying from Copenhagen to Stockholm, seated next to a man with a disturbing nervous twitch. Something went wrong. The de-icing system failed, and the pilot apparently lost radio contact with the ground. He dropped down to try to find his way visually.

Suddenly, with a tremendous crash, we hit the ground, a tyre burst, the lights went out, and we slithered and screeched to a stop with all the parcels and blankets on the overhead racks tumbling down on us.

Women and children were screaming, and in the midst of this frightening scene, something even more macabre began to happen to me. I felt the twitching man at my side clutch at my shoulders, and then in the darkness his hands tightened around my throat.

Earlier I had ordered a bottle of mineral water, which was on the seat in front of me. I managed to reach it, and frantically used it as a club on his head until his grip loosened. Apparently the terror of the crash had thrown him into an epileptic fit, and he might have strangled me.

We scrambled out, sliding down the chutes, and began walking through knee-deep snow towards Stockholm. I was wearing idiotic little French shoes made of thin straps. They were useless and soon I was barefoot. It was night before we reached the airport. There was a large convention in Stockholm, so all the best rooms in my hotel were taken. As I had not shown up on time, they had given mine away, and all I could get was a tiny room at the top. Its window did not close properly, and I slept in a draught.

For three days I had a dreadful sore throat and a high fever. I realised I would never get better if I did not move, so I asked the receptionist to find me something better. He began telephoning other hotels for me. A guest standing near the desk had heard the whole conversation, and said to me:

'I feel guilty because I arrived last night without a reservation and was given the suite you should have had. I'll take the little room and you take mine.'

I declined but he insisted. He introduced himself as an American television producer, Sheldon Reynolds.

Shelly, as his friends knew him, had just become the wonder-child of American television. He was only 27 but had been assigned to write, direct and produce a pilot film for a new series called 'Foreign Intrigue'.

I liked him immediately because, like all the men to whom I have ever been attracted, he was witty and had a brilliant and daring intelligence that would have taken him anywhere his ambition pointed. It was easy to see how his natural talent and his devastating charm had combined to get him most of the things he wanted in his career—and in life.

He had the charisma of Frank Sinatra at the peak of his career. The same grin, the same chin. When Shelly entered a restaurant, heads turned and women went limp.

This, then, was the man who sent me flowers the day after we exchanged rooms, with a note asking if I was feeling better. At first I was too ill to take particular notice of him, but a few days later some friends invited me to a cocktail party at which Shelly was present. Perhaps it was then that our chemistry began to work.

I was tired and my throat was still sore, so he offered to take me home. We stopped for a drink in a restaurant. There was a form of prohibition in Sweden at that time, and the only way to get a drink was with a meal or by registering as an alcoholic.

We sat at the restaurant table and asked for sandwiches, and I ordered a grog, or hot toddy. This seemed to baffle the waiter. He came back a moment or two later and said they did not have any grog.

I said 'Surely you can make one?' He looked doubtful. I explained that it was made with hot water, lemon, sugar and rum.

The waiter returned shortly to ask whether they were supposed to put in the sugar or whether I wanted to do so. I said it did not matter. Ten minutes later he returned again.

'Do you want the lemon squeezed or do you want it sliced?'

All these interruptions were making me impatient, since I was totally absorbed in Shelly's account of his television assignment. Once more the waiter sidled over to our table.

'Do you want it served in a glass or a cup?'

By this time I was really annoyed, and with a straight face, I said:

'Will you please give it to me in a soup plate with a spoon?'

Unfortunately, he took me at my word!

Shelly invited me to visit the set at Per Schueltz's Europa Studios in Sölna where the late King Gustav V used to play tennis. A stone silhouette of the king in a tennis stance marks the spot. I had never been to a film studio.

The double doors were open, and as I walked in, I saw the great lights, 'the brutes' as they are called, the blue-overalled technicians swarming on scaffoldings, and the intent group of Shelly, the director, cameramen and assistants clustered around the camera.

I had never felt so thrilled and excited, and there and then began my mad love affair with television and films which was finally to make me the first woman producer in the world.

I went to the studio manager and asked permission to study the studio's workings. He laughed as though he did not believe I was serious. But I convinced him, and spent two months sampling all the various jobs of a studio—cutting, dubbing, mixing, script-editing and so on.

In June, when I returned to Paris to vote in the election, I went of to the library and took out 37 books on the technical aspects film-making. I saw all the films I could see, and applied what I had read. At the same time I was still selling my designs for printing, and the English in my first film report was corrected by Eric Lingard of the Calico Printers Association.

When I had completed my homework, I felt I was ready for work, and wrote to Shelly saying I would like the opportunity of organising his productions in Paris. He replied that he and his team would be filming in Paris between July 13 and 16. I telephoned to remind him that July 14 was Bastille Day, virtually a three-day national holiday, with parades and dancing at every street corner until three o'clock in the morning. He answered that they wanted this day specifically because of the crowds and processions, but the Préfecture of Police was adamant—I could not have a licence to film on a holiday.

'You're going to get me fired before I really have the job,' I said reproachfully.

The official sucked his pipe and with Gallic logic replied:

'I will not give you a licence because I cannot. But I will assign two policemen to patrol near you, and all the other policemen will think you have a permit. In that way we will both be satisfied—you will be able to film, and I will not have to establish a precedent.'

I went looking for film equipment, and it was a ghastly moment for me when the supplier asked: 'Do you want a 300 or a 120?' I had no idea what he meant, but rather than lose face I said with a conviction I did not feel: 'Bring both.' When the day came, I discovered I had given the right answer. A '300' is a sound camera and a '120' is a silent camera—and both, as it happened, were needed.

Shelly's plane arrived on the night of July 13, and I went straight to the airport from the Bal des Petits Lits Blancs, a glittering annual charity affair at the Opéra to raise money for hospital beds for children. I was one of the organisers, so I arrived at Orly Airport wearing a beautiful Grecian dress from Madame Grès in blossom-pink silk jersey. Shelly looked at me and shook his head:

'I thought you were a working girl,' he said. 'I don't think you will do for the job.'

He changed his mind when he saw how minutely I had followed instructions and tracked down the exact locations needed for the film—including a particular kind of Métro station, and a square with two benches and four trees.

In October the J. Walter Thompson advertising agency notified Shelly that the series had been sold to an important sponsor—the gold accolade of success in American television.

In those early days television production was spontaneous, exhilarating, challenging, and not the commercialised sausage-machine it is today. Shelly would write the script at night for the next day's shooting. We would hire actors in the morning for scenes to be filmed in the afternoon. We were lining up scenes as the sets were still being finished. We helped paint scenery, sewed costumes, and helped swell out the crowd scenes. Nothing was impossible. I lost count of the number of times I was the back view of a spy speeding in a Citröen through the streets of Munich, Naples, Hamburg or Vienna—I simply changed wigs or hats to suit the particular episode.

If for nothing else, that first 'Foreign Intrigue' series is remembered because it introduced the trench-coat as the uniform for actors in television thrillers. Shelly was probably the first director to improvise the story to fit the scene our cameras had caught. We developed the technique of putting stories onto film at the rate of one complete episode every three or four days, a speed then unheard of.

They were marvellous days, when nothing seemed impossible. I was not yet 30 years old, and looked 25—slim and blond—and it was difficult for hardened businessmen to take me seriously when I said I wanted to rent a studio for ten months. One of the first executives I saw acted nervously as though he thought I might become violent at any moment, and seemed relieved when I left.

But Jacques Mathot of Epinay Studios had confidence in me and gave me carte blanche to modernise his studio for our type of production. It was like fixing up another apartment: we constructed a new stage, put in new sound-proofing, built new offices. It was a happy and fruitful association, and 'Foreign Intrigue' won an 'Emmy' award, the Oscar of American television.

By the end of 1952 I was a fully-fledged producer, dividing each day between the studio and my family. I would be awake by 7 a.m., and spend some time with the children. Then I would collect Shelly from his apartment, and on the way to the studio I would tell him what we had arranged for that day, what actors we had hired and what problems, if any, were still unsolved. He would go to the set and I would go to the office. At the end of the day I would drive him home and discuss en route anything that had happened during the day.

One of the few sad events in those early satisfying years of my relationship with Shelly was the death of Borrah Minnevitch, the harmonica virtuoso and inventor of musical devices who was, in his way, as unique and flamboyant a character as Philippe de Conninck.

He came to live in Paris after years of topping the bill in vaudeville in the United States with his famous troupe, 'The Harmonica Rascals'. He was, by now, very rich—royalties poured in from all over the world. His friends knew that under the practical joker was a brilliant technician—and a fine judge of theatrical talent.

It was Borrah, for example, who was the first to see the genius of Jacques Tati. But how could one take him seriously? He lived in a beautiful apartment on the elegant Avenue Foch, where the police were constant visitors because he claimed he could concentrate only when he had the record-player turned on full blast—generally in the middle of the night.

He also had one of the most unusual country houses I have ever seen—a converted mill near Orleans. The dining-room floor was a thick sheet of movable glass over a trout pool. Guests were frequently given a rod and told to fish for their dinners.

Borrah had a girlfriend in Paris with whom he frequently quarrelled, so he secretly wired a refrigeration device to the bed-springs and then pressed her body down on it until her derrière

Ronquerolles, our paradise full of freedom and laughter

Growing up

The sitting-room at Ronquerolles which the children decorated themselves during a rainy Easter

Proud mother again—at Didier's wedding

My actor son Gilles as Brigadier Gérard in a Napoleonic film

The girls. Caterine and Anyes making an advertisement for a hair product

Madame Producer!   'The female Mike Todd'

With Shelly, who introduced me to films

A perfectionist—filming in the Royal Palace in Stockholm

The party I gave for Bob Mitchum's birthday which moved him to tears

With Ingrid Thulin making 'Foreign Intrigue'

Left—Ronnie Howard as Sherlock Holmes. *Centre*—F. Marion Crawford as Dr Watson

On the right, America's 'Mr Television'—the comedian Milton Berle, with his wife Ruth, my best friend

'Would you like to come to the theatre?'

was nearly frozen solid. He released her only after she promised to study Chinese grammar with him.

I was a guest in his house that night, and from the screams, I thought the girl was being strangled. But the next day she carefully explained that Borrah simply wanted to ensure that she did not doze off while he was reciting Chinese verbs. She was so used to the most bizarre behaviour that this episode seemed quite normal to her.

Borrah had absolutely no respect for that sacred American television institution—The Sponsor. In Britain television shows are produced by special programme contractors. An advertiser has little or no say about the programme during which his advertisement appears. In the United States the advertiser often financed the programme and thus controlled its content. If a man made his fortune in, say, garbage disposal and decided to advertise on television, all of a sudden he had the right of veto over trained professional writers, producers, directors and actors who had spent their lives in show business.

It was a stupid system that fortunately no longer exists, but it used to irritate me to see how genuinely talented people like Shelly had to defer to the wishes of The Sponsor (always spoken of in capital letters), and indeed very often The Sponsor's Wife.

One night we took one of our Sponsors to dinner, and we invited Borrah and his girlfriend Lucille to join us at one of the Left Bank institutions, the Procope, which was founded in the eighteenth century and was the first of the Paris coffee houses. Some friends of mine had turned the upper floor into a private club that attracted a sophisticated crowd of artists, writers and journalists. That night there was a good deal of television shop-talk, and Borrah was bored. A witty conversationalist when he wanted to be, he claimed The Sponsor's attention and, as he spoke, he began buttering a slice of bread. Then, still talking, he started to butter his sleeve from cuff to shoulder. The Sponsor's eyes bulged. Borrah continued as though nothing had happened. Scattering bon mots, he then took Lucille's beige suede gloves, which he washed in the finger bowl, using the slice of lemon as though it were soap. Carefully he squeezed them out and hung them over a glass to dry.

The Sponsor was beginning to look so worried that we decided to leave. On the way out, there was a table fully laid for about 30 people. As we passed it, Borrah did one of the trick falls he had learnt in vaudeville, dragging the tablecloth and everything on it down with him in a tremendous smash.

One could hardly blame The Sponsor for wondering what kind of people he was associated with—especially when Borrah also insisted on trying to drive him home through the forbidden centre of the Arc de Triomphe—until the police intervened.

Some of the fun went out of Paris when Borrah died at the wheel of his car not long afterwards.

I used to have an open table at the Procope, and one night one of my protégés, a young photographer from *Paris Match* magazine, Michou Simon, brought a sweet and rather shy-looking girl. At the end of the dinner I said to Michou:

'Your girlfriend is very pretty.'

The girl retorted in a small but firm voice:

'I am not Michou's girlfriend. I am going to marry Roger Vadim' (then one of the writers on the magazine) 'and he will give me the cover of *Match* and I will be a big star, the biggest of all, because I know how.'

The girl's name was Brigitte Bardot. She did indeed marry Vadim and she became a big star, just as she had forecast. She was 17 years old at the time! She is still amazingly beautiful. She has an astonishingly sensual figure, and each January when she is resting in Meribel, we can see her in and out of the piste, still a glorious 17-year-old apparition.

22   *'She's a Square'*

EARLY IN 1953 we decided that I ought to spend some time in New York studying that end of our television operation. I was anxious to see the country that had produced Shelly and so many of my friends.

My arrival in the *Ile de France* in March that year was less than auspicious. An immigration officer checked my French passport and, on hearing that I had only a few dollars with me—I was going to draw some from our agency—looked me straight in the eye, and slowly and distinctly asked:

'Are you alone?'

'Yes,' I replied.

Still pronouncing every syllable, he went on:

'I want you to understand that prostitution is not permitted in the United States.'

'I ought to slap your face,' I shouted. Furiously, I snatched back my passport. The delegation of advertising and Press people who had been told they would be meeting 'a charming Frenchwoman' were astonished when I came storming down the gangplank.

I was still sizzling when I registered at the St. Regis Hotel. Howard Reilly, of J. Walter Thompson, suggested a drink might calm me down.

I drank whisky. He kept me company with martinis. He almost passed out, and I went on to dinner at the '21' with some friends. En route we saw a policeman chasing, and shooting at, a bandit. I was assured that this was not an everyday occurrence, but New

York is a violent city, filled with tension and unbelievable beauty. Many foreigners hate it because it can on occasion be tough and hard. I can be tough too, and I get along in New York.

I loved the skyline—giant blocks of ice melting into the sun. I found the air as bracing as the first run on skis down a mountain. I loved Broadway with its bawdy, brutal lights that blind the eyes, and the softness of a Manhattan dawn with mists floating round the skyscrapers. I enjoyed the vitality, the harshness, the urgency, the brashness. It was so different from the dilettante spaciousness of Paris. I kept looking up for patches of blue sky between the tall columns of buildings. To drive through Central Park, bordered by twinkling lights, was like Christmas every night of the year. I was like a child in wonderland.

One night, the Vice-President of J. Walter Thompson, Ed Rice, and his wife invited Shelly and me out to dinner. I suggested Chinese food, which is marvellous in New York. Mrs. Rice picked up the telephone to book a table.

'Could I book a table for four tonight? The name is Rice,' she said.

'Yes, we have some rice,' the Chinese voice replied.

'No, it is the name that is Rice.'

'Yes, we have boiled and fried rice. Very nice.'

By then I was in hysterics, and we were all shouting, 'For God's sake, call yourself Smith.'

Mrs. Rice also made me smile one day when she said:

'Nicole, you cannot be French, you must be American. You look so clean.'

I have a saying that always angers Ian: When I am in New York I feel 17; I want to lose weight; I want to be beautiful; I want to be loved; I want to do things. When I am in England I feel 65; I want to hibernate like an animal in winter; I want peace. When I am in Paris I am just a woman; I have no age.

I have never had occasion to change my favourable opinion of New York or of most places I have visited in the United States. But I disliked Hollywood, the Suburb of Nowhere, and I found Miami Beach tawdry and vulgar.

On a trip to Miami with Shelly, the J. Walter Thompson

representative booked us in a 'restricted' hotel. This meant that Jews were not allowed. It was my first experience of this sort of segregation, unheard of in France. I did not like it—nor did Shelly—and we moved to another hotel. I actually saw two women in bathing suits wearing mink coats on the beach!

One of the characteristic stories about the place—too true to be funny—is about the woman who asks her friend the time. Consulting her wrist watch, the friend replies: 'It's two rubies past three diamonds.'

On our return to New York I met Matty Fox, and all the characters in my private gallery had to move to make room for a real original. Matty had been the boy financial wizard of Universal Pictures and had gone on from one extraordinary promotion to another.

He once had a deal to receive part of the customs receipts of an entire country—Indonesia. He was always involved in some spectacular transaction or other, and if only half of them had worked out, Matty would have been the richest man in the United States. As it was, he lived in a magnificent glass-enclosed penthouse on top of a skyscraper, and slept in a bed that he could rotate so that he could look out in any direction over New York.

Matty was twice as large as life in his dealings and in his physique. He did most of his business in bed, and hated wearing clothes. I have seen him more often in shorts than in any other costume. Once he came to Paris from New York, registered at the George V, took off his clothes and walked around the suite in his shorts for a fortnight. All his meals were brought up, and his business associates visited him in his room. When it was time to return to the United States, he put on his clothes and left for the plane. Not once in between had he set foot in the street.

Matty married Yolanda, a beautiful brunette, who was Miss America of 1952. We drove in a party that included a Boston banker, who discussed with Matty a deal involving millions of dollars.

'I'm glad we've gotten together,' said Matty, 'now I won't have to go to London.'

He ordered the car to stop at the next drugstore and telephoned the airline to cancel his ticket to London. I thought he behaved in more of a hurry than the occasion seemed to warrant, and I asked why he could not have waited to telephone from home.

'My dear girl,' said the man who had just been talking in millions, 'that airline ticket is cash!'

I made some friends—and enemies—in American show business because of my incurable habit of speaking my mind. One of the friendships I value most is that of Mrs. Frances Lastfogel, whose husband Abe is head of the William Morris Agency and a leader of the entertainment industry. Our relationship started disastrously. Shelly and I had been invited to dinner, but I was not yet used to formidable American women, and when Mrs. Lastfogel complained bitterly about our table at a nightclub, and then insisted on taking a table reserved for someone else at the Stage Delicatessen, where we had gone on to eat, I just could not contain myself.

I turned to her and said: 'Are you always that forceful? Don't you ever smile?'

Shelly turned pale. Abe held his breath.

'What's the matter with you?' said Mrs. Lastfogel. 'Do you want to be killed, or something?'

I said: 'No, but I think you are ruining everybody's evening. You are so much prettier when you smile.'

Suddenly Frances Lastfogel smiled—and she has a beautiful smile—and we had a delightful dinner at what I consider to be the only place to eat well in New York City at 3 a.m.

From then on the Lastfogels were my friends, and when I parted from Shelly they were among the few who gave me comfort. I suppose no-one had ever spoken to Frances like that before. I found her to be the kindest and nicest person. She was terrified of generosity. I sent her a pair of Dior gloves from Paris because she had admired mine. She promptly sent them back to me.

On the other hand, the same forthrightness in Hollywood earned me the enmity of the wife of an important agent. She had once been a star, and constantly sought the limelight. We put up with her because we liked him. In the middle of dinner she would get up and demand:

'George, drive me back home.'

Everybody would plead with her to stay—which was what she wanted. One night I got fed up with this performance and said:

'Give her the money for a taxi, and send her home.'

There was dead silence.

'Well,' I said, 'if you don't, I will.'

I opened my purse and said to the wife:

'Goodnight, my dear, it is past your bedtime.'

She stormed out of the restaurant and never spoke to me again.

One evening, on my return from swimming at Malibu Beach, I had a telephone call from fascinating Harry Cohn, then head of Columbia Pictures, saying he would be along to pick me up for dinner. I had asked a few journalists in for cocktails, and I let my Press agent take over as host while I went to dress. There was sand from the beach in my hair, which I decided to shampoo. I came out of the shower into my bedroom, towelling my hair, and looked up to see a man standing there. I grabbed the towel and held it in front of me, thinking that one of the newspapermen had wandered into the wrong room.

'What are you doing here?' I demanded.

The man said, 'I am looking at this camera. It's rather a strange one. Swedish, isn't it?'

I said: 'Yes, it is Swedish, a Hasselblad. Now will you please get out of my room?'

He went. When I looked for my jewels I discovered that they had gone too. I telephoned the hotel manager, who arrived with the police. I described the man—he was short and might have been a double for Charles Boyer. The policeman said: 'It's Dusty again.' They recognised him from my description.

I was pleased to leave Hollywood.

Frances sent her chauffeur and car to take me to the airport. I was queueing for the Las Vegas plane when an agent rushed up and said he had missed me at the hotel.

'You are in the wrong queue,' he said. 'This plane is for Las Vegas.'

I said that was where I was going.

'You can't go there alone,' he said, 'it's a dangerous city.'

At that moment he spotted Frank Loesser, the famous song-writer and dramatist, and his business manager, Herb Eiseman. Taking me by the hand, he led me to them.

'Fellows,' he said, 'this is Nicole. Don't let her out of your sight. You're responsible for seeing that she leaves Las Vegas in three days for New York.'

Frank, who wrote the score of 'Guys and Dolls', 'How to Succeed in Business Without Really Trying', the Danny Kaye picture 'Hans Christian Andersen', and the book and score of the operetta 'The Most Happy Fella', took his instructions literally. He did not let me out of his sight for three days. I hasten to say that I did not go to bed for the whole of that time, which was spent in a wild and enjoyable round of nightclubs and gambling, in the company of the most frantic assortment of people—stars of stage, screen, and the underworld.

I sat one night with a group of the richest and toughest and, withal, most amusing racketeers in the United States. The subject of conversation was sleeping pills. All those tycoons of the slot-machine suffered from insomnia.

'Nicole,' said one gambling chief, 'I have to take four pills in order to get any sleep. Now you, being French, must have something special.'

I replied: 'When I put my head on the pillow, I fall asleep immediately. No pills. No nothing.'

With a look of supreme disgust, the gang leader said: 'Clear conscience. How dull!'

Sugar Brown, as sweet a man as his name, once took me on a walk around New York. Every now and then he nodded at the shadows, and a man would slip out.

'This is Nicole,' he said by way of introduction. 'She's a square. If she needs anything, let her have it.'

The next day I was strolling around roughly the same route with Hervé Alphand, the French ambassador to the United States. One by one from their posts, characters with names like 'Boston Louie' and 'Horseface Howie' came over to us, looked

Hervé coldly up and down and growled 'Anything we can do, Nicole?' After a while Hervé simply commented:

'You have some strange friends, Nicole.'

It was an understatement worthy of that true diplomat.

The night before I was due to leave New York for Paris, I suddenly remembered that my uncle had asked me to go to Abercrombie and Fitch to buy him a tiny handwarmer to slip into his glove. It was to keep him warm while he played golf. The store was closed, and I knew he would be terribly disappointed if I went back without it. I beckoned one of my mysterious friends from the shadows of a Broadway niche, told him my problem, and asked whether he could help me.

The next morning, as I checked out of my hotel, the doorman handed me a parcel. It contained the little handwarmer. I would rather not know how it was acquired.

I once spent New Year's Eve in New York and wound up in a party to remember. It was given by Abe Burrows, the famous comedy writer and librettist. Among the guests was Leonard Bernstein, then, as now, a conductor, but not yet the composer of the music for 'West Side Story' and so much else.

At that time he was writing the music for the Jean Anouilh play about Joan of Arc called 'The Lark', and since I did not know who he was—and perhaps even if I had it would have made no difference—I stated flatly that the music as he played it to us that night was entirely the wrong type.

Bernstein seemed angry, and a running argument raged between us throughout the party. I maintained that, because of her family background, Joan of Arc was not likely to be familiar with the music of the minstrels of the inns, and the only music she would have known would have been the Gregorian music of the church or children's songs.

I must have argued better than I thought at the time, for Bernstein's score took account of my ideas.

23 *Sherlock Holmes*

I WAS NOW totally hooked on producing films. I wanted to experiment in every avenue of television, and suggested to Shelly that we did a period series.

Bob Cinader, our guardian angel from the William Morris Agency, had suggested 'The Adventures of Sherlock Holmes', and Shelly flew to Tangier to try to secure the rights from Adrian Conan Doyle, son of the author. The terms proposed were quite impossible for us, however, and Shelly returned to Paris.

In the meantime I had hired the Victorian costumes from Monty Berman, and it seemed as though a lot of time and money would be wasted. Then I remembered that Conan Doyle had two sons, and I decided to solicit the help of Dennis, who at that moment was shooting tigers in India. We located his wife at the Trianon Palace at Versailles. Born Princess Mdivani, Mrs. Dennis Conan Doyle had the most beautiful collection of turquoise in the world. The dashboard of her Rolls was entirely in mahogany and gold, and each knob was set with a turquoise. She was an extraordinary, eccentric woman, who padded around bare-legged and wore a black satin pleated skirt like the French flower-sellers. I liked her.

A week later her husband returned and we were invited to lunch at the Trianon Palace. I explained that I might be late, and when in fact I arrived, everyone was on the cheese course. I was seated between two maharajahs. Perhaps because of my late arrival, the maître d'hotel appeared to ignore me, and it was not until Nina Mdivani caught his eye that he turned to me, and said:

'The only thing left is cold meat.'

'I am hungry and would like something hot,' I told him.

'It is too late, madame. You can only have cold meat—or steak,' he added as what seemed to me a grudging afterthought.

The Trianon Palace is a luxurious hotel and one expects better service. I said, sweetly, but angry inside:

'Fine. I'll have the steak. But please note exactly the way I want it. It must be precisely seven inches long, five inches wide and two inches thick. I want it from between the fourth and fifth ribs and I would prefer it from a steer not more than three or four years old. And I want it charred outside and rare inside.'

By now even the maharajahs had stopped eating and were listening. The head waiter made a note of my order, and I added solemnly:

'Before I eat it, I want to see the meat, so will you present it to me?'

Some time later he arrived with a silver dish. He whipped off the top with a flourish, and there was my steak. I could see the chef peeking from the kitchen to get a look at the impossible customer.

'Good,' I said, glancing briefly at the dish. 'Now chop it up and give it to my dog.' I seldom lose my temper!

We were eventually able to buy the rights to the Sherlock Holmes stories, and cast Ronald Howard, son of the late Leslie Howard, as Holmes, and another British actor, F. Marion Crawford, as Watson. This series also won a television Oscar and gave me an even greater sense of achievement than 'Foreign Intrigue', for Shelly applied himself mostly to creative thinking and I had to take on all the varied jobs of production—from the first line of the script, casting, choosing sets, and editing, to the finished product.

We had a few minor problems. One of the least troublesome was that Archie Duncan, who played Inspector Lestrade, insisted on stopping for tea every day at precisely four o'clock, even if we were in the middle of a scene. He would look at his watch, say 'sorry', and work stopped for the next fifteen minutes. He had his tea specially blended in London. I am afraid I caught the habit, and now carry my own Earl Grey or Lapsang Souchang tea everywhere I go.

We had Dawn Addams in one of the episodes, and I remember that Prince Massimo, her husband at the time, came to the studio with her and was kind enough to run errands for me. He wore jeans and a turtle-neck sweater—which I thought a strange style of dress for a member of the oldest Italian aristocracy. He was charming, and drank from a beautifully carved silver flask. Now their son Stefano has married Atlanta, the daughter of Lady Edith Foxwell and her husband Ivan Foxwell, another film producer.

We shot one of the episodes in London after I had had my hair rinsed red, just to see how it would look. I went out to the location a redhead in a white jersey. It rained all day, and I came home a blond in a red jersey.

Among other stars we used was Paulette Goddard. She detests the colour green and made us repaint her dressing-room. She also had a horror of cemeteries and her chauffeur had to make a three-mile detour every morning so as not to pass a burial ground.

We wound up the first series of 26 films with a tremendous party at Ronquerolles.

I invited 150 people, but about 400 turned up. With my passion for organisation I had cleared three rooms on the first floor and two on the second. The garage had been turned into a nightclub and the loft into a discothèque. We set up a huge buffet in the garden under the trees, in which we had placed hidden lights, but there were fool-proof plans in case it rained.

The guests began arriving at three o'clock in the afternoon, and by six o'clock, when the party was really beginning to swing, the rain indeed came down.

My staff knew what to do. Everything was quickly carried inside; the food was spread around the house, and three huge barrels of wine were put on the marble floor of the hall. The red wine began to leak, but nothing dimmed the joy of my guests —the house was full of happiness. Everywhere there were people carrying food and drink, and wading through the red puddles into the garden in between showers, until the hall was a mixture of mud and wine.

There was a fireworks display and we had an orchestra, but some Brazilian friends quickly formed their own band with kitchen utensils. The noise, the fun, the uninhibited joie de vivre continued until dawn. At one point the master of the local hunt, of which I was president, was found in the garden calling a 'tally ho' to the moon.

By the morning some of the guests were asleep in bedrooms piled high with champagne bottles, while others just lay where they had fallen. One man had turned up in a London taxi and spent the night in it. Some decided that, since it was by now Sunday morning, they would enjoy another day in the country.

I crawled into my bed exhausted and happy. It had been a good party for everyone. I had sent the children away for the night, the girls to some friends and the boys to a farm.

Suddenly at 9.30 in the morning, I was woken from a deep sleep by a loud banging on the front door, and the arrival of my faithful Geneviève, who announced:

'Madame and Monsieur Milinaire are here. They are downstairs, asking for you.'

I leapt from my bed and peeped out of the window. My mother-in-law and my husband were both dressed in severe black. Henri looked solemn, as always. I froze in horror. I just did not have the nerve to face them with the shambles downstairs. My courage completely failed me, and I sent Geneviève downstairs to tell them I was not there.

'So this is the way she brings up my grandchildren,' my mother-in-law snapped as she swept down the garden, fully aware that I was there somewhere, and probably thinking that this was the life I lived every single day in my strange world of filming.

I sat on my bed and laughed and laughed and laughed.

After the Ronquerolles party, however, I decided it was time to take stock of myself. I had every reason to be satisfied with my career, but I was worried about the future.

Shelly and I had been among the first in television, but it takes as much effort to stay at the top as it does to reach it, and I could not convince him of the urgency of always moving upwards and onwards. I am one of those people who always think years ahead, and perhaps Shelly's first success had come to him too easily. This disturbed our personal relationship, and I decided I had to get away to think things over.

I mapped out a holiday route through Spain and Portugal and took with me only my secretary, Dorothy, an Anglo-Italian girl who was so romantic that I had to put a clause in her contract that she was not to flirt during production hours.

When we arrived at the Palacio Hotel in Estoril, we found that Shelly had flown in from Stockholm with a suitcase full of scripts. He was in a black mood. He said he did not like the country, the city, the hotel, the people, or the food. I loved the place, but to avoid bickering I suggested we went somewhere else. We agreed on an hotel in the Canary Islands—which in those days attracted fewer tourists than now. The hotel was magnificent, and the people exceptionally handsome.

I had a chambermaid, Prudentia, whose gleaming teeth I envied. I asked her how she managed to keep them so white. She said her toothpaste was a family secret. Later she brought me some, and I discovered the secret—it contained sulphuric acid!

We did not have much of a holiday because Bob Cinader and Lew Blumberg flew into Las Palmas to discuss future productions. We hardly saw the miles of lovely beaches, the pool, the tennis courts and the brilliant sunshine because we spent most of our time talking business indoors under electric lights.

When I sailed back to Cadiz I telephoned the children and instructed Caterine, now aged 10, and Didier, 12, to fly to meet me. I had always made a point when travelling to have the children fly out to meet me, and had trained them from an early age to be independent—to make plans on their own, to check into hotels and to understand foreign money.

I remember the first time I took Gilles and Anyes to London. It was still in the days of pounds, shillings and pence. During our flight we had played shop so that they would understand all the different coins—sixpences, shillings, two shillings, half-crowns, pennies and halfpennies—and I had given them one or two of each coin.

We arrived at the Berkeley Hotel, had dinner and went to bed. The next morning I called the children for breakfast, but Anyes came alone. I asked where Gilles was.

She replied: 'He has been out a long time.'

I was in a terrible state as he was only 9 years old at the time, did not speak one word of English, and had never been to London before. I called the hall porter, my old Swiss friend: 'Have you seen my son?'

'Oh yes, Madam. He left about two hours ago.'

I was now frantic, thinking of calling the police, but he added:

'He told me that you were expecting him at 9.30 for breakfast, and that he would be back.'

I looked at my watch. It was only 9.25. My confidence somewhat restored, I decided to wait, and indeed at 9.30 there was a knock on the door, and there was Gilles.

'Where have you been?' I almost screamed.

'Oh,' he replied calmly, 'I took the 25 bus, went down to a place full of banks, then took the 9 bus and went to a street full of shops. I bought myself a cake—and these are for you.'

From behind his back he produced some flowers. What I will never understand is that he had more money than when he left.

To get to Cadiz, Caterine and Didier took a plane to Madrid, stayed overnight and took a connection to Seville, where I met them. I was proud of them—already such complete individuals.

24   *'I shall not return'*

'JE NE REVIENDRAI jamais.'

That is what I felt, and what I suddenly said to my husband at luncheon after I returned from my holiday.

We were sitting as usual, hardly exchanging a word. My nerves were on edge, and perhaps this communicated itself to Henri, who banged the door as he entered the dining-room. The unnecessary noise made me tense. Then as the maid passed a dish, Henri banged the table and spoke to her sharply for no apparent reason.

Whether or not he was at fault, in my mood at that moment I thought his behaviour unpardonable. I suddenly asked myself 'Why do I put up with it?' I placed my knife and fork very quietly and calmly on the plate.

'I am leaving, and I shall not return.'

I pushed back my chair, gently opened the door and closed it so quietly that I could hardly hear the click. I went into the hall. Through the open doors of the library I could see my books. I loved those books, and for a second they almost held me back. I loved that apartment too. But, as in every crisis, I do not act; I react. I could still hear Henri shouting.

I put my hands on the cold marble under the looking-glass, and stared at myself. My pallor astonished me, for I was not even angry. Just very calm. And very sad.

In that second, I knew that I was creating my own destiny. I felt exhausted and empty but curiously light-headed. There were

no heartbeats, no thundering in the mind, only a profound dis-
taste, a desolate emptiness. On the spur of the moment, I had
taken the decision that probably, unknown to me, had been
lingering inside me for months.

Outside the sun was blazing. Inside, in the coolness of that
beautiful apartment, there was nothing for me. Nothing, that
is, that I could endure without losing my self-respect. I went
down the five floors towards the Faubourg St. Honoré in a daze,
wondering what to do next. I passed the concierge's little glass
den, crossed the stifling courtyard, and stepped over the sill of the
big double doors into the street.

Immediately all the warmth and colour and magic of a
summer's day in Paris enveloped me. I began walking. I had no
idea where I was going.

I walked instinctively towards the Champs Elysées, in the
direction of green trees, water and fountains. Water and trees
mean a great deal to me. As I walked, I passed an hotel. Almost
like an automaton, I went in and booked a room, but I did
not inspect it, and instead went out again, and continued
walking.

That day I walked for hours on end. I saw no-one. I spoke to
no-one. It was almost as though I were sleepwalking. I am
normally an extrovert, people often say I am quite noisy, but
that day I was silent. I remember walking as far as the Boulevard
Montparnasse, and crossing the Seine at the Ile de la Cité by
Notre Dame, all the time trying to work out how to arrange
my life: what was best for me to do, not only for myself but for
the children. I adored them. They loved me. They were my
responsibility. I felt I had to educate them, bring them up, start
them in life, somehow. Their interests were all-important.

By the time I had reached the end of my tether physically, I
had also reached Les Deux Magots. I bought a newspaper and
sat at a table but I could not read.

Eventually I left the place, bought a toothbrush and walked all
the way back to my hotel. By then it was about eleven o'clock.
I went to bed, tried to read my paper, and fell into a deep,
exhausted sleep.

Thus was I reborn. From that moment, from that lunchtime, I reshaped my world, my life. I remoulded myself, I created my own destiny. I refused to be stifled by convention or squashed out of existence by fate, or life, or luck, or whatever most people call it.

Curiously enough the family motto of the Dukes of Bedford is 'Che Sara Sara'—what will be, will be—a dogmatic statement that is the precise opposite of my own violent, rebellious philosophy.

I believe that anyone can become anything—at least if you know what you want—which most people do not. I believe that chimney sweeps can become prime ministers, little ragged boys with dirty noses can become great, chic couturiers, ugly graceless little girls can become great actresses. So long as you work hard and have courage, everything is there for you. If you think that you cannot fail, then you will not. If you think you are going to lose, then you will lose. It is up to you.

My first thought was for my children—their happiness and security. My two maids Geneviève and Annette collected them from their boarding-schools and took them to Ronquerolles. Dear Ronquerolles with its shuttered windows, secret rooms and funny attics was meant for children. I knew they would find happiness there as only children can—running through the grass, climbing trees, roaming the surrounding park, rolling, tumbling, laughing, swimming, riding.

This typical eighteenth-century farmhouse, with clumsily added nineteenth-century additions, had a kind of magic about it. It was a dream house. When we first arrived there, it was falling apart, and there was no water and no telephone. We gave it a new life. We dressed it up in yards of toile de jouy. I cut the material; Anyes tacked it with her small, firm hands; Caterine diligently sewed it together on the machine, Gilles glued the braiding; and Didier nailed it in position. Everyone worked hard, and if the shepherdesses seemed to be approaching too often, and if every goat had two noses, we did not mind. The children felt it was their home. They had brought it to life.

After the separation from Henri, I took a small apartment in

Paris, but every hour I could manage I would jump into 'Rosalie', my small car, and drive out to see them. There were shrieks of joy as we met. Every time was a new adventure. As many families are separated this way in the summer months, the arrangement did not seem strange to them. They assumed that their father was away on a business trip, and they knew for certain that they had me. Children are like animals—trusting.

I used to collect my apples to make cider. For years I produced a superb Calvados.

One day there was a knock on the door. Two gendarmes stood there, one of whom said:

'We understand, Madame, that you make your own Calvados.'

'Oh yes, would you like to come in and have some?' I replied.

'We are here to arrest you,' they said. 'It is illegal for you to distil Calvados.'

Having no idea that it was illegal, I was flabbergasted, particularly since my brew was of a very good quality, which all my friends enjoyed. I was fined, of course, but I was more sorry that the gendarmes had not tasted it first.

Ronquerolles is near Chantilly, and it was strange that my children should be living so near the place where I spent the only happy years of my own childhood, with my grandmother.

Years later, in 1960, when I left Ronquerolles to live in England, I received a letter to say that an autoroute was to pass through my back garden. Ronquerolles could no longer be my private retreat. It would never be the same again. But by then I had no regrets.

Every girl should have a guardian angel, and mine was Pierre Lazareff, the newspaper and magazine publisher. Ever since we had met in 1952, I had always found him to be a friend to whom I could turn, no matter what the need or crisis. I cannot begin to count his kindnesses to me or to pay adequate tribute to the sure direction of his advice. I called him 'Dieu le Père'—God the Father. I consulted him on every important matter. He was small in stature but he had an enormous heart, and I have never heard anyone speak other than well of him.

I buried myself in work, as one always does when emotionally disturbed. Then I had to make a major decision. Shelly asked me to get a divorce and to marry him. When I recovered from this surprise, I went to see Pierre.

Shelly and I had been working in close collaboration, and we had become more than a team. Pierre was not enthusiastic at the idea of my remarrying, but he said that if Shelly would take the responsibility for a divorce, I ought to get one, since I was miserable with Henri. Strangely, if Shelly had not asked me to divorce Henri I would probably have remained married to him. Divorce does not come easily to Frenchwomen.

I wrote to Henri, believing that my decision would not affect him too much. Shortly afterwards I took the children to the Russian circus. We were sitting at the end of a row when suddenly, at the beginning of the bear act, Henri came and sat by me. He suggested that if there were to be a divorce, he should keep the apartment and its contents, and said that I should look after the children. I shall always remember that discussion in such unusual surroundings.

I opened legal proceedings in 1955, and the divorce was eventually granted on August 23, 1956. Once we were divorced, I looked at Henri and said: 'How will you get back home?'

He had not thought about it, so I offered to drive him back—which I did, through the gay summer streets of Paris. We spoke politely to each other about nothing. I felt sorry for him.

Meanwhile Shelly had written a feature film script to cash in on the 'Foreign Intrigue' vogue. It was a spy story set in the French Riviera, in Vienna and Stockholm, and Robert Mitchum was signed as the star.

Mitchum is one of the most unusual actors in the business. He has a photographic memory, and does not have to study his lines. He never looks at the daily rushes of scenes shot the day before, and rarely ever sees his own completed films. He does not especially like acting—in fact I cannot think of anything he really likes except sipping brandy, eating cheese and talking about girls. I say talking about girls, because, his charming wife apart of course, that seems to be as far as his interest extends to the opposite sex. He has the reputation of being rough and tough, and on occasion he can punch as hard as a heavyweight fighter. But inside he is sentimental, and this soft streak must be the source of his genuine acting ability. I liked him and his wife Dorothy, and wish I had known him 20 years earlier.

While the shooting was in progress, his two sons came to live at Ronquerolles. Wild as unbroken horses, which astonished my children, these high-spirited boys got into my wine cellar and drank or poured away half my wine stock, tossing the empty bottles onto the lawn from the second-floor window. Another night, one or both of his boys went to the kitchen, took the tube of silver cream that is used for burnishing the stove, and polished everyone's shoes that had been left outside the bedroom doors. When we awoke, we found to our horror that we all had silver shoes. Jimmy Mitchum was only 16 at the time, but very likeable and already a full-size carbon copy of his father. Christopher was 13.

The shooting of the picture ran over into 1956 and was marked by a couple of notable parties. I gave one for a host of stars including Audrey Hepburn, Mel Ferrer, Jean-Pierre Aumont, Gérard Philippe and Françoise Prévost—a close friend and then one of the top French stars.

I also arranged a surprise birthday party for Mitchum at Epinay Studios. The question in his case was what to give a man who already had everything.

His craving for cheese provided the solution. Mitchum would eat whole meals of cheese, all kinds of cheese, and carried cheese with him on the set. I knew a shop in Paris where the cheeses of the entire world were stacked on four floors. I went there, and chose 39 different varieties. With the help of the prop man, I arranged a huge board on which I fixed the cheeses, each with one candle and a little identifying label. We converted a sound stage for the party, and set up trestle tables to hold the glasses and the casks of wine—and, for Mitchum, a cask of brandy.

The most difficult part of the surprise was to get Bob to come to the sound stage from the stage where he was filming. He wanted to go home to take a shower. I said that the art director was worried and wanted him to look over the set for the next day's shooting, in which Bob would have to jump through a window, hang from a balcony and drop to the ground.

'Aw, I can do that,' Mitchum growled. 'Tell him not to worry.'

I was not doing too well, so I said: 'I hate to be a bore but I honestly think you ought to see the set.'

He wrapped one great arm around me—he is twice my size—and said: 'You are a tiresome girl, aren't you?'

The sound stage was darkened.

'Why no lights?' he asked.

'There are stars in the ceiling,' I replied. 'Look up.'

'You must be nuts,' he said, but he looked—and slowly, from the ceiling, descended the cheese board and its twinkling candles.

The hard-boiled exterior cracked wide open. He tightened his arms around me and wept softly into my neck. The crew, who adored him, gave him an inscribed gold cigarette-lighter.

I also cast an actress, completely unknown at the time, who is now Ingmar Bergman's favourite star—an engaging Swede, a half-Eskimo from the Northern wilderness, named Ingrid Thulin. She was a wild and lovable individualist. She refused to shave under the arms, and had to play a love scene with Mitchum with her arms held against her sides.

She seemed to me to be a certainty for stardom, although she went to live with the gypsies in St. Germain des Près and refused to attend cocktail parties or take part in publicity stunts. I was pleased when she was picked as the star of the remake of 'The Four Horsemen of the Apocalypse'.

It is a wonderfully rewarding experience to discover talent.

25   *Hollywood*

GOOD AND BAD, 1956 was an exciting year. Professionally I was mentally stretched, which I enjoyed. I had put on my own shows in a legitimate theatre in Paris, shares of which I owned, and still do, with the poet Georges Charaire.

Then came another trip to the United States to help with the publicity for the 'Foreign Intrigue' feature.

Shelly had already announced in *Variety*, the show-business weekly, that we were officially engaged. I was the only person who did not know.

Maybe it was the novelty of a woman producer, but my personal appearances were packed with fun.

In Dallas there was a convention of Shriners at the hotel—funny men with funny fezes. One day, on the fifteenth floor, I pressed the button for the lift. The doors opened and there stood a horse, neighing in my face. So this was Texas.

In one big southern city the mayor introduced me at a dinner party to his wife. Then he turned to another woman, and in a slightly lower tone said: 'And this is Mrs. So and So, my mistress.'

In New Orleans I was made an honorary sheriff in a ceremony that was televised. At rehearsal, the sheriff pricked my skin as he tried to pin the badge on my flimsy silk dress. At the actual ceremony, he was so anxious not to repeat his error that he carefully slid his hairy paw down the decolleté of my dress, in full view of the television audience. The television viewers were probably just as hysterical with laughter as the live audience in the studio.

To save time, Shelly and I had divided the United States for promotional purposes, and we were to meet in Beverly Hills in California when the tour was over. I was delighted at the publicity, which just poured in. Shelly's first words to me when I came down the steps of the plane were:

'I see you had more publicity than I did.'

Paul Benson was our Press agent during this trip. He met me in New York at the airport, and told me he had a fabulous surprise.

'Here it is,' he said, handing me an envelope. 'Don't open it until you are in your hotel.'

By the time I reached the hotel I had forgotten the envelope. I went out to dinner. Later I discovered that the envelope contained tickets for the opening night of 'My Fair Lady', an event that had been anticipated with something like madness in New York. Tickets for any performance fetched astronomical prices. Seats for the opening night had been sold out months in advance or had been changing hands on the black market at vast sums.

Paul and his tall, red-haired wife had a poodle called Monsieur. They had a baby-sitter for the dog during the afternoons while they were both working and another in the evenings if they went to a theatre or restaurant.

There were 15 coats for the poodle, including a mink coat for evenings, and a party collar of real pearls. When Paul had to go to Europe with his wife, he left the dog with a relative, with full instructions how to care for it—what to do in the case of illness, and according to the weather. There were washing and drying instructions, and of course the menus—the breast of chicken had to be cut into squares of a particular size, and no larger.

The story is that after he had finished dictating a four-page foolscap memorandum of instructions, his secretary got up and said: 'I will type all this out for you but after that I quit.'

I came to realise that the Hollywood I was now exposed to was light-years away from the sophisticated French world in which I worked. Hollywood both tantalised and repulsed me.

It was then that I met Ruth and Milton Berle, now two faithful friends.

Milton is one of America's greatest comedians on stage, screen and television. He used to be called 'Uncle Milty' and 'Mr. Television', and he had a show that ran for an enormous number of years. In his youth he was sometimes called 'The Thief of Baghdad' because his competitors claimed that he borrowed their material. But even if he did, he made the jokes ten times funnier than the originals. He has an incredible brain-file of gags, with instant recall. I have yet to mention a subject that Milton could not illustrate with dozens of jokes, all of them funny. Like many stars of his calibre, he is an exhibitionist. So what—he has more to exhibit than most. Whenever he travels, he carries with him two pillows in a special case, together with his own sheets and wads of cotton wool.

I was prepared to dislike Ruth because I had heard that she was tough, but instead I found her to be one of the brightest people in the film colony, where a good brain is not the best recommendation for popularity. I liked her enormously, and soon learnt to accept her advice, even when my own inclination was to do the opposite. She is a remarkable woman.

It was Ruth who was responsible for my using makeup for the first time in my life. She taught me to use a brown tint to give my skin more colour, to pluck my eyebrows, to do my eyes and use lipstick. There was a decided improvement in my appearance.

The Berle home, one of the finest in Hollywood, is like a club for the stars. There I used to meet such people as Kirk Douglas and his French wife, Anne, a friend of mine from Paris; Dean Martin and his pretty wife; Gloria and Sammy Cahn, the Academy Award winning songwriter; and dozens of others.

One day we were sitting around the Berle pool, and the usual crowd were dropping in and out—Sammy Davis, Jr. and Gene Kelly among them. The Berles had a rare cactus Century Plant, which supposedly blooms once every 100 years. The beautiful flower lives only one day. That was the day. A pinkish mauve colour, it was 18 inches in circumference and was as fragile as a

dandelion clock, but with the prickly character of a cactus. Everyone gathered round to examine it and take photographs. A well-
known actor arrived at that moment. He was in riding boots, and
carried a riding crop. He made his entrance—his on-stage entrance
—cross-eyed, knock-kneed, stumbling. We told him about the
flower. He went over to look and suddenly took his crop and
slashed the stem. The flower fell on the grass.

Thinking that he had done it deliberately to attract attention,
I hated him for what I considered to be his wanton destruction
—for decapitating this wondrous flower that nature had given us
supposedly for one day. I was so enraged that I grabbed him and,
with one of my Judo holds, spun him fully clothed into the pool.
The antiseptic in the water turned his white shirt green. I was
delighted.

Ernie Kovacs was one of the highest-priced actors in the film
business. His home, which cost 600,000 dollars with its indoor
waterfall and driveway turntable for automobiles, was the most
bizarre in the movie world. The carpets were so thick that it was
safer to take off high-heeled shoes rather than risk a twisted ankle.
The fireplace was in the middle of the living room, and the
dining-room was built around the rim of a steaming swimming-
pool, the water in which was kept as hot as a bath with gaslight
torches flaming in the corners. After a swim, we would lie on
polar-bear rugs alongside the pool while the men played cards
in a separate room—the typical American domestic practice.

The entire house was wired for sound and the hi-fi was on
continually. There was a duplex room stacked with guns from
floor to ceiling, including elephant guns, and Ernie spent $13,000
a year on cigars alone.

Frank Sinatra also became a life-long friend. He is com-
passionate, warm, thoughtful, gentle—not at all the Sinatra one
reads about in the newspapers.

One day we were lunching, and people were thrusting pieces
of paper under his nose to sign—any piece of paper, from
cigarette packets to the backs of bills. He signed continuously but
the queue was ceaseless. We could not even talk. Eventually he
became so exasperated that in the middle of the meal he stormed

out to his car. The crowd followed. And then Frank was rude. My God, was he rude, and did I agree with him! Those people would have been furious if someone had pushed bits of paper in their faces. Private life is private.

On another trip to Hollywood, Ruth Berle decided that I must lose weight.

'I have some fantastic pills. Instant slimming. It is all so simple,' she explained.

Ruth had not yet tried them but they had been prescribed by her doctor. Gleefully we took three or four and went out to dinner with Milton, Frank and another couple. I love Dom Pérignon, which that night was in plentiful supply. Suddenly I was on top of the banquette and shouting at Frank:

'You have a dreadful reputation. It's terrible, and you must do something about it. You should stop knocking photographers about, because really underneath you are such a nice man.'

I then turned to the restaurant and began haranguing the diners:

'This man is nice. You have no right to treat him the way you do. Shame on you . . .'

By then Ruth had joined me on the banquette. Gently and firmly, the men led us out and took us home.

Next day I woke in a terrible state of embarrassment. It was so unlike me to have done such a thing—so desperately unlike me. But Frank was marvellous about it. I wrote him a letter, and he telephoned back, came to see me and laughed:

'Little girls should not take slimming pills.'

He was so understanding, so gentle. Another evening, dinner at his home was composed of exactly all the things I most like. He had remembered every single dish and drink. It is that kind of caring that makes him so special.

Rubirosa was another man who knew about women. He had a chameleon character that he would adapt to suit the woman he was with. He remembered what you liked, what scent you wore, what was your favourite colour. He seemed to understand your pace of life, your various moods, and knew how to mould himself to the need of the moment. He had that kind of perfectionism that a woman wants from a man—and so rarely finds.

Ruby had a little private plane, and it was not unusual, when in France, for him to telephone:

'Nicole, what are you doing for lunch? Let's go to Nice or Cannes.'

Off we would go to lunch in Cannes and dinner back in Paris. All the time Ruby would be charming, flirting, attentive, totally beguiling. It is no wonder that some of the world's most spoilt women fell in love with him.

At that time in Hollywood Shelly and Milton were discussing a film to be made in Paris. Shelly seemed tense and irritable. I decided I needed a brief change of scene, so I hired a car and chauffeur, Roberto, and set off for a holiday in Mexico where Suzy de Gilly, a French friend, had invited me to stay.

From there I went to Tasco where I spent a whole day studying the cathedral, as large as Notre Dame, which dwarfs the tiny village of about 200 little houses. It was built by a Frenchman who went to Tasco and made a fortune by working Mexicans to death in the silver mines. Towards the end of his life he began to regret his skinflint past, and spent all his money building the cathedral in the hope that God would accept it as penance for cruelty to his fellow men.

I was invited to the home of Bruno Pagliai, who was married to Merle Oberon. Straddling the top of a hill with long, wide views, it is one of the great houses of the world. The soft Mexican night was filled with the scent of flowers, and after dinner we danced outside. Bruno was mildly flirtatious and told me I had pretty legs. Quite suddenly he said:

'I must show you my wife's legs. They are beautiful. That was what first attracted me to her.'

He then swung me across the floor to where Merle was dancing, and lifted her skirt like the sail of a boat. She was not amused.

I also went to Guernavaca where Jack and Natasha Gelhman not only receive you superbly but also have a magnificent collection of Impressionist and modern paintings and pre-Columbian gold masks. The house was pretty. They were chatty. I was happy.

I then went to Theotihuacan and climbed the tombs of the

early Aztecs. I was sorry that I did not have the children with me. They would have been fascinated by that ancient culture of the Sun God.

Didier was now 17. He had finished his French schooling and was now studying in England. I had promised that I would go and see him play cricket.

Caterine and Anyes were at the Convent des Oiseaux, both doing extremely well; Gilles was at the Ecole des Roches, where he created for himself a world of fantasy.

26   *The will to fight again*

BACK IN PARIS I had to organise the shooting of a television pilot film with Milton Berle as the star. Shelly had arrived—irresistible as always. He tried to persuade me that quarrels, like hangovers, are best forgotten. Our life more or less resumed its old pattern, but he was incapable of understanding that each scene, each black mood, destroyed something inside me.

Almost from the first, Milton and Shelly did not hit it off, and usually when Shelly had something to say, he relayed it through me. It was not the happiest of working relationships. Milton is not difficult; he is simply a perfectionist who insists on the high standards from others that he expects from himself.

I wonder what we would have done without the understanding of Ruth Berle. As soon as the pilot film was completed, she insisted that I accompany her on a holiday to Capri. At that point Shelly and Milton were barely speaking to each other, and we were exhausted by the strain. I was emotionally upset by Shelly, and Ruth nursed me like a baby, chiding me for taking things so much to heart, reminding me that life was for living. It was an Indian summer, and we spent most of our time sunbathing at Gracie Fields's swimming-pool Canzone del Mare. At Christmas Ruth and I went to Megèves with the children, and we had a happy family party.

After Christmas Ruth and I flew back to Hollywood. Shelly and Milton had still not reconciled their differences, and the air was full of tension. Shelly said that he had missed me and suggested that we fly to Acapulco for a few days.

When we arrived, we dashed to the beach and into the water, not bothering to read a sign in Spanish which warned against swimming in that particular spot, where there was a strong undertow.

We were promptly drawn under. Even with all my years as a competitive swimmer behind me, it took every ounce of strength to fight my way to the beach. I swam out towards the horizon and then diagonally for it is fatal to try to beat a strong undertow head on. I kept turning and shouting to Shelly: 'The other way!' —meaning that he ought to go out to sea beyond the undertow and come back across it.

Shelly kept swimming directly into the undertow, and went under, pulled by the current. I was afraid he would drown, and shouted for help to our chauffeur, who unhesitatingly plunged into the water with all his clothes on. A waiter was passing, and I snatched the tray out of his hands, and said: 'Into the water— man drowning!'

An elderly man, also fully dressed, tried to help Shelly but was himself caught by the undertow. I had recovered sufficiently by then to go to the man's rescue. Shelly fought the waves for an hour and a half, his head bobbing in and out of the sea, his face getting greener by the minute. Many people now were helping with ropes and life saving gear.

Eventually the chauffeur, the waiter and I managed to get him ashore. I shouted for a doctor to come to give him a heart stimulant, as he was deathly pale. Shelly seemed irritated by all the attention.

'Why didn't you let me get out of it by myself?' he fumed, spluttering water.

I had him carried to bed, where he fell asleep immediately. In the evening I ordered bouillon and buttered noodles. Shelly practically threw them at me.

'Do you think I'm an invalid?' he stormed.

He dressed, went downstairs, and ordered pork chops with hot Mexican sauce, washed down with wine and later brandy. I kept saying gently that pork was too heavy after his ordeal, but he ignored me. Of course he became ill that night, and we had to call the doctor again.

The next morning, still sullen, Shelly roughly told me to 'get lost'. I took him at his word. When I returned to find him packing, I started packing too, but he said he did not want me along this time and he would return in a few days. I was worried about his condition, so I asked a friend at the hotel to accompany him.

Shelly went to Los Angeles, from where he telephoned me, but I refused to take the calls. I had come to a decision. Our love story was finished. I was determined to find peace of mind again. By nature I am independent, and find temperamental people tiring.

I spent my time swimming and water-skiing. One day I was skiing behind a boat driven by a boy named Pedro. The waves were higher than usual, and I was pitched off balance into the water. I opened my eyes and there, only about a yard ahead of me, was the ugly, slit mouth of a big shark. I was so shocked that I was unable to move. The monster must have been equally surprised, for he did nothing for a moment or so, and in a flash Pedro jerked me bodily out of the water and into the boat.

'You are all right,' he said, cheerfully. 'But last week a shark bit off both legs of an English girl.'

I had friends in Acapulco who saw to it that my time was filled after Shelly left. On July 14, Bastille Day, I found the hotel dining-room decorated in my honour in blue, white and red. The Australian proprietor had found a recording of the 'Marseillaise' which was played so often during dinner that I was bouncing patriotically up and down like a yo-yo. Afterwards I was taken to a party on top of a mountain, in a terraced garden studded with little bungalows. An exceptional number of pretty girls all in white topless crinoline dresses with blue and red accessories, added an intriguing touch. Red and blue ribbons criss-crossed the garden. A somewhat older woman addressed me.

'Madame,' she said, 'this is a French evening, so will you give us a lesson in French love?'

Only then did I realise that this mountain-top Garden of Eden was a 'house' . . . not a 'home'.

All over the world the idea exists that Frenchwomen know everything about love. It amuses me. In fact an Englishwoman's attitude to sex is much more liberated. I should think most French girls are virgins, which I doubt is true of English girls. Personally, I dislike virginity in women; it is a hindrance.

I had been away for a month and I was missing the children. We wrote every day to one another, but it was not the same as discussing all their little problems with them, so I flew back to Paris.

It was a dull February, cold and windy after Acapulco. I visited the children in their different schools, and decided that it was time to organise an apartment I had bought on the Quai d'Orléans.

It was empty, dusty, desolated. There was practically no furniture but a bed, on which I sat and looked at the pouring rain falling in the Seine. I felt unhappy indeed. I loved Shelly deeply and of course missed him terribly, but enough is enough; when you have a gangrenous leg, you cut it off.

I had pushed myself hard since the war, and everything was hitting me at once—the divorce from Henri, the quarrel with Shelly, and the indecision about my future. Deeply disturbed, I wandered round and did not go out of the flat. I drank quantities of tea. I would not eat. I could not sleep. I went to ground like a wounded fox.

Among my friends then was Henri Vidal, the French film star and husband of actress Michèle Morgan. His laughing attitude to life always lifted my spirits. He was good-looking, virile and incredibly 'sympathique'. He made you feel a woman —a person. He was also an expert on furniture, antiques and interior decoration, and always said that had he not become a film star, he would have gone into that field.

Vidal died suddenly in 1960 at the height of his fame. He was only in his forties.

He knew I had bought the place on the Quai d'Orléans. His own apartment was nearby. During a chance meeting when he said he would like to see the flat, I said he could do so any time, as I would appreciate his advice on decorating it. I told the concierge, Madame Cute, to give him the key if he came by, as I was not yet living there. One day, soon after I moved in, Madame Cute saw Vidal go into a flower shop on the Ile St. Louis, and said to him:

'I think it would be nice if you would go and say hello to Madame Milinaire. She does not look well. I think she needs a friend.'

I doubt if there is anything in the world like the French concierges. They are not only the guardians of their buildings, but take a dedicated interest in the daily lives of their tenants, and often know as much about them as members of the family.

Madame Cute was an angel to me. Before my return from trips, she would have the flat cleaned, buy flowers, and put butter in the refrigerator and bread in the bin. She answered my mail or forwarded whatever needed my personal attention.

Her remark to Vidal was not presumptuous, but made through intense interest in one of her flock.

Vidal bought a bouquet of roses, and called on me.

'You idiot,' he said. 'What are you doing in this dusty place, crying into your tea? Here are some flowers. Stop crying, and get dressed.'

He was such a happy and vital person that I found myself laughing. We talked till he had to go to the studios where he was filming 'La Parisienne' with Brigitte Bardot.

I then took stock of myself in the mirror. I was pale, my eyes were swollen, my hair unkempt. I looked a mess.

Every morning before going to the studios at Boulogne-sur-Seine, Vidal brought me something to eat—perhaps a slice of ham, a little éclair au café, or some gruyère cheese. That is true friendship. I am very lucky that, throughout my life, I have had friends who helped when they were needed.

'I know you don't want to eat,' he would joke, 'but you can always give it to the pigeons.'

'I am not going to the studio today as they are not shooting my scene. I am going to take you to the park for some fresh air.'

I started to protest, but he said:

'I am not asking you. Get dressed or I will carry you out like that!'

I was so low and tired that it was easier to go than to argue. I put on trousers and a pullover, and combed my hair, but I put on no makeup. We drove in Vidal's Lancia for some 15 minutes, into the suburbs of Paris.

'Where are we?' I asked.

'We are going to see a friend,' he replied.

We went through a door into a garden. I was rather frightened when two women passed by, one looking straight through me, the other staring vacantly at the sky. Then some men wandered along, singing and muttering to themselves. I was wondering what sort of place this was when I saw a nurse and realised that I must be in a private hospital.

'I don't want to stay here,' I cried.

Vidal laughed.

'You couldn't get out if you wanted to,' he said, 'because all the doors are locked and you haven't got a key, and you cannot telephone anyone because you will not have a telephone. Nobody knows where you are, so nobody will be able to find you. I will tell everyone that you are in the country with friends.'

He put me into the care of Dr. Moran, who ran the clinic. I was given a pretty room, decorated with ivy-leaf wallpaper. He had thoughtfully sent along a very large rose-bud. I did not leave that room for a fortnight. The shutters were closed and the doors were locked. I tried to persuade Dr. Moran to release me, but he insisted gently that my health was in a precarious state. He gave me pills and syrups, and I was asleep or only half-awake throughout the two weeks.

Vidal had told my production manager, Sacha Kamenka, where I was, and, when it was considered all right to let me leave, Kamenka came along to take me home. I still felt fragile. A letter was waiting from Gilles—who was then at the Ecole des Roches in Normandy—saying that he was going to sing in a Latin version of Bach's 'Magnificat' at a Paris concert hall, and I insisted on going, taking the other children to see and hear him.

I sat in the hall, feeling as though I had had too much to drink, and trying not to doze off in my seat. When the little boys in white came on the stage, I searched for Gilles but could not at first see him. Suddenly, through the group, like a little angel in his white surplice and shining face, Gilles appeared. He walked slowly, all by himself, to the proscenium to sing one of the solos.

I had no idea he could sing so well. As his beautiful, sweet voice rang through the hall, the need to live was restored to me. I found the will to fight again—to fight for that beautiful, angelic face, and for my other children.

27   *'Duke who?'*

So once more I found myself taking stock, laughing at my misjudgment, and losing my private problems in work. I never look back. I am uninterested in the present, and only look into the unknown years ahead.

In 1957 I was back in Nice, organising a new film studio, and happily absorbed in all its problems. My brain functions better under pressure.

Shelly telephoned and begged me to come to London. My first reaction was to say 'no'. I had had enough. But he tempted me, as always. He wanted me to set up the production of 'Dick and the Duchess'—a television comedy series. The story was about the adventures of an American insurance broker, Dick, working in Britain. His screen wife was a beautiful scatterbrained English girl from an aristocratic family, known as 'the Duchess.' Dick was played by Patrick O'Neal, who later starred on Broadway with Bette Davis and Margaret Leighton in Tennessee Williams's 'Night of the Iguana'. 'The Duchess' was played by Hazel Court—ideal with her beautiful porcelain skin and fine bone structure—and we used that marvellous British comedian, Richard Wattis, as the foil.

I had not planned to be part of this venture. I was quite content in the south of France. But Shelly was persuasive, and when he insisted that he could not cope without me, I put aside my own project and joined him in London.

I did not like the British climate and did not understand then what I thought was the aloofness of the British people, who appeared to me to be Francophobes.

I rented a vicarage at Totteridge, and brought the children and Geneviève over from Paris. The vicar and his family were in Cornwall for the summer. I found it pleasant to live in the ambience of an English vicarage, with its garden of roses and the peaceful cemetery next door. Besides, Metro-Goldwyn-Mayer were close by.

Geneviève, who did not speak one word of English, was clearly unhappy. When the lavatory became blocked, I telephoned for the plumber before going to the studio; later, when two men appeared at the door, Geneviève ushered them into the bathroom, jiggled the chain and insisted in sign language that they look into the bowl. They were interested but unresponsive. They had been sent by the bishop to see the vicar!

We ate as a French family. I told Geneviève that I wanted boeuf à la mode, one of my favourite dishes—beef, pigs' trotters, carrots and herbs cooked for hours so that it jellies when cold. It is a delicious dish, which I often have at Woburn.

Geneviève went to the butchers, and not seeing any pigs' trotters, tried to explain by pointing to her own feet. The butcher seemed to understand, and gave her a name and address on a slip of paper. Geneviève, thinking that perhaps in Britain pigs' trotters were sold in a separate shop, went to the address—a chiropodist!

Another time I asked her to prepare cassoulet—made from pork, goose or duck and haricot beans. I could not eat the concoction she placed before me.

'What beans are these?' I asked.

'I could not find the kind we use in France, Madame, so I thought these might be the English version,' she explained.

I looked at the packet. They were sun-flower seeds.

Three weeks after we arrived Geneviève telephoned me at the studio in tears.

'It is bad enough, Madame, that you ask me to live next to a cemetery, but some men have just delivered a coffin, and they insisted on putting it in the hall. I will not stay in the house while that thing is here.'

'Calm yourself,' I said.

When I returned, I persuaded Geneviève that it had to stay in the hall until the vicar returned. The children were delighted, and naturally played hide and seek in it. They adored the vicarage, and used to creep up to Geneviève's window and make ghost noises at her.

It was all too much for her. She packed her bags and went back to Paris.

I thought I had made it absolutely clear to Shelly that I would assemble the staff, arrange the schedule, and once everything was neatly tied up, I would return to Nice. Meanwhile Shelly had retired to the comfort and seclusion of Ronquerolles to turn out the scripts.

On June 27 I telephoned him to say that I had completed my part of the arrangement. Two days later he flew into London. I am incurably romantic, and as June 29 was my birthday, I thought he had come over to help me celebrate it, as in other years. We took one of the writers, Ray Allen, to dinner. In previous years Shelly had always ordered a birthday cake for me, but this time when the meal ended there was no cake . . . no lighted candles. I then realised that he had forgotten.

'Why are you so sad?' Allen asked.

I shook my head. My throat was dry and lumpy. I was sad—for the miserable frailty of human relationships.

'It's my birthday,' I said.

Allen struck a match, which he lit, into a piece of gruyère cheese. The gesture was charming. I smiled my thanks.

Back at the hotel, I told Shelly that I was returning to the south of France.

'You mean you are not sticking with the production?' he countered.

'That's exactly what I mean,' I replied.

He stomped out of the room. Half an hour later, Allen rang to say that Shelly was upset by my decision, and could I not see my way clear to stay? The production needed me.

I was still adamant. Shelly arrived, metaphorically banging on my door.

'I'll give you the whole damn production. It's your show,' he shouted.

My inner self told me that this was a typical Shelly exaggeration, but the idea of my own series was tempting.

'Fine, I will stay,' I said, 'but I cannot stand any more emotional crises. You have killed something inside me. It is no longer the same. 'Dick and the Duchess' will be our last collaboration.'

And it was. I have always had the highest regard for Shelly's talents as a writer and a director. At his best he was brilliant and adorable. We are still friends, and there is no bitterness—I loved him too much for that.

In mid-July our publicity man came rushing into me. I was knee-deep in budgets and schedules at the time, and when I am totally absorbed, the outside world does not exist.

'Listen,' he said, 'since we are calling the series 'Dick and the Duchess', why don't we get a real live duke and have him pose for pictures with our duchess?'

'All right, then, find a duke', I replied absent-mindedly.

Slightly aghast, he said, 'It's not that easy with an English duke. I've looked it up, and there are only 27, and four are royal, so they are out of the question. Five live abroad, some are gaga, and the others would never dream of visiting a film studio. How about a French duke?'

I thought of the dukes I knew in France. There was the Duc de Brissac and the Duc de Maillé. They certainly would not do. I realised that he was right.

'Well, let's forget it. It's not that important anyway,' I said, returning to my charts, budgets and cast lists.

A few days later the publicity man came in again.

'I've got one,' he said.

'Got what?' I asked.

'A duke,' he said. 'This fellow's family goes back to the fifteenth century. As far as lineage is concerned, he's fantastic—great background. He lives in a wonderful house, Woburn Abbey. He's opened it to the public to try and keep it in the family, and he needs publicity. He does anything for publicity and loves being photographed.'

'Duke who?' I asked, my mind on the financial report I was compiling for CBS.

'The Duke of Bedford,' he said.

'Fine,' I replied. 'We'll fix something up. Meanwhile I have a lot of work. . .'

A few weeks later the publicity man rushed straight into my office. 'His Grace,' he announced, and promptly disappeared.

Before I could say anything, a tall, shy, smiling man in a grey suit was in the room, looking down at me. I never connected the words 'His Grace' with a duke. In France we call a duke plain 'Monsieur'. I thought this must be either an actor coming for a job or a salesman with a new product called 'His Grace'. I was about to ask the stranger what he wanted, when a girl arrived with a tray of tea and cakes. The publicity man returned, obviously flustered.

'This is terrible', he said, 'The photographer has had trouble with the flashgun. Could you please entertain the Duke of Bedford for a few minutes?'

At last I understood. The Duke gently took my hand as we introduced ourselves.

That superb English custom—afternoon tea—bridged the awkward silence. I did not know then that the four o'clock tea-break was one of the contributions of the Duke of Bedford's ancestors to gracious living. We spoke of course of the weather, the traffic, the time of year, and suddenly I was out of polite conversation.

The wall of my office was covered with a huge historical map of Paris. To make small talk I showed the Duke where I lived on the Ile St-Louis.

'This is the oldest part of Paris and my house was built in 1640,' I said.

'My house was built in 1626,' he replied with that firm assurance I was to come to know so well. He then began on his favourite subject in the world—Woburn Abbey.

'All right, you win,' I laughed, when he stopped for breath.

The photographer was now ready and waiting. The CBS people had long wanted a photograph of me, and the publicist suggested that now was the time. He said it would make a superb news picture if the Duke would inscribe to me, the producer of 'Dick and the Duchess', a copy of his new guidebook to Woburn. The Duke handed over one of the guidebooks, which he always conveniently carried round on such occasions, and we spread it on the desk. I sat down and pretended to read it.

As the flashbulbs popped, instead of writing 'Best wishes' and his name, he wrote 'Would you like to come to the theatre?'

I was amazed. Until that moment I had believed that Englishmen, and particularly English dukes, were generally stuffy. This one behaved in a very French way, I thought. I looked at him, and he had laughing, smiling eyes.

Underneath his question, I scribbled 'Yes'.

Little did I know then how many times I would help to rewrite and design that guidebook until it became the best in England, and perhaps in the world, winning an award from Lord Snowdon's Design Centre.

There are many things the Duke could have written, but nothing could have pleased me more than an invitation to the theatre.

I did not think about him again until some three weeks later, I was walking towards the studio restaurant for lunch, deep in thought, when I noticed the doorman trying to attract my attention.

'I have His Grace at the door,' he said in that special voice of awe which the British reserve for royalty, peers and archbishops. 'What shall I do with him?'

'I don't know,' I said. 'He surely cannot have come to see me? I was certainly not expecting him.'

The doorman looked confused and embarrassed. I walked to the gate and found Ian there, smiling as always, leaning nonchalantly against his black Lincoln Continental.

'How about lunch?' he said. No wasting of words. I liked that.

'I am too busy to go to London,' I explained.

Instead we lunched at a quaint and chilly little pub near the studio. I was not in a happy mood. I had been a month and a half away from Ronquerolles. I missed the children. It was summer but everything was cold and unfriendly. I had not wanted to come to England, and now I was regretting bitterly that I had done so. In the eyes of most people I had a glamourous job, but my life, as I saw it consisted of long hours at the studio and dinner on a tray in front of the television in my rented furnished flat. Somewhere my personal philosophy that life is for living had got bogged down. My life was smouldering away.

'You look like the saddest person I have ever met,' the Duke said.

I looked up. 'You are very perceptive. I am sad—terribly sad,' I answered.

'I did not mean to pry. I only knew you were because at the moment I feel like that too,' he said.

He then proceeded to tell me all about the break-up of his marriage. I was rather embarrassed, for it was only the second time we had met. I could only say 'Be patient' or 'I'm sure she still loves you' when tears came to his eyes. This was too much for me, and I made a mental note not to see him again.

But some days later I was lunching at the Mirabelle when the maître d'hotel came to my table and said:

'His Grace the Duke of Bedford is at the door, asking for you.'

I invited him to join me, puzzled as to how he knew I was there. He had apparently asked my maid where to find me. Strangely, effortlessly, we picked up the conversation almost where we had left off in the pub.

We talked about the production, and then in that disarming, penetrating way of his, he asked whether I was still sad.

'My marriage has broken up,' he said. 'I've done everything to try to save it, but nothing seems to work.'

What does one say at a moment like that? In any case I was not exactly qualified from my own experience to advise on marriage. We dropped the subject.

A week later Ian—by now he had told me that he was known by this name rather than by his given name, John—took me to the theatre, as promised at our first meeting. I found him witty, wise, attentive—a wonderful companion for a deflated ego.

We did not see a great deal of each other during the next few weeks, as I was thoroughly engrossed in launching the television series. I was interviewed on radio and television. As I did not speak English until I was an adult, I still have a heavy French accent that to English ears sounds very funny. It baffled the interviewers, and for a while even baffled Ian.

Once during a conversation he thought I remarked that I liked the plays of Mozart. 'But Mozart did not write plays, he was strictly a composer,' he said.

'Not Mozart,' I explained, 'M–O–S–S H–A–R–T.'

Wherever I was in the world, part of me always remained where the children were. The moment the series was launched in September, I dashed back to Paris to prepare them for the winter term at school. There were new clothes to be bought, private confidences to be listened to.

Didier, now 18, was going to a catering school in Lausanne—a strange wish on his part, as no-one in the family had ever been involved in that sort of business. Caterine was 15 but looked 18; she had a fantastic beauty that made my men friends gasp; but she was still a child and a terrible tomboy. By now she had been bitten in the cheek by a Doberman, had a skiing accident, had all the skin taken off her bottom when being towed on roller skates by Jonathan Sieff's car, and had fallen off a galloping horse and gashed an arm. The boys were perfectly quiet, but I was forever concerned about Caterine's new exploits.

Gilles was 13, and when I went to fetch him for the holidays, he had two suitcases and a bag. I put them in the back of my big American station-wagon, and I saw him in the rear-view mirror unzip the bag and let out a jackdaw ready to take flight. When later I opened his suitcases, they were full of books and records—but not an article of clothing.

Anyes was 12, and brilliant at school. She had those huge turquoise eyes, and her lashes were so long that a friend asked me if they were real.

When the children were safely back at school, I flew to Hollywood to discuss a picture deal, and returned to London on October 2.

I arrived back desperately tired. I wanted to shut out the world, take a bath and go to sleep. The doorbell rang. No one knew that I was coming back except my secretary, so I had no idea who it might be. I opened the door gingerly. It was the Duke of Bedford. I was amazed to see him, because at that point we were acquaintances rather than friends.

Looking back through my diaries, I see that in August I referred to him as the Duke of Bedford. In September I was a little less formal, and wrote Bedford. It was not until October in fact that I wrote Ian.

Holding my robe around me at the door, I said:

'It's nice to see you again, but how did you know I was back?'

As if it were the most natural thing in the world he said: 'I checked with your secretary.'

I liked his direct approach.

'Well, come and have a drink.'

I noticed for the first time that he had an enormous bouquet of white lilies half hidden behind his back.

'What is so special about today?' I asked.

Ian looked down at me with a singularly tender look. He has an almost superhuman gentleness when he wishes, and in his slow, hesitant way, he said:

'I have come to ask you to marry me.'

In crises, in embarrasing moments, in moments in great joy, I laugh. I have laughed since I was a child. It is something I know about—my own secret weapon to protect me from being hurt. Once again, I laughed and laughed, and parried:

'Won't you settle for a drink instead?'

He said: 'No, I have been thinking of marrying you since I met you. You are everything that I have been looking for.'

'Marriage is a pretty serious affair, and I am against it. Besides you don't even know me. Let's talk about something else,' I said.

Ian shrugged and settled for a drink. He did not mention marriage again that day.

28   *'What's all this about Ian?'*

BY NOW THIS persistent Englishman, whose charm and enchanting smile hid an iron determination, had become a part of my life. I accepted him as someone I liked to be with outside my frenzied working life.

I returned to New York, where I spent several months working on scripts. One day I was going over a story called 'As Dark as the Night' with a writer I found difficult and stubborn, when my telephone rang. It was Ian. I thought the call was from England.

'Where are you?' I asked.

'Downstairs,' he replied.

'Downstairs! What are you doing in New York?'

'What are you doing for the weekend?' he countered.

I had been invited by Ruth and Milton Berle to Atlantic City, where Milton was starting a nightclub engagement and Sammy Davis Jnr. was closing one. I telephoned to ask Ruth whether I might bring a friend from England—whom I did not identify as the story was too long and complicated for a telephone call— and of course she agreed.

Ian was hungry. As I had a lot to do, I sent him to the Stage Delicatessen for lunch. He rang from there to ask whether I wanted him to bring some salami along for the journey and I told him I had just heard that the friend who was to drive us down could not hire a car, as it was the Labour Day holiday weekend. Gentle and generous Max, the owner of the Stage, offered to drive us himself, and off we set with Mickey Hayes, a dear friend and practical joker, as a member of the party.

When one is on holiday and light-hearted, everything seems funnier than it really is, but it seemed at the time the funniest trip ever. Max speaks with a heavy German accent. I speak with a heavy French accent. Ian speaks, when he speaks, in his best aristocratic manner, his mouth half-closed. Mickey lisps. There was a Marx brothers zaniness about the journey.

While queueing to get into the Holland tunnel, a carload of Mexicans drew up beside us. They were all singing Mexican songs, and we applauded. In the same holiday mood they passed us a bottle of Tequila, which we immediately began to drink. This, added to our own joie de vivre, made the rest of the trip quite hilarious. When Mickey told us how he and some friends had gone fishing in a rowing boat in top hat, white tie and tails, using lines too short to reach the water simply to confuse the crews of a fishing-boat fleet, we thought it was the funniest thing we had ever heard.

When we reached the hotel in Atlantic City, I telephoned Ruth and asked if I could bring some friends up for a drink.

'I've just had a bath and I've only got a towel round me and curlers in my hair, but come up,' she said.

The Berles' suite was enormous, with large terraces. Ruth met us in a bathrobe. I introduced Ian as the Duke of Bedford. In the States, titles are sometimes used as Christian names—Duke Ellington, Count Basie, Earl Wilson spring immediately to mind. No-one queried Ian's name. They simply called him Duke.

Americans accept people at face value. They seemed to have an idea that Ian was in show business, possibly another David Niven.

Before I could explain further, a new group of showbiz characters came bubbling in, and a party was born. One man, a music publisher and Yoga addict, stood on his head with his legs crossed. Milton and Mickey tried to imitate him, but Mickey found that his pot belly got in the way, so someone suggested that he and Milton should be massaged. They were tumbled on the floor, and the guests took turns, to hilarious laughter, in kneading their stomachs.

Ian was slapped on the back and called 'Dukey'. No-one asked any questions, and he was accepted for what he was—'a good guy'.

That night we went to the last performance of Sammy Davis's nightclub act. Milton joined him on stage, and they improvised as only two such fantastically talented and professional people can do. The audience loved it. Then, without warning, Milton said:

'Tonight we have two distinguished members of royalty with us. The King of the Salamis—Max of the Stage Delicatessen, and the Duke of Something-or-other.'

Whereupon, to the accompaniment of laughter and applause Max and Ian went onto the stage and themselves did an impromptu act.

Ian astounded me. This was a totally different side to his character. I knew that he had enjoyed working on newspapers, that he would have liked to have been an architect and create handsome buildings, but I had never thought of him as an entertainer. With complete self-assurance, this shy man took the microphone and began telling funny stories, with talent and style. As with many famous comedians who are shy introverted people in their private lives, when they are in front of an audience they expand and take on a different personality. I fully understand why Ian is called upon so often as an after-dinner speaker. He is both witty and charming. He blooms with an audience.

It was 4 a.m. before we returned home, and I was beginning to feel ill. I developed a high fever almost certainly from a smallpox vaccination I had had a few days earlier when I flew into New York from Athens. I had to call a doctor, who put me to bed for three days.

During this time Ian was at the mercy of my rumbustious friends. They still did not believe that he was the Duke of Bedford —and he did not try to convince them. They still kept calling him 'Dukey'. At one party, the wife of a comedian called Jack Carter hit him in the face with a blueberry pie, which she said was good for the complexion.

Ian's adventures in Atlantic City made hysterical listening when I recovered from my illness. At lunch one day with the entire group, I said:

'Well, I am sorry you did not believe me when I said that Ian was the Duke of Bedford, but here is a copy of his autobiography 'A Silver Plated Spoon', and you can read it and be ashamed of what you have done to the poor man.'

My friends were suddenly serious and genuinely shocked. They began to apologise to Ian, who shrugged it off and thanked them for making him laugh.

It was an extremely happy time for us both. Ian then went to Canada for a lecture tour, and since I was going to Boston, I stopped off at Harvard to meet his eldest son, Robin, Marquess of Tavistock. Instead of going to one of the Establishment universities in England, he had decided to complete an international education in America. He had been at school at Le Rosay in Switzerland as a boy.

I found him an attractive young man, quiet, well mannered and serious for his 19 years. I liked him. Robin is my husband's son by his first wife, who died in 1945. There is also another son by this marriage, red-headed Rudolf, four years younger, and the image of his father in looks and personality, which is probably why I like him so much.

I returned to France briefly for Anyes's first communion at Maintenon—a serious and important occasion for a French girl. In her long white dress, and with a veil covering her fine brown hair her large eyes serious and wondering, she looked innocent and strangely appealing. I prayed that life would not hurt or destroy her.

She had developed into a studious, intelligent girl, as good at mathematics, painting and petit-point as she was at swimming and riding. She was already showing that gentle, almost Victorian beauty that she has today, so different from the sixteenth-century Madonna looks of Caterine.

Didier was beginning his career in the restaurant business, Caterine lived with me in London and attended the Lycée Française and Gilles was at Romsey College, near Lord Montagu's stately home of Beaulieu. Every Sunday, Gilles and his friends used to pay their fee to enter Lord Montagu's grounds.

None of us thought at that time that one day I would be at the receiving end, and immersed in the stately-home business.

At this time, I was seeing Ian quite often. We laughed a lot together, and to this day I tell him that that is why I married him. It was obvious to most of our friends that ours was more than a casual friendship—obvious to everyone but me!

My birthday came round again, and Ian flew to Paris to help me celebrate. I invited a few friends to my apartment before dinner. I was with my two Pauls—Paul Auriol, the agreeable son of the ex-President of France, and Paul Chalant, a caustic wit who has written many charming funny books. I suddenly noticed that Ian had left the room. Had we all been too noisily French?

I found him leaning on the balcony that overlooks the Seine behind Notre Dame. Below, the Paris of Camille Pissarro slumbered in the dusk. I leant over the balcony next to him:

'What is the matter? You are so quiet,' I said.

He did not even look at me, but replied slowly:

'I would like very much to marry you.'

'Let's not talk about it now,' I said quickly, 'We can discuss it after dinner.'

He dropped the subject. Perhaps he detected a note of panic in my voice. My unhappy marriage with Henri had given me a subconscious fear of being tied down again. I enjoyed my freedom and resented the idea of being attached to any man. The end of my romance with Shelly, with all its hurts and disappointments, was also still too fresh in my memory.

The birthday dinner at Maxim's was gay and amusing. Again I had managed to avert the issue of marriage, and Ian did not return to the subject.

I had to go to Italy to look for suitable locations for filming 'Two Faces to Go', which had a marvellous script by that first-class writer, Dale Wasserman, author of 'The Man of La Mancha'. It happened that Paul Getty, who had made his home in England, at Sutton Place near Guildford, had an Italian property near my hotel. He had persuaded Ian to fly down to look at a motel that might be a suitable model for a development at Woburn. Ian naturally came over to see me—I was seeking locations on a mountain—and offered to drive me back to my hotel.

We were driving along, and I was chattering about my project when I realised that something was wrong. I looked ahead—there were two cars in front of us and three approaching in the other lane. A motorcycle had just pulled out into the middle of the road, coming towards us, and yet Ian was also beginning to move into the middle.

I could see he had his foot-brake hard down on the floor, and he was trying to change gears. Something was obviously wrong with the hydraulic brake system. We flashed past the motorcyclist with an inch to spare. The heavy car had gathered such tremendous momentum down the steep gradient that Ian had been forced to move out to keep from crashing into the cars directly ahead of us. Now he had to jerk back into our own lane to avoid the oncoming cars, and he did so at such speed that it was a wonder we did not overturn.

Down the hill we raced at a crazy speed, Ian concentrating on keeping the car under control. We reached the bottom, where the car automatically slowed down before going up the next hill. There was a field on the left. Pulling the steering-wheel hard round, Ian turned off into a ploughed field. We came to a halt in soft earth. We were both shaking. My legs were trembling. We got out of the car and stood for a moment in complete silence, neither looking at the other.

'Perhaps we had better have lunch,' he said.

We found a small trattoria nearby, and telephoned a garage. The car was collected and it was discovered that the wrong fluid had been put in the brakes. We were lucky. We were meant to live.

While the car was being repaired, we went to a hotel in a small seaside village to swim and sunbathe.

The news of the near-accident reached the local press. We never knew how. I suppose I had made the error of using the Duke's name when summoning the mechanic. That evening, as

I came out of my cottage to cross the grounds to the main building of the hotel, Ian shouted to me from the door: 'Watch out.'

From behind every rock and tree, from behind every bush and piece of furniture, came photographers. They rushed at me, exploding their flash bulbs in my face, grabbed me by the arm, swung me round, and shouted at me hysterically. I had never been submitted to anything like that before. I could not understand what had happened. I jerked my arm free, and covering my face, ran to my room and locked myself in.

Outside, Ian was trying to cope with the reporters. He explained that we had simply stopped there for a day or so en route to Rome. But the Italian paparazzi were not to be put off so easily.

I stayed in my room and had dinner on the balcony, convinced the fuss would all blow over by the morning, but next morning a face appeared at the bathroom window while I was taking a shower, and a camera pointed my way. I was furious. The ludicrous siege continued and by the fourth day I could stand it no longer.

Ian and I agreed on a rendezvous. I climbed through the terrace window unobserved, made my way to the kitchen, and asked the cook to take me down to the village in his car. He hid me under a blanket on the back seat, and drove me along the twisting mountain roads. The suspicious photographers followed us for a while—would they link me with the bundle on the back seat?

Ian had set out in his own car. He is a fast, experienced driver and he soon lost the Press. We met at our rendezvous and later talked about the incident. I was worried what my children might think of the publicity, which had by now spread to France and England. I flew back to Ronquerolles immediately, and the children demanded:

'What's all this about Ian?'

I said: 'Don't believe the newspapers. There has been nothing scandalous, nothing to be ashamed of.'

Ian telephoned to say that the British Press were very interested in us. I went to my room to think. I knew I had to be in England for several months to shoot another picture. I now had to face the problem of whether to give up Ian or to continue to see him, knowing that there would be incessant publicity.

I knew suddenly that my life without him would be empty. He had become so much a part of it, with his gentle manners, his soft sense of humour, his wit, that when we were apart I missed him not a little, but very much. It was as simple as that. He had become indispensable to my happiness.

He had worked a miracle in me—slowly, subtly—by persuasion, by suggestion, but never by force. Life had made me dominant, if not domineering. I was used to making decisions, to fighting for what I wanted. I always knew where I was going. I had to know, since my responsibility had been thrust upon me in the bringing up of my children and in the competitive world of the film industry. I prided myself in being super-efficient.

'Stop being so efficient,' he said to me one day. 'Let me do the organising.'

He began to take a practical interest in my appearance. I was a blond with short boyish hair for convenience. I have not much patience with all the paraphernalia of hairdressing. Ian asked me to change back to my natural auburn, to grow my hair longer, gently to wave it. It looked better. Ian advised me to lose some weight. I did, and looked better for it. He took an interest in my clothes, which none of my other friends had done. If I wore something he liked, he told me so. His was a positive approach, and it worked. I began to enjoy dressing up for him.

Having altered my physical appearance, he began to remould my personality. I was being reborn as a woman, and that is a feeling that once experienced, can never be forgotten.

I felt cherished, wanted, needed. I blossomed. He had given me a new dimension.

A friend said to me after I had known Ian for some time:

'You look different, Nicole. You look like . . . like a woman.

29   *'Cheap at the price'*

By now we had known each other nearly three years—years full of fun and laughter, and meetings in faraway places. We had mutual friends all over the world and we were invited everywhere together.

During one visit to the south of France, we stayed with some friends in their house overlooking the sea. After lunch our hostess went shopping; I preferred to stay in the sun. Ian went with her instead, and I lay reading a book at the side of the pool.

Some time later, I was lying on my stomach when I heard my name called. I looked up. There, in the middle of the colonnade at the end of the pool, was our host, looking like the statue of a Greek god, completely naked.

Just at that moment, my future husband returned. He appeared from the steps behind, and saw the whole extraordinary scene. I stood up and went to meet him. Our host, as if he were completely dressed, carried on a normal conversation with him, asking him whether he had seen anything he liked, discussing rising prices, commenting on the weather, and so on.

This required enormous panache, and for that I will respect him forever. At the time I merely thought it terribly, terribly funny—as did Ian.

Being French, the fact that Ian was a duke meant little to me. I thought of him simply as a man. He assumed an important part in the lives of my children. They adored him—and still do. No other man had meant more to the children especially as they saw so little of their own father. Ian listened to them, joined in their games, made them laugh. He was a perfect subject for their practical jokes. As he is rather vague he was always taken in by the squeaking Camembert or the unmeltable sugar.

I had spent the summer holidays at Ronquerolles with the children determined that I would not see Ian for some time, but he telephoned every day.

By now the British Press were driving me insane. One paper had a reporter outside the gates for two weeks. Every time the children went down to the village, he spied on them. I felt a prisoner in my own house. In desperation, I asked him in for a cup of tea one day. He was a pleasant man, who explained that he was only doing his job and could not go away.

I telephoned Ian in despair.

'If you want to avoid it, marry me,' was his laconic answer.

He had asked me to marry him in England, France, Italy, the United States and Mexico. Perhaps I should. I loved him with all my heart, and I missed him terribly when I was not with him. I cannot remain with anyone long who does not have a sense of humour and a quick brain, and Ian had both. In fact I explained my marriage to him by saying that he made me laugh. But in reality, the gentlemen of the Press finally decided me.

I felt it was wrong for our children to have every movement spied on and reported in the gossip columns. I did not want them to be exposed to cruel taunts from their friends. No child wants to read a headline about his mother or father.

It was the last day of the holidays and I knew that I had to say something. I was really scared. Nothing must go wrong with this intimate and decisive moment. I was as nervous as a girl talking to her parents about her fiancé. After dinner I asked the children to come to my bedroom.

I have always had a feudal bedroom. Wherever I have lived, it has always been my place—full of my pictures, my photographs, my books on a large table by my bed, my boxes and trinkets. I call it my organised mess. I do not have to look for anything: I just stretch out my hand. The children came and sat all over the place. Didier perched on top of the bed, Gilles picked up a new book, Caterine tucked her long legs under her on a bergère, and Anyes sat at my dressing-table and sniffed my scent.

'Darlings, you have all known Ian for a long time now,' I began. 'Do you like him?'

'Very much,' they said in chorus.

'Well, he has asked me to marry him,' I blurted out. 'What do you think?'

There was complete silence. Didier, the cautious one, was the first to speak:

'Oh, he's nice and he rides very well, but I would like to know him a little better.'

Caterine was the next, and said very forcefully:

'Well, if you marry him, it will have to be for ever. You cannot change your mind, so you had better think about it twice.'

'He's adorable. He makes me laugh,' Anyes whispered.

'Does it mean we will have to go and live in England?' asked Gilles.

I did not want thoughtless, superficial answers to something that would affect our whole lives. I respect my children too much for that. I had to give them time to think.

'You are all going back to school tomorrow and you have a whole night to think about it. Of course it will mean a great change if I marry Ian. I will have to go and live at Woburn, and that will mean the end of this house where we have been so happy together. Think about it. Talk it over together and let me know in the morning.'

I lived on the first floor of the house and they lived on the second. I always have breakfast in bed, and the next morning they each came separately to my room.

They had talked long after bedtime, and decided that I should marry Ian. One by one they told me so.

That settled it. I picked up the telephone and called Woburn.

'Darling,' I said, 'if you still want me, I will marry you.'

Once the news was out, there was a terrific blast of publicity. We got the full treatment. In the midst of everything, a well-known English Duchess cabled Ian from the United States:

'Cheap at the price'

'Why marry her when you can have me?'

I wanted a quiet wedding at Ronquerolles with only the immediate families present. Ian's children would fly over. I would wear an everyday dress, the mayor would perform the ceremony, there would be a family luncheon in the garden—and there would be no reporters.

Of course it did not happen that way. I knew we would be married from Woburn, but I was the last to know the actual wedding-date. I am a poor liar—my face blushes and my nose twitches—and I had asked Ian not to tell me until everything was set, so that I would not have to lie.

Ian had asked me to keep September 3 and 4 free, and to meet him in London. As he always telephoned to let me know what days he would be free so that I could arrange to be available on the same days, I suspected nothing, although it was arranged that the children would accompany me.

In order to avoid photographers, we arrived in England on the midnight plane on September 2, and went straight to a house in Mayfair that I had rented. At eight o'clock the next morning, there was a ring at my door, and I opened it to find a battery of television cameras, photographers and reporters.

'What is all this?' I asked.

'You are getting married,' they said.

'Not for a week at least,' I parried.

And I meant it. I took the children shopping, and when we returned, the photographers and reporters were still at the door. Ian telephoned and asked us all to meet him at the Connaught Hotel for lunch. In order to avoid the Press, we hurried out through the back garden, climbing into the garden next door. I knocked on the window of a house where a painter was decorating a ceiling. The man, somewhat astonished, climbed down from his ladder and led us through the house and out into a deserted street.

At the Connaught, while the waiters were bringing lunch, Ian took my hand under the table and slipped a ring on my finger, saying, 'A bit of glass for you.' I blushed furiously. The children asked what was the matter with me. I lifted up my hand and gave myself, and them, a first look at my engagement ring—a solitaire diamond. I wear it constantly and never take it off.

I decided to return to the house. I was certain the Press would have gone by now, but as we approached, I saw several hundred people and two television cameras. I told the driver to go round the block. I knocked at the door of the house where my painter friend was working, and we went back the same way as we had left.

We waited inside for the crowd to go away, but if anything it seemed to grow as darkness approached. I looked across the garden. The painter had gone. The offices of Harper's Bazaar also backed onto our garden, and I asked the children to go across and see if we could get permission to go through their building.

Didier did not see that there was a goldfish pond in the middle of the garden, and suddenly found himself knee deep in water. It was all part of the fun, and the children enjoyed it thoroughly.

I knew the wedding was approaching, but I had no idea when exactly it would take place. We had our ordinary Sunday lunch with friends at Woburn, and then I went into the drawing-room. The guests had coffee, but by now I had acquired Ian's habit of drinking China tea. He came over to me as I was pouring it, and said:

'Darling, you had better get ready. We are getting married at five o'clock.'

Now that the moment was at hand, I felt weak—limp—shaky.

'Poor darling,' he said. 'It's not as bad as that, is it?'

I went upstairs thoughtfully, and found Anyes in hysterics. In the excitement she had doused her hair with bath-oil instead of shampoo, and now it was a greasy mess. Despite repeated attempts, she could not wash out the oil, her hair looked lank and terrible. We telephoned downstairs to the kitchen for some detergent, and I began washing her hair. It took six shampoos.

The bride was too busy to think about herself.

I then went to my bedroom to put on my wedding dress designed by Pierre Balmain. I had told him: 'All the ceilings, furniture and picture-frames at Woburn are gilded. Please design me something to go with them.'

So he designed me a dress and coat of gold lamé, with a large mink collar. It was beautiful, and of such good quality that I still wear it today. Madame Nicole of Franck had made a large Ascot-style hat in toffee-brown piqué satin, from a Paulette model.

As I was crossing the bedroom in my bare feet, I trod on a wasp. I am highly allergic to wasps, and a year earlier had nearly died after being stung by one inside my throat.

I telephoned down to Ian, who said: 'You must be joking!'

'It's true. I am serious,' I wailed. 'My foot is already enormous.'

All our combined children piled into the room with Ian to examine the foot. Everyone began to laugh hysterically. A doctor was sent for who gave me an injection and said that I was to lie still for two hours and have no excitement! The poor man, had no idea why everyone was laughing. My wedding was to take place in half an hour!

By walking, or rather limping, through the back garden on the arm of Ian's valet, Finlay, we were able to sneak into the cars unnoticed. My husband's Lincoln Continental— with its DOB 1 number plate—had been sent in another direction as a decoy. We slipped into the blue sports car belonging to Henrietta, who was engaged to Ian's eldest son Robin. The children all went in the mini-bus that normally brought the cleaners every morning.

Ian had sent armfuls of flowers to the Ampthill registery office, including of course lilies, which had become our leitmotif. Even our wedding-cake from Floris was decorated with white sugared lilium ruberosum.

The ceremony lasted six minutes. When the registrar, Mr Harry Robinson, asked Ian what his father's name was, he replied 'Hastings, William, Sackville, Russell.' Having expected him to say the 12th Duke of Bedford, I looked at Ian in astonishment.

Mr. Robinson then suggested that he be married in the name of Ian, the name he uses rather than his actual first name, John, which he dislikes.

Ian gave me a diamond and platinum wedding-ring like a cluster of little roses, and paid Mr. Robinson £3.6s.9d. 'Cheap at the price,' he remarked. And so finished the most publicised hush-hush wedding of the year.

Next day one of the newspapers, reporting the wedding, said I had 'wiped a tear with a beautiful lace handkerchief'. I suppose it would never have done for a duchess to use an ordinary paper tissue—which was exactly what I did.

After the ceremony we all went back to Woburn to have dinner with the children, and at midnight, with children and friends throwing rice, we drove off on our honeymoon. On the car seat we found a baby doll with a note signed by all our seven children:

'We love you. We want you to be happy.'

30   *'Here we go again'*

WE ONLY HAD a short honeymoon in Europe before going to America. We flew first from Heathrow to Venice. I was distraught when I discovered that there were a reporter and photographer from a national paper on the aeroplane who had elected to come on honeymoon with us. This was too much.

I was exhausted when we arrived. The lagoon smelled of refuse, and the day was grey. The Cipriani Hotel was asleep and unwelcoming. When we reached our bedroom I burst into tears. I begged Ian to take me to a place where we could be unrecognised and alone.

We found a little Yugoslav boat to take us down the Adriatic along the beautiful coast past Dubrovnik to a small island named Sveti Stephan, which has a romantic history. In the eighteenth century, Yugoslavian soldiers routed a Turkish invasion army, capturing a boatload of gold and jewels. With the gold they bought the island, fortified it, and built 112 houses. Sveti Stephan still has 112 houses. A few years ago Marshal Tito converted the entire island into an hotel.

Almost as soon as we arrived in America. I began to find out that being a duchess 'on duty' had its own liabilities. One of the attributes I have always admired in Queen Elizabeth, the Queen Mother is her ability to put people at their ease. Getting strangers to talk is a matter of strategy.

I learnt my first lesson in New York. We were having dinner

with Earl Blackwell, and seated on my left was Pierre Schlumberger, the French industrialist and patron of the arts. Unfortunately, for some reason, he was not very talkative. Facing me was Clare Booth Luce, of the lucid brain and lily-cool looks. I was interested to watch how, with her ambassadorial experience, she would handle the situation.

Suddenly, in a moment of desperation, she said:

'Have you ever spent a weekend in a submarine?'

That did it. Mr. Schlumberger raised his head and said: 'In a submarine?'

'Yes,' she continued, 'don't you think it's chic? I always do so when I can.'

Learning from her, during the next hiatus in the conversation I took advantage of an earlier discussion on my right about the difference between American, French and English women, and asked Mr. Schlumberger:

'What's your type of woman?'

He considered for some time, and replied: 'Naked and round.'

'Then should I take my clothes off?' I suggested.

'Yes,' he said.

When I began unfastening my buttons, his eyes opened and he began to laugh.

Pierre has an enchanting wife called Saõ. She is Portuguese and some years ago gave a ball in her house 'Quinta da Vinegra' to which people fought to be invited, even going as far as to steal tickets.

I once sat next to another silent man—the President of the English-Speaking Union. On this particular occasion, he refused to speak English or any other language throughout dinner, until I was getting desperate, having tried the weather, his hobbies, the culture of roses, and so on. Suddenly I said to him:

'Do you roller skate?'

He looked at me in bewilderment, and said:

'Yes—I used to.' And for the rest of the meal, he hardly stopped talking. It was very touching.

For some reason my husband's face registers with people, but it is my voice that people remember. I was fitting a dress in a shop when a woman said:

'Oh, the Duchess of Bedford is in the next cubicle.'

'Yes, it is me,' I called. 'How did you know?'

She replied: 'I recognised your voice from the television.'

Another time I got into a New York taxi, and the driver said: 'I know your voice, you are the wife of that chap from England who has a big house open to the public,' and he would not let me pay for the journey.

We were asked to dozens of parties. Earl Blackwell asked us to one at ten in the evening, so we decided to have dinner and go to a cinema before hand. Unfortunately I chose 'I want to Live' with Susan Hayward, the story of Ruth Ellis, who was condemned to death for murder. Each time it was thought she might be reprieved, they brought her two-year-old son to see her. By the end of the film, I had cried so much that I had no makeup left. My face was swollen and red like a tomato—I was a mess.

When we arrived at Earl's party, people rushed up to me saying 'Is he awful to you? Is your marriage breaking up?' This made me laugh, for the first time that evening, and I reassured everyone.

At that time Marlene Dietrich was appearing in New York, I knew her from Paris, and have always admired her complete integrity. She leaves nothing to chance or to last-minute improvisation. Everything in her performance is carefully calculated; the position of the shoulders, a leg turned forward just enough to tease, and a throaty voice to move you down to the middle of yourself.

We are both perfectionists. We demand perfection from the people we work with and from ourselves. She achieves it all the time. I do sometimes.

What is really so marvellous about Marlene is her contrasts of mood. On stage, in her sensuous, flesh-coloured gauze dress that looks as if champagne has been poured over her slim body, she is diaphanous—a translucent, shimmering personality. But take her out to dinner after the show and she is very earthy and gutsy.

We went to Sardi's after her performance. She was ravenous, and devoured a corn-beef hash with lots of potatoes, topping this off with chocolate gateau. Her slimness is miraculous.

My best Dietrich story concerns Scott Carpenter, the American astronaut, who met her after her astonishing success in New York with the performance we were later to see in London. He said:

'I have been into space. I have been to the bottom of the sea. But I have never been as moved as by you tonight.'

Marlene cried.

There were parties every night in New York. While we were staying with Titi Hudson at Sutton Place, she suggested one night, as we were leaving for a party, that I should put some more lacquer on my hair, because it was windy outside. When the wind is fierce in New York, whistling down those narrow streets between the tall buildings, it is almost unbearable.

Since it meant walking down a long corridor to get to our bathroom, she told me to use hers. She had some lacquer in her cupboard.

As we were late and I was in a hurry I did not bother to turn on the light but, in the half light, grabbed a pretty gold container. I sprayed myself lavishly. When I returned to the hall, they all screamed in horror. I had used shoe-polish instead of lacquer, and I was speckled all over with a thousand spots, as if I had black measles. It was a long and terribly painful business to remove the polish with turpentine.

At a New York party one Tuesday, Eileen Plunkett, one of the Guinness girls, asked us to dinner the following Thursday. Her husband passed by a little later and said something about taking her to the airport. Slightly amazed, I said: 'Where is she going?'

'Paris,' he said.

'But she has just asked us to dinner on Thursday.'

'Oh yes, she'll be back. She's only going for a hair-do.'

I discovered that it was part of her regular routine to fly every Tuesday to Paris for this purpose, and return on Thursday.

It reminded me of Ian's aunt who went annually to Paris to buy black safety-pins. On the first day she rested; on the second day she made her purchase; and on the third day, she packed to return home.

Marriage is an emotional affair . . . my paper tissue became 'a lace handkerchief' in the newspapers

She: 'John Robert Russell—who is he?'
He: 'Cheap at the price' . . .

'Thank God it's over'

Happiness is D O B 1

Venice on the wall—4 September 1960—dinner in the Canaletto dining-room at Woburn

Venice in reality—bliss, bliss, bliss despite photographers, grey skies and the smell of refuse

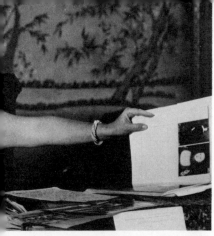

Executive Duchess: 'I wish I could join a union!'

Their Graces! Our first official Ducal photograph

Happy families. Left to right: Didier, Ian,
Fernanda, Anyes, a glimpse of Robin, Gilles,
Nicole, Caterine, Henrietta

Chef de cuisine, David, with his crew

Amethysts and ancestors

Riding a rhinoceros can be dangerous

'I love animals, any type of animal, even the human ones!'

Melchior

My private sitting-room with a view. Rembrandt was tiny and fierce. Cleopatra looks like a mop and has the brain of one

'I come to the conclusion that philosophy is a very silly subject . . .' said Bertrand Russell to Freddie Ayer

Flamboyant Barbara Cartland with the Duchess of Leeds and her husband Peter Hoos

Miss New Zealand in the Long Gallery at Woburn with Paul Getty and Nubar Gulbenkian.
They may have been rich but she had got it all!

I must like or attract the bizarre, because so many of my friends behave unusually.

It was in New York, too, that Aleko Papamarkou gave a large dinner party for us at the Grenouille, which I think is the best restaurant in the city. The proprietor, Charles Masson, is a genius with food. He is also very generous, as he always gives me recipes when I ask him. I think it silly when people cherish their recipes like gold.

It was a very fine dinner, attended by a couple of kings, destitute of course, a number of senators, and some government ministers. I was sandwiched between a king and my host, and as we had such lovely food and wine, the evening went very well. After dinner, for some odd reason, people changed places, and I found myself talking to a stranger.

'I understand that you and your husband are visiting 37 cities in the United States,' he said.

'Yes, we are,' I answered, somewhat puzzled.

'Do you know that you could be a tremendous help to us?'

'What for, doing what?' I replied, still more puzzled.

'When you go on your lecture tour in these cities, all you have to do is say at the end, 'We think Mr. Nixon is a very nice man. He is honest and trustworthy and worth voting for, and if we were American, my husband and I would both vote for him.'

I looked at the man, astonished. I was simply bewildered.

'Well, my husband is English and I am French, and I do not think it is either of our businesses to interfere with American politics.'

The man then looked at me straight in the eye, and said:

'I see that you have a very nice mink coat. What about a sable one too!'

Only then did I realise what it was all about, and that my charming friend was part of Nixon's entourage.

At the same table there was also a blonde woman who came and sat next to me, with a purposeful look.

'I understand that you are coming to lecture in Orange County,' she began.

'Yes', I replied, 'we are speaking in the morning.'

'That's exactly why I wondered if you would like to sleep at my house, so that you will not have to get up early.'

Ian agreed that we should take advantage of this very kind offer, so it was arranged that a car would be sent for us.

When we finally arrived at the house, we were greeted by the housekeeper and told that our hostess had a migraine.

We were both relaxing after a bath when we were informed that dinner would be a black-tie affair—which I thought strange for a simple foursome—and we were asked to be' downstairs by seven o'clock. The husband was there to meet us. Then the guests began to arrive, and we were moved into position by a draughty door to shake hands with perhaps 200 people. Our hosts had invited all their banking friends to meet the Duke and Duchess of Bedford. I was livid.

After we had been shaking hands for some time, I said: 'Let's go on strike.'

Ian is much more patient, and in his gentle way, said: 'Let's carry on. Never mind, it won't be for much longer.'

We continued until 9.30 without a single break or a drink. When all the guests had gone, we were given a whisky and soda.

By this time the hostess had appeared, and she announced:

'My migraine is terrible, I think I will go to bed.' With that, her husband added 'And so will I', and disappeared with her.

We were left standing there, without any dinner. Ian made the most of it by saying that it would do me a lot of good to go without dinner for one evening.

We left as soon as we could the following morning, and went to our lecture.

When we returned, I was told:

'A woman has telephoned several times. She'll be calling again soon.'

Sure enough, she did. 'I am a friend,' 'she said,' 'of your hostess last night. I would like to arrange a party with the trustees of a very nice museum we have.'

I said, 'No, thank you.'

'But they are very special people and would make a charming party for you.'

'No, thank you,' I repeated.

'Why won't you let me arrange a party for you?'

'I do not like parties,' I said, replacing the receiver.

I had learnt my lesson the night before, and knew what might be in store for us.

Still the woman persisted. She wrote a letter, which was delivered by a chauffeur, naming all the people she intended to invite. I did not reply. But the lady was not to be put off. She telephoned once again, and asked what kind of people I would like to have invited.

She was so persistent that I wrote back, saying: 'If you want to give a dinner party for eight, but no more, we will come, explaining that eight or ten are nice numbers that enable people to speak to each other comfortably. I find it extremely boring standing with a drink in my hand for hours on end.

She replied with a list of ten people she would invite—all from the art world. On the given day, we were collected, and to my dismay I could see that there were already more than ten people present, so I said to my husband: 'Oh God, here we go again.'

I found myself chatting with the Belgian consul, who was most charming, and asked him: 'Are you having dinner here?'

He answered 'Yes.' This reassured me, so I began circulating among the rest of the guests. But by ten o'clock there was still no sign of food. I went back to my friend, the Belgian consul, and asked:

'What is going on? What time is dinner served in this house?'

He laughed. 'Have you not been told? Do you not know that all the staff walked out an hour before dinner and our hostess is in the kitchen now, trying to cook the dinner, and she cannot cook?'

'Oh, my God, the poor woman. I must go and help her, because at least one thing I can do is to cook.'

I was wearing a lovely peach crêpe-de-chine dress, but I took my Belgian friend with me into the kitchen. There was the poor lady, surrounded by meat, onions and mushrooms, totally bewildered.

I decided to make a fricassée, and asked someone to put on some hot water for the green beans. Tying a kitchen towel round my

lovely evening dress, I began frying onions, adding a little of this
and that, while our hostess took the ice cream out of the refrigerator. By this time Ian had noticed my absence, and poked his head
into the kitchen.

'I am cooking the dinner because the staff has walked out. Come
and make the salad.'

He took off his dinner jacket and started preparing the salad the
way we do it at Woburn, with all kinds of lovely things like walnuts, chives, radishes and mixed herbs.

Eventually we served dinner to about 40 people, seated at about
half a dozen separate tables. The evening ended enjoyably, and
our hostess was charming and delighted.

For years, as a career girl, housewife and mother of four children,
I had trained myself to exist on three or four hours' sleep a night.
Now I was being put to the test, and I found that I was able to
carry on our whistle-stop tour of America and do our nightly
party round without wilting.

Phoenix is a delightful place, and its dry Arizona air attracts old
people with rheumatism and arthritis. We were due to lecture at
a club in the evening, but were rushed off the aeroplane.

'Why the hurry?' I said. 'The lecture is at eight tonight.'

'Oh no, you have to come to a luncheon first.'

Once more it seemed we were the prize possessions to be displayed to the organisers' friends. How I resent being used just
because of our title! However, my temper improved when I met
a charming Mexican who told me where to find the Indian
Reserve where all the beautiful silver and turquoise jewellery is
made.

We went back to our hotel before setting out for our evening
lecture. We were collected by one of our sponsors who took us
into the lecture hall, and announced:

'Here we have, in our good city . . . *the Duke and Duchess of
Windsor* to speak to you.'

In Miami there was more handshaking when we had to stand
for three hours at a reception arranged by the English-Speaking
Union. I was beginning to understand the occupational hazards of
being married to a publicity-conscious duke.

From Miami we flew to Texas, where we were made honorary citizens of Houston. From there the handshaking never stopped until we felt like touring actors at one-night stands.

In Dallas we were invited to an exclusive club. They knew all about the 'red carpet' treatment, but, being Texas, the carpet was not only red but made of thick fur.

The women guests wore long dresses and high heels, and we stood at the end of this 65-foot carpet to receive them. It was hysterically funny to watch them topple over when their heels caught in the fur, but of course we had to keep absolutely straight faces as befits a duke and duchess. I was less amused, however, when I realised we had been standing in front of a fountain and that my backside was dripping with water.

This was an entirely different America from the one I had known in my film-producing days. Seeing it through Ian's bemused eyes was both pleasant and revealing.

At one dinner party, all the 12 guests were multi-millionaires. On my left was a man reputed to have 600 million dollars. On my right was a man worth 400 million. At the end of the table was a man who had only 100 million! Everyone referred to him as 'Poor Joe'.

I met one very funny multi-millionaire, Henry Clay Koontz, who owned the H.K. range where they raise Brahmin bulls—those golden Indian animals with long horns and great jowls of loose skin. He was with a friend who could not read or write. 'Why should I?' he said. 'Someone can always do it for me.'

On another occasion we were driving with Henry in a Jaguar. After a long silence he said: 'This is a beautiful car.'

A woman with us began commenting on its powerful motor, when Henry interrupted:

'I don't care about that. It's the sliding roof I like. I could shoot doves on the telegraph-poles.'

On our trips to America, we always try to take in California, which during my film days became a second home to me. Back in Los Angeles we stayed again with Ruth and Milton Berle, who lent us a guest-house in their garden.

In the Sixties Hollywood still had panache. There was still a mystique about such names as Sunset Boulevard. Crouching in the hills surrounding Los Angeles were the large houses where the big-name stars still lived in their droll, larger-than-life style. Important pictures were still being made and the real drift away to the Continental studios and more cultural climate of Europe had not begun.

Hollywood was Hollywood was Hollywood.

The life-style of Beverly Hills was so totally different from that in France or England. For instance, very few people owned their own houses. Everything was on hire purchase. If you had a huge house and two Cadillacs in the garage, everyone knew you were doing well. Even the Impressionists on the walls were on hire purchase. A bad film or your star's illness, and overnight you might lose everything and move to a small apartment on a back lot. People who were on top one day were down the next. No-one minded.

'There but for the grace of God go I' was their philosophy—not so different from my husband's motto 'Che Sara Sara'.

When we arrived, the film city was in a ferment with the campaigning for the presidential election. The Berles and many other stars seemed to be for Jack Kennedy, who was of course elected.

Typical of the kind of Hollywood madness at that time was an election-night party to which we went at the home of Tony Curtis and Janet Leigh. Before their divorce, they had a very spacious, modern and beautiful house. I have never seen such luxurious confusion.

On the night of the party, a television set going in each room, a fair-haired man arrived and made two telephone calls—one to his sister in Hawaii and another to his brother in Paris. In the confusion no-one took much notice at first, until suddenly we realised he had been talking for hours.

The host and hostess circulated through the rooms, asking first one guest and then another who the man was and who had brought him. None of us knew. Finally, when Tony Curtis asked me for the third time, I said:

'Why don't you ask the man himself?'

The man turned out to be a complete stranger who had gate-crashed the party merely to make his telephone calls. As silently as he arrived, he disappeared.

Janet Leigh was a compulsive cleaner. She went round all night with a silver container into which she emptied the cigarette-ends. In her pocket she carried a chamois leather with which she polished the ashtrays. If a spot of ash fell on the floor, she rushed in with a brush and pan to clean it up. I was fascinated watching her.

At one stage of the party, Frank Sinatra, at that time one of the most vociferous Kennedy campaigners, got on the telephone to the Republican candidate, Richard Nixon, and shouted—almost screamed—at him:

'Make your concession speech. Make your concession speech.'

I cannot imagine any French star talking that way to a candidate for the Presidency of France.

That night I witnessed one of the most moving moments ever on television. When Richard Nixon made his speech conceding the election, his wife Pat stood behind him, absolutely erect, statuesque—without moving a muscle, like a figure from Madame Tussaud's. Two enormous tears sprang from her eyes and rolled down her cheeks. I felt nothing but compassion for her.

Sammy Davis Jr., who was also present, told us he was getting married the following week, and invited us to the wedding. I have known Sammy a long time. He is a complete perfectionist, rehearsing and rehearsing until everything is exactly as he wants it.

We went to his wedding reception at the Beverly Hilton Hotel. Downstairs in the lobby, we gave our names, which were checked off against a master list. Upstairs, our names were again twice checked off against different lists and we were ushered into a large room that overlooked the city.

Maj Britt, Sammy's blond Swedish bride, was not present, but Sammy was not perturbed. Indeed he was exuberantly happy, and explained that Maj was emotionally exhausted and had gone to bed. We later learnt that she was expecting a baby and Sammy was telling everyone about his child to come.

I met Elizabeth Taylor for the first time. Despite what many people say about her and her flamboyant Press image, I like her. She is a realistic woman of good judgment who from the age of five has been surrounded by sycophants and yet has remained with her two feet on the ground. She has also remained a very good and attentive mother, throughout her turbulent life. Everyone jokes about the way she travels in her private plane with her 60 suitcases, numerous cats and dogs, and an army of personal staff. Why not, if she can afford it?

I think she has an impossible life. Every time she cries, sneezes, smiles, somebody takes a picture. She behaves very well in the circumstances. In her personal life she is very much a real woman. She told Richard Burton that she would leave him if he drank again. That takes guts.

I have my own personal memories of Miss Taylor which are indicative of her character—her generosity and her sense of reality. She was to dine at Woburn, but at the last minute had to cancel to fly off somewhere. She sent me a bouquet—all white flowers —large enough to fill half the drawing-room.

Soon after Mike Todd died, she went to a dinner party, and in doing so offended some of her sanctimonious friends who were shocked that she was about so soon after her husband's death.

She retorted: 'Mike is dead and I'm alive.'

I thought that made a great deal of sense. Why flaunt your unhappiness at people. She really did love that man, but why wallow in self-pity? When you go out and meet other people, it takes you out of your own sorrow and misery—which is sound therapy.

I was to meet her at a dinner in the British Embassy in Paris given by the then Ambassador, Sir Pierson Dixon. Enchanting-looking Elizabeth was placed between two French Government ministers, who, under General de Gaulle, were rather grand, bourgeois, stiff and formal. At the end of dinner, she pushed back her chair, and in a loud voice said to Richard Burton across the table:

'Now I'm going to the can.'

The horror on the faces of the ministers had to be seen to be believed. I just giggled quietly.

It was in Hollywood that I received the biggest compliment any man has ever paid me. It came from Tony Bennett, the singer. I was coming out of the swimming pool with my wet hair glued to my sunburnt face. I was slim, athletic and golden brown. I lifted myself up in one movement from the side of the pool. Tony just stood and said:

'You are the earth.'

31   *Ways of living, ways of dying*

W HEN I MARRIED my husband Ian, the 13th Duke of Bedford, he made it imperatively clear that his house, Woburn Abbey, came first, but I loved him immeasurably and I understood his love for his ancestors and their legacies.

Had I known the hard work, the long hours and the tremendous task involved, I certainly would not have married him. Woburn has been a devouring duty, swallowing nearly 14 years, my health, my happiness, my friends, my hobbies.

But I regret nothing.

Ever since I had walked out on my first marriage, I had been making decisions on my own. I had gone where I wanted, done what I pleased, chosen my own friends. My single enduring responsibility, joy and love was for my four children.

I had led a fascinating life because I decided what I wanted and went out to achieve it. Contentment is happiness. Happiness is to have achieved and brought to life one idea or thought—and I had done that.

Now, at Woburn, I was forced to take a new bearing on life, both as a duchess and as a wife once more. I had also to share with my husband the immense burden of a role in society, which has never interested me, and to live in a house that could never be as much a home as a national institution. It is one thing to have a kind and loving husband, but to become the chatelaine of a vast stately home, which the public has grown to regard not so much as your home but as their heritage, can never be other than a hard job.

Life is for living, and whatever I do, I invest it with all the enthusiasm I have; with all the will I have; all the skill I have. So Woburn became my life, too. It was just like having another child to raise.

My husband says: 'Being a duke is no fun any more. You cannot live on the same scale as your ancestors. You cease to see the beautiful things around you, only the repairs of 300 years and the problems of running the estate.'

Being a duchess, one only sees the 12, 14, 16 hours of work each day during the summer season to keep the place alive, beautiful and rewarding for our visitors.

Even after I had been married for six months, I would still ring up for an appointment and find myself saying:

'Nicole Milinaire speaking.'

One day Ian was not amused to hear me, and said:

'Darling, you are married, you know.'

Being a duchess is merely an occupation to me. I treat it as a career, much as you would say someone is a teacher, a secretary or a journalist. I seldom use the title myself and prefer to sign 'Nicole de Bedford', which is how I would be known in France.

Customs of course differ from country to country. I have noticed that the former Duchess of Leeds uses her title when she signs our guest book, despite the fact that through remarriage she is now Mrs. Peter Hoos. And when I was doing a charity show one day with Lady Lindsey I was surprised that everyone referred to her by her former title, the Duchess of Westminster.

'You get more if you are a duchess than a plain lady,' she explained very sensibly.

When I knew that England would be my home for many years, I decided to join a club. In Paris I had belonged to The Racing Club de France, which of course has nothing to do with racing, but is a superb sports club.

I decided to join the Hurlingham Club at Roehampton on the outskirts of London, thinking it would serve the same purpose. I remember, when I entered the office, being asked:

'Oh, you are the Duchess of Bedford?'

'Yes,' I answered.

'Which one?'

'What do you mean?' I countered.

'Oh, he's been married more than once.'

I stood up and left.

When it is my job, and I am appearing as a duchess, then I accept the anachronism 'Your Grace'. At first that appellation made me jump out of my skin, because the word 'grace' to my French ear sounded exactly like the French 'graisse', which means fat. Through the years as 'graisse' has invaded me, it is even more painful.

But when it is a matter of my own choice, I do not see why I should bother with a title. A great part of me is Republican. Royalty has survived in England only because the Royal family work at it. The Queen is such a remarkable dedicated person, and Prince Philip is so progressive, that they have achieved the wonderful balance of a charming family able to live their own lives and to command respect. It must have been tremendously difficult, and I do not think the public realise quite how remarkable their achievement is.

I was against inherited privilege. I saw it as part of the mentality of the English, who have little imagination and like established order. But seeing Woburn growing more beautiful through each generation of the same family, I am not sure that Ian is not right.

The lack of rapport was one of the many things that I found most difficult when I moved into Woburn. The house is so vast that it is almost impossible to maintain human relationships. I found myself using the house-telephone to speak to the children, or going out to the terrace to see which cars were there so that I knew who was in.

When I first arrived, to get a cup of tea (and I drink many during the day) took one and half hours. First I had to tell my personal maid, who telephoned the butler, who told the footman, who took the instructions to the chef, who in turn asked the under-chef to boil the water. The tea was made, and then the whole procedure had to be reversed once more until the Lapsong Souchong arrived tepid. This is why now we have a kitchenette next to our private apartment on the second floor. When I want a cup of tea, either my maid or I make it.

In London, when I am exhausted after a day rushing round, my wonderful Ellen, who has been with me for 18 years, understands when I say: 'Taxi-driver tea, please.' She then brews a pot full of Indian tea that is dark brown, bitter and reviving.

For some strange reason, I do not crave tea at Woburn in the same way. When I have had a day of pressure and am expecting guests for dinner, I get into my bath and reach for the decanter of my husband's best port, which I keep by the side, and which I sip as I eat gruyère cheese. This is most invigorating and immensely sensuous, with the steam bringing the bouquet of the port to full bloom.

There are 120 rooms at Woburn, 97 telephones, 13 miles of walls, 565 windows, and thousands of pictures—so different from my human Ronquerolles that I had left behind.

Ronquerolles was a happy house of laughter and joy. The very first week we lived there, one of the children broke the lock. We never repaired it, and the front door remained unlocked summer and winter for the many years we were there.

At Woburn my husband and I are not even trusted with a key. No matter what hour we arrive, night or day, 365 days of the year, we have first to ring the bell, and a security man admits us.

I had, of course, married into the most extraordinary family. The Russell history is provocative, stimulating, whimsical—totally bewildering. England has always cherished its eccentrics, of whom the Russells have provided plenty.

By marrying the 13th Duke, I became the 15th Duchess in this complicated family tree.

When my husband's grandfather was hanging the pictures in the Dukes' Corridor with Gladys Scott Thomson, then the librarian, he began with the 1st Earl and ended up with himself. When he reached the end of the corridor, Miss Scott Thomson suggested:

'Now you have all the husbands on one side, let's put the wives opposite.'

'They are not even of the blood,' the Duke snorted, and walked away angrily.

[227]

I think that was a marvellous remark when one considers that each Duchess was the mother of the future Duke, but that is the way that all the Russells seemed to think about their wives. 'They are not of the blood', so they do not exist, except as objects to be used for child-bearing, housekeeping, entertaining.

The women in the family have always been strong characters. They had to be in order to survive. My husband accepts that I am the noisy extrovert, and he the introvert, but in fact he is the strong one of the family. I may make the noise, but in fact he does exactly what he wishes.

He has a rare and gentle charm, and like all the men in the Russell family, is tenacious, stubborn and implacable behind a façade of inertia.

The famous Sydney Smith, said at the time of the 5th Duke: 'A peculiarity of the Russells is that they never alter their opinions— they are an excellent race but they must be trepanned before they are convinced.' How true!

The Russells have never been shy of marrying, and if they have not been entirely satisfactory husbands, they have always intended to have a family life at Woburn.

Many of their marriages turned out to be prudent investments, for their wives added considerably to the family fortunes. When the 1st Earl married Anne Sapcote in 1526, he was 40 years of age. His wife brought the manors of Thornhaugh in Northampton-shire and of Chenies in Buckinghamshire into the family. The Earl had a son at the age of 42, and was the first Russell to adopt the motto 'Che Sara Sara'.

The 2nd Earl, Francis, was the godfather of Sir Francis Drake, and known as the ugliest man in England. It was Lucy Harrington, wife of the 3rd Earl, who was responsible for obtaining the famous Armada portrait of Queen Elizabeth I by George Gower. Lucy was not only vivacious but level-headed, and Woburn owes so much to her for her good taste in collecting paintings.

The wife of the 4th Earl was Katherine Bruges, who had a family of ten children. The 5th Earl—who became the 1st Duke— fell madly in love with a neighbour, Anne Carr, an orphan who had been brought up by her grandparents in Northampton. His father was violently against the marriage because, unknown to little Anne, her mother was a criminal—a murderess in fact.

Her mother had been married to the Earl of Essex when she was 12 years old, and as was the custom of the time, the bridal couple went back to their parents until the age of consummation. When she was brought to meet her husband, she took one look at him and said 'No, never', and then proceeded to fall in love with the Earl of Somerset.

She asked her husband for a divorce, and the marriage was eventually annulled, but she went too far when she murdered her lover's secretary, Sir Thomas Overbury, who objected to the liaison with his friend and employer. The Countess was sent to the Tower, but by that time she was carrying Somerset's child. And that was how little Anne Carr came to be born in the Tower of London, but died before her husband became the 1st Duke.

Rachel Wriothesley, wife of William, the Earl's son, was a formidable woman. This daughter and co-heiress of Thomas Wriothesley brought into the family the very profitable districts of Bloomsbury and St. Giles with Southampton House and an estate in Hampshire. It was considered at the time that she had the worst of the bargain, and as my husband's family lived off the proceeds of the Bloomsbury estate for many years, her contribution was indeed of great value.

The 2nd Duke—known as the Good Duke—made the most remarkable marriage of all the Russells. At the age of 14 he married Elizabeth Howland, who was just 13. She added Childs bank and the districts of Putney and Streatham to the family fortunes.

The 3rd Duke married Anne, the granddaughter of the famous Duke of Marlborough. They had no children, perhaps because he died very young. His brother, the 4th Duke, was one of the best in the family of Bedfords, and married twice. His first wife was Diana, granddaughter of the Duchess of Marlborough who when she visited Woburn was totally unimpressed and called it 'a gigantic ruin'. That was 300 years ago, and we still live in it today.

Diana died of consumption when she was only 25. For his second wife the Duke chose Gertrude Gower, whom I love because she had such good taste. When her husband was sent to Versailles, she gathered magnificent paintings, furniture, objets d'art and porcelain for the embassy. She used the best cabinet makers—Roger van der Cruse la Croix, who is known by connoisseurs as R.V.L.C., Gaudreau and Topino. My private apartment on the second floor is entirely composed of the furniture Gertrude commissioned.

She is also responsible for the magnificent Sèvres service in the State Dining-room. In the crypt I have made a special pavilion, set as if the King of France were coming to dinner, for the set of Sèvres which was a personal gift from Louis XV to the Duchess. In 1763 the 188 pieces cost 18,374 livres—the pounds of that period—and of course today it is priceless.

Gertrude also loved clothes, and was painted by both Reynolds and Gainsborough. She and her daughter wore a blue and white riding habit that so took King George II's fancy that he appointed it as the uniform of the Royal Navy. The bill for Lady Caroline's habit fascinates women visitors to Woburn.

The 5th Duke never married. He lived with his grandmother, but as soon as he inherited, he brought his beautiful mistress—'Anybody's Mrs. Nancy Parsons'—to live in the house. As his mistress and grandmother were of similar age, the two ladies did not get on. It was a permanent fight until finally poor Gertrude, then 71 years old, was moved out. She died nine years later. The 5th Duke came to a sad end. He had a hernia, and one day when he was playing tennis too strenuously, he dropped dead.

The 6th Duke had two wives, both called Georgina and both beautiful. The first was Georgina Byng, who gave him three most distinguished sons—the 7th Duke; Lord William, who married the beautiful Elizabeth Rawden; and Lord John, who became Prime Minister.

The second wife was Georgina Gordon, who left her mark on Woburn by introducing tea instead of beer at breakfast. Each member of the household was given his own vermeil teapot. We have 12 left of these elegant French eighteenth-century silver-gilt little pots with ivory handles. They are in daily use.

Georgina had thirteen children and my husband is apt to remark that a few of the children were by Landseer, the painter, who came to Woburn to paint the deer.

The 7th Duke's wife, Anna Maria Stanhope, daughter of the Earl of Harrington, was one of the ladies-in-waiting at Queen Victoria's coronation, and her daughter was a bridesmaid. She also attended the Queen when she married Prince Albert, and a sprig of orange blossom plucked from the Queen's bouquet is in the special display showcase I have made in the crypt. The bridesmaids' gift of a golden bracelet with a miniature of the Queen set in diamonds is also there.

Because of the family's new business interest in shipping tea from China, Anna Maria popularised the custom of afternoon tea to popularise the habit. She already had the right commercial approach for Woburn.

The 8th Duke was a bachelor. In a portrait we have at Woburn, the wife of the 9th Duke, the former Lady Elizabeth Sackville-West wears the famous Bedford pearls. I wear only five strands, for they are heavy, and alas because pearls need skin warmth and constant caressing to keep alive; many of them are dull and dead.

The wife of the 10th Duke was Lady Adeline Marie Somers-Cook, daughter of the 3rd Earl Somers. The wife of the 11th Duke, Mary Du Caurroy Tribe, was the daughter of the Archdeacon of Lahore. She was far in advance of her time and would have made a career-woman had she lived today. We still have on the staff Miss Amy Pilgrim, who remembers the Duchess vividly. 'Oh, she was lovely. Strict, mind you, but we all loved her and admired her.'

Despite the fact that she had a personal income of £30,000 a year, and four maids into the bargain, my husband says that she was always badly dressed. As the 11th Duke insisted on taking over the running of the household, which included drawing up the luncheon and dinner menus, and only spoke to her during their half-hour's walk in the park every evening, she had plenty of time to develop her own interests—including painting, wood-carving, needlework, bird-watching, butterfly-collecting and skating.

She was a member of the Skating Club in Knightsbridge, and when she heard that the owner proposed to sell the rink, she persuaded her husband to buy up the lease of the club so that she could go on skating for another 11 years.

It was while she was at school at Cheltenham Ladies' College that she had secretly attended Red Cross lectures and become fascinated by medicine and science. She then founded a hospital at Battlesden, outside the village of Woburn. Amy Pilgrim remembers that whatever hour of the day or night an operation was performed at the cottage-style hospital, the Duchess had to be informed. She would dash over, scrub up with some of the best surgeons from London whom she had persuaded to come and operate, and be present in the theatre. The patients were poor people who needed special treatment which they would not have received in the ordinary hospital.

She continued to work at her hospital even after it was turned over to the army at the outbreak of the First World War. She often worked there 16 hours a day, much as I have done to help my husband save Woburn.

She also climbed to the top of Mont Blanc with her long skirt sweeping the top of her lace bottines. By sheer application she became a remarkable shot, and once bagged 272 pheasants in four and a half hours. She was the first society woman to wear an astride riding habit, and insisted on driving herself in a large, high Rolls-Royce. She always motored without a chauffeur, and carried out her own repairs, including changing the tyres at the side of the road.

At the age of 61, because of an incessant buzzing noise and increasing deafness, she decided to take up flying, and had a private airfield built, complete with hangar, in the park at Woburn.

She became known by everyone as 'the Flying Duchess', and with co-pilot Captain C. D. Barnard, the man who taught her to fly, they broke air records to South Africa and India. She was made a Dame Commander of the British Empire.

In the Flying Duchess's room, which my husband has created at Woburn, there are porcelain animal figures, a case of butterflies she collected, models of her de Havilland Gipsy aeroplane, the strut of the plane in which she last flew, bird paintings by Peter Scott, her skating boots, guns, and samples of the fine embroidery she did in her many hours of solitude.

I am not sure that she would have approved of her name being given to the buffet for visitors at Woburn. But she was human and liked people, and it seemed right.

When we decided to create the buffet, I wanted a building that would be in keeping with the Chinese dairy, and I made a scribbled drawing of what I had in mind. The trustees' architect, Mr. Frost turned this into a most attractive design, with the same kind of red trelliswork and colonnade as the dairy, but topped with a beautiful modern roof with no support whatsoever which is called a hyperbolic paraboloid.

When it was built and opened to the public, we pasted a sheet of paper and placed a pencil on the door, inviting visitors to suggest an appropriate name. There were some amusing ideas like 'Nicole's Café', 'The Duchess's Folly' or 'The Duke's Retreat', which were all inadequate, until Francis, my husband's third son, came up with 'The Flying Duchess'.

When she was 71 years of age, in 1937 the Duchess took off to complete 200 hours of solo flying; she was short by only 55 minutes. A 68-mile course was plotted which should have taken just over an hour. She put on her flying helmet, buttoned up her leather coat, and set off.

A snowstorm blew up, and she was never seen again. My husband has a theory that the combination of her failing faculties and the imminent closing of her beloved hospital may have led her to seek an end in the clean skies she loved to explore. Who knows? Her plane was washed up on the shore at Yarmouth.

My husband's mother, Crommelin, wife of the 12th Duke, was a neglected and sad woman. Daughter of an Oxford professor, she did not want to marry the Duke, and prayed that he would propose to her sister. Instead she was pushed into the marriage by her mother, and spent her married years with a man who rarely spoke to her.

Her death is poignant. She lived in her own dower house, and one Friday evening after her maid had gone, she felt a terrible pain in her head. Stretching for her pills, she fell on the floor due to a stroke that left her paralysed. She was not found until Monday morning when the maid arrived, and she died shortly afterwards of double pneumonia.

My mother-in-law was a kind woman who gained little from her marriage except worldly comforts. In her will, she asked that her ashes be scattered over the hill where she lived and which she loved so much. My husband's sister Daphne took the ashes in a car, but she did not take account of the direction of the wind. The ashes blew back into the car, and she was combing her mother out of her hair for weeks afterwards.

The few times I met my mother-in-law I liked her. Even Annigoni, who painted her, could not make her look very much different from a farmer's wife. After our first meeting, she said to Ian: 'She is the best one of the three.'

My husband has been married three times. His first wife was Clare ('Brownie') Holloway, a dazzling asset to the pre-war London social scene. She was 13 years older than Ian, and theirs was a flamboyant passionate romance that defied his parents' consent. She died in tragic circumstances following an infection that would probably have been cured quite easily in the age of antibiotics.

His second wife, who is very pretty, with huge turquoise eyes, and with whom I am very friendly, was Lydia, daughter of the Duchess of Leinster, the amazing and fabulous Jessie Smithers who had crashed London society by way of being a George Edwardes beauty. Lydia's first husband had been Captain Ian de Hoghton Lyle, who was killed in the war, and she is the mother of Francis, who is the sweetest of all my husband's sons. He does not seem to have the typical Russell characteristics, but has inherited from Lydia a gentleness and an emotional attitude towards life.

I love his coming to Woburn. He puts his two arms around me and bends his tall figure—he is taller than my husband—and gives me a big affectionate kiss. He has enormous charm and a kind of puppy quality. The only thing that I find unnecessary in Francis's attitude towards life is his delight in gossip, but in that at least he follows the family trait.

When he was only a few days over 21, he married the woman of his choice, as his father had done before him. Sweet Anak, who has the gentleness of the Orient, has brought to Francis a ready-made family—bright Patricia, and silent, handsome William. They are all very happy and have made a home where it is a pleasure to visit, for Anak is a superb cook.

My husband's three wives—myself, of course included—had the common denominator of dedicating their lives to that very special Russell, my husband.

As he is born under the sign of Gemini, you never know which personality you awake with—the enchanting, amusing, beguiling, witty human being, or the moody, silent, stubborn, detached man. Life is never dull with him, and I am grateful for that.

He has had three wives—a brunette, a blond and a redhead—so his next one will have to be bald. That is, if I die, of course!

When I came to Woburn, I was distressed by the muddle in the rooms—eighteenth-century pieces side by side with Victoriana, for example. My husband has such a deep sense of heredity that when I wanted to move something, to keep in the room only the bare necessities of the highest quality, he always answered by telling me which Duke had bought the object in question, saying that it had to remain.

I first conducted a big search for pairs, and put them together. Then I started doing one room in completely English style, and one in French, but each time it involved an aesthetic argument with Ian.

Then a young friend called Claude Serre came from France for the weekend. He had acquired a great knowledge of the eighteenth century. I asked him to advise me about the Blue Salon, where the superb Montigny desk with the Cartonnier clock stands under a Claude Lorraine. He agreed to stay for a time to help my 'de-junking' campaign. We had to make a journey to South Africa. As we were leaving, Claude said 'What about bringing the Roman Emperors and their columns into the West Hall?' 'What a good idea,' I replied lightly, as I got into the car and waved good-bye.

We boarded the ship at Southampton, and were at sea for three weeks. When we arrived in Cape Town, we found frantic tele-grams: 'Both lifts broken, three workmen in hospital with bad backs, all household staff resigned, please send instructions what to do with Claude Serre.'

My husband was furious. 'He can't move my ancestors,' he said.

But when we returned to Woburn, we had to admit that everything looked so much better than before. I was delighted, and I carried on from where he had left off, to the despair of the trustees and their inventory.

To the first Countess of Bedford the family owes its burial ground, which was part of the estate of Chenies. For many years this was the main family seat, and now still holds the family mausoleum where the tombs of all my husband's ancestors still exist.

When Ian dies he will be buried there, although I have made other arrangements for myself.

In the winter, we often visit Chenies for burials, as my husband is the head of the clan. In bad weather, the cousins seem to drop off one after another.

Once I was there and saw a van from Harrods standing at the side entrance. It looked so odd in the centre of the secluded churchyard.

'What is a Harrods van doing here?' I asked.

'Oh, they always organise the family funerals,' Ian replied.

Only the Dukes and Duchesses are buried in the fantastic chapel which contains all kind of monuments in all shapes and sizes. One cousin liked foie gras, so his ashes are in a foie gras jar. They had to seal the lid of my father-in-law's urn five times. Every time we passed it, Ian would say: 'Oh God, the old man has popped out again.'

Downstairs, in what at first glance looks like the luggage department of any big department store, there are coffins on the shelves, one on top of the other. They are all covered with red felt, and have brass knobs. On top, there is a coronet, or a sword for a military man.

As my husband passed a beautiful silk coffin one day, he said: 'Hello, dear.'

I asked who was buried there.

'My first wife,' he replied.

I did not like the thought of being buried inside this forbidding place, away from my children. It was then that I had the idea to ask Ian for his heart if he should die before me.

'If you want that piece of old muscle, of course you can have it,' he said.

Once I knew that he had put in his will that his heart was to be buried with me, I then proceeded to organise my own future return to France. I did not do so in a rush. Such matters must be done rationally and with thought. I just waited for a convenient time.

One day, shopping in Harrods, I bought a collection of delicious French cheeses—Camembert, Brest Bleu, Caprice des Dieux. Then I went to the delicatessen counter and bought some good garlic and Rosette de Lyon salami. Continuing my shopping I suddenly found myself on the top floor near the funeral department. I went in and asked to see the manager. I was taken into a very small office, to a Mr. Chambers. I sat at the desk in front of him, and put my carrier-bag on the floor.

'I have come to see you about a funeral,' I began.

'Yes. Perhaps we should decide on the coffin first.'

'What do you offer?'

From his drawer he brought a selection of woods. I decided on teak because it is a nice strong wood.

'And now for the handles.'

'I do not want anything fancy. Silver metal will be all right.'

'Would you like a cross on top?'

'All right, put a cross on top.'

I have an excellent reason why I want Harrods to do the job. I have put in my will that when I die, I do not want my husband, children or any friends to see me. Once you are dead, it is finished. It is over. I am very firm about that. People should be remembered alive, in action, laughing, walking.

I think dead people are a bore, and that tiptoeing in silently to see a dead body is all very morbid and in bad taste.

That is why, everywhere I go, I now carry a card saying that in the event of my death, Mr. Chamber's department must be contacted immediately and before anyone else. Whether I die in a road accident, or an operating theatre or in my own lovely bed, Harrods will come and collect me pronto.

[237]

Then I want my body stuffed with herbs, or whatever they do, put in the coffin I have chosen, and sent to France.

Even arranging that was not easy. First I had to find a burial ground. The family one at Creil is full, but in any case I do not want to return there. Creil belongs to my youth. Ronquerolles was where I had been happiest, where the children had grown up, and that is where I wanted finally to rest.

Still, there were difficulties. I was no longer domiciled at Ronquerolles, so the cemetery could not have me.

I enquired at Meribel in the French Alps, where I have my joyful mountain-house. The man in charge of the cemetery happened to be my carpenter. Yes, Meribel was right. Now there are ten rooms reserved for me and my children and grandchildren—and my husband's heart.

I was discussing all this with Mr. Chambers, and he showed me what it would all cost.

'Will you send it to me in writing?' I asked. He agreed.

Then I wrote out my deposit cheque, and bent to pick up my bag.

By now the whole of that little room was invaded by the pungent smell of cheese and garlic. It was so strong, it almost made you sneeze. If Mr. Chambers noticed, his funeral manners forbade him to comment. Instead he asked quietly:

'When do you expect the person to die, or is there a deceased body already?'

'You have it facing you in the chair,' I replied.

Poor Mr. Chambers turned very white, and looked at me in horror, as if I were going to commit suicide there and then.

Every year I send another hundred pounds to keep up with the inflation of dying, and nightly I sleep safe in the knowledge that Harrods never lets a customer down.

32   *Duchesses may come and go but . . .*

MY HUSBAND WAS playing golf in South Africa when he heard of the death of his father, the 12th Duke. He and his wife Lydia were then living on their 200-acre fruit-farm 'Waterfall' in the Drakenstein Mountains about 40 miles from Cape Town. He was extremely happy there, and enjoyed the life.

The 12th Duke had been found with gunshot wounds in his head. The coroner's verdict was accidental death, but the Duke was a very experienced shot, and the opinion has been expressed that his death was the result of the acute depression from which he had suffered during the last months of his life.

Ian returned at once to England to attend the funeral and to look at his inheritance, which included a dilapidated Woburn Abbey. He felt totally ill at ease with his new responsibilities as the 13th Duke of Bedford.

His first glimpse of the Abbey was distressing and depressing. He told me that it looked as though a bomb had fallen on it. The Secret Service had used part of the house during the war, and rooms had been cleared to provide the needed space. No redecoration had been done for 100 years. All the main reception rooms were piled high with furniture, paintings were stacked against the wall, and great areas of carpet were rolled up in the entrance-hall. The impression was of a series of bankrupt auction-rooms rather than one of England's great houses. Everywhere there was a smell of damp, dry rot, and death. It was a house without spirit, without hope.

Only a man like my husband, with his own private well of determination and inflexibility, would have undertaken the task he did in restoring Woburn to its former dignity and glory.

Ian's problem was how to restore the house as a family home and how to finance its costly upkeep.

His father, who had withdrawn from the outside world, left a chaotic financial mess for his son and the trustees to sort out. Had he lived another three months, the financial settlements he had made for his son, and other members of the family, would have been legally acceptable. As it was, his total estate of £8,600,00 was subject to a tax of £4,500,000.

There seemed only one way to keep Woburn alive—to follow what other families had done in the same situation, and open it to the public.

Once Ian had made this decision, characteristically he set himself what seemed the impossible task of having the house and grounds ready in six months.

We have a wonderful staff at Woburn. I call them my 'Woburn family' because it is the way I feel about them. They speak about 'the Woburn Way of life'. In a crisis, we all pull together, working for Woburn. Through weeks of 17-hour days, the staff worked with Ian, sorting, cleaning, painting, polishing. Every day brought new surprises. The fabulous gold and blue Sèvres dinner-service, for example, was discovered lying on the cobbled floor of a loose-box. Lydia and Ian took on the enormous task of washing each of the pieces themselves, on the theory that if anything was broken, the responsibility should be theirs.

At last the great day came when Woburn was opened to the public. It was an immediate success. With Ian's flair for publicity—which still irritates many of the other stately-home owners—he obtained tremendous Press coverage. Today, 20 years later, with its handsome rooms, priceless works of art, beautiful grounds and safari park, it is still number one in the stately-homes business.

Just four years after she moved into Woburn, Lydia made the heart-breaking decision to lead her own life, so she and Ian were divorced. The house remained without a châtelaine until I arrived in September 1960. Duchesses may come and go, but, thank God, Woburn goes on forever.

Tolerance unfortunately has never been one of my endearing virtues. Among intelligent people, I find it a waste of time and emotion. On my fiftieth birthday, however, I promised myself that I would learn to be tolerant, otherwise I will end up a cantankerous old lady. I am never knowingly unkind, but my straightforward approach is sometimes misunderstood. I had been a guest at Woburn many times, but now, as the new mistress, I knew I must tread warily.

Besides I was French—and, therefore, under suspicion.

Six months after I arrived, we had a crisis in the kitchen when the chef broke a bone in his foot. I looked among the staff for a temporary cook. One of the women we used as guards on public days said that she knew how to cook plain English food—as indeed she did. Appropriately, she was called Mrs. Cook, and I superimposed on her cooking my own French style. It was a good combination. She was wonderfully quick to learn, and made the best puff pastry I have ever tasted, so light and flaky. She remained as our cook for several years. My husband is willing to try anything new in the food line. There is hardly a new restaurant in London that he does not test. Once I persuaded Mrs. Cook to make a complete Chinese meal. She prepared it with authenticity and style. It looked superb. She stood back, looked at it, and announced disdainfully:

'I would not touch a single dish of it for a million pounds.'

Between us—Mrs. Cook and I—we began to persuade the staff to become more adventurous and experimental in their taste. We cooked meats in their own juices, banished forever those heavy floury English gravies that cover the meat like a blanket of brown fog. We introduced veal, which had never been eaten at Woburn, and the first time I ordered it from the butcher I had to buy a complete half animal. We ran the range of herbs from tarragon to garlic.

Today, instead of the dreadful odour of boiled cabbage, a visitor to the kitchen is more likely to smell the fragrance of onions or garlic sizzling.

I gradually persuaded the staff that simple, well prepared, fresh food, as the French farmers eat it, is really the best. It took me years to get an artichoke served perfectly plainly with vinaigrette, or to have courgettes sautéd in butter and served with Parmesan cheese as a special course. Guests always enjoy our salads with crisp lettuce heads, radishes for colour, and spring onions for tang.

The day I saw Mrs. Cook preparing an enormous ratatouille—tomatoes, aubergines, onion and garlic—*for the staff*, I knew we had succeeded.

I made other changes in the menus. I had cheese served before the pudding or fruit because I do not think it is pleasant to leave the table with the taste of Stilton or Camembert, still in the mouth as is the English habit.

I insisted—and Ian agreed—that we should not tolerate the bizarre separation of men and women after the last course. Why should women be herded upstairs just when the port arrives and the conversation sparkles? It breaks the rhythm of the evening.

I am always amused by the look of total bewilderment on the faces of our foreign guests when they sit in the Canaletto Room and find five forks on their left. The reason is that fish-knives had not been invented in the eighteenth century—the family silver is Georgian—and my husband would not dream of eating with a Georgian fork and a Victorian fish-knife. Even when we have dinner in a restaurant, my husband asks for two forks. Habit is second nature. I soon discovered to my amazement that it was much easier to eat a sole with two forks.

Our troubles began when Mrs. Cook slipped in the bath and hurt her back. I was dining at the American Embassy at the time. It was a Friday night, and at about eleven o'clock the butler told me that I was wanted on the telephone. I immediately thought something was wrong with one of the children, but it was Woburn calling to say that Mrs. Cook was hurt and that there was no-one to cook for a weekend full of guests.

I said: 'What do you expect me to do at this time? Should I walk into the Embassy kitchen and tell the chef to follow me?' I then asked them to telephone all the big hotels in London to enquire if one of their chefs had the weekend free and could come and help.

Indeed, the next morning I found a fresh-faced 22-year-old assistant chef called David Coyle. I showed him the rather elaborate original menus, but said: 'Of course, we will change all the menus and you will choose something that will be easier for you.'

As soon as David spoke, I knew at once that he would do the job well. He had the right ideas of what is essential in cooking, and he was interested. Now he appears on television, and was even chosen for the 'Cooking with Wine' demonstration at the first London International Wine Festival. I asked him to return the following weekend. I liked his creativeness and his enthusiasm, and I decided that I would teach him French cooking. We had a two-hour lesson every Monday morning, going over everything that had gone wrong. Sometimes he wept or raged when things had not gone to his liking. I always complimented him when he was right.

I asked him to stay, and he has been with us now for nine years.

One of the first things I did when David took over as chef was to go into the kitchen and say: 'David, look what I'm going to do.' I took all the artificial flavouring and gelatine and colourings, and flung them in the dustbin, saying: 'I never want to see them here again.' I explained that if he wanted gelatine, he could get it by cooking pied de veau—calf's foot, and he could get colouring from natural things, not from a bottle.

When there are no guests, I have by me a pad with the menu on one side and space on the other for my comments—'Not enough onion', 'Too much salt', 'No flavour', 'Try again'. I send it back with the coffee-tray to the kitchen.

I was very unhappy about the food for visitors to Woburn. It was done by concessionaires and became, by my standards, so bad that I eventually inserted in all our literature: 'If you are a gourmet, we recommend that you go to the following restaurants after your visit to the Abbey . . .' and named several good restaurants in the district. One day I said to David, 'How would you like to be in charge of the restaurants?'

David, who is very adventurous, was excited at the prospect. Ray Beardow, one of the 'Woburn family', would, I thought, work well with David in this project. He would provide a perfect foil for David's Irish temper, for Ray has an even, smiling temperament and never gets flustered. I am very fond of him. He had arrived at Woburn 17 years earlier with a pregnant wife and an old jalopy packed to the brim. He had suggested that a roundabout would be popular with children while their parents absorbed culture in the house! Although by now he knew a lot about entertainment, neither he, David nor I had any experience of catering management.

My husband said we were mad to enter a field about which we knew nothing, but we were all enthusiastic and hard working, and keen to make a success.

We now not only have two restaurants and a buffet but also a banqueting department, which gets booked up months in advance.

Today we have Joel, our charming French chef, but we still follow the same routine that I planned with Mrs. Cook. Every Monday morning, we meet to consult on the week's menus. I have my own system. I have a wide printed sheet of paper, divided into days and then subdivided into morning and evening. We put a complete menu into each square, and we indicate the number of people who will be present. At the bottom there is a space for the wines. These are kept on a special slanted shelf in the kitchen.

In the pantry, on the household board, there hangs another sheet of paper, listing the names of the guests and the bedrooms they have been given, with the name of the newspaper they would like in the morning.

I also keep an alphabetical book of the guests with special requirements—vegetarians, practising Jews, those with allergies, those on diets.

Naturally I am more concerned with the inside of the house than with the 13 miles of wall that need to be kept in constant repair. In 1960, Ian installed upstairs an elaborate self-contained kitchen with ovens, grills, hotplates, refrigerators, and a deep-freeze. It is there in case one day we are without staff. Today the vegetable compartment of the refrigerator is filled with cigars, the shelves with champagne, the grills used for breakfast toast, the oven is virgin new, and the hotplates are used for warming up croissants. It is a strange luxury when you think of the large kitchen and the staff three floors below, but we like it that way.

For breakfast, which we prepare ourselves, we normally have Muesli. My husband shreds the apple with a machine, and I put raisins, walnuts, hazel-nuts and almonds into the bowls with the milk. We change apple for raspberries or strawberries in the summer—and, of course, we both drink Earl Grey or Lapsang Souchong in bed, each carrying his or her own tray in dead silence.

We then sit up in bed with the papers. I read the *Daily Mail* and the *Guardian* while my husband prefers the *Daily Express* and *The Times*.

When I was first taken round to meet all the staff, I was intrigued with Mrs. Houghton. A lively woman with bright eyes and a fast tongue, who remembers the days of Herbrand, the 11th Duke, for it was she who used to prepare the consommé that he had as a first course every evening. As she explained:

'It took 19 pounds of best shin of beef to prepare a day's supply of two cups of beef bouillon.' At today's prices, one cup of Herbrand's beef elixir would cost at least £5! Nevertheless he insisted that he lived in only 'modest comfort'.

I am a practical person. Life has made me that way. One of my earliest observations was that Englishwomen need to powder their noses, or whatever else they do, twice as often as French women.

To have an attractive ladies' room therefore seemed terribly important. Our 'Ladies' at Woburn was uncomfortable, dreary and depressing, and if it did not smell sour, it looked it.

Wandering round it one morning, I pulled away the window curtains and discovered that I was looking at some Roman-style arches that supported a terrace built by the 5th Duke. Clearly this was where to begin. I covered the arches with white trellis and planted ivy all over them. Up in the Sculpture Gallery I found a seven-foot-high statue of an angel. Ian was not too happy about my choice. He said:

'I am not worried about the humidity, but an angel looking into the ladies' loo sounds improper.'

I was adamant. It took seven men three hours to bring the angel from the gallery into my arcade. When it was finally in place, I shone a spotlight on it. It was incredibly beautiful. Back I went, and found four more neo-Classical sculptures to keep it company.

We were short of money for such trivial things as a cloakroom dressing-room, so I covered the walls with red velvet paper to give it an intimacy, and I used the same red toile de jouy as at Ronquerolles for the long dressing-table and built-in cabinet for the coats.

When I had finished, I invited Ian to the opening. 'It is pretty enough to use as a sitting-room', was his verdict.

That was also the opinion of Charles, known by everyone as Charlie. A fastidious white and butterscotch cat, half Siamese, half Abyssinian, he immediately installed himself there as if in his own private apartment! Whenever he is not hunting, he is invariably to be found sleeping on the chair in the cloakroom.

One night soon afterwards, several women guests went to the new loo. As they entered, Charlie raised his head from the red velvet armchair, got up, arched his back, and disappeared under the dressing-table to reappear with one of his hunting trophies— a half-eaten rabbit, dripping with blood.

Tiaras toppled as one friend of mine fell back into the curtains in a dead faint. Another jumped up on a chair. Long dresses were snatched up around knees as Charlie took his trophy and showed it to each woman. There was complete chaos.

One morning, I was looking for some appropriate pictures as a final touch for the walls, when Mrs. Pepper, our diligent house-keeper, heard me laughing almost hysterically. She thought I had gone mad, until I told her:

'The 4th Duchess brought back many treasures from France. The 7th Duchess was a close friend of Queen Victoria's. One after another the Duchesses have added beauty and fame to Woburn. I hope I shall not be remembered only as the Duchess who decorated the ladies' room.'

My husband says that the stately-home owners belong not only to the smallest and most exclusive club in Britain but the bitchiest. This could be true.

The whole stately-home business has its own hierarchy. We come at the top of the list simply because we attract most visitors. Then come Beaulieu, Chatsworth, Blenheim and Castle Howard, and on down to the other 995 houses open to the public.

Meetings, if you can call them that, are usually informal—just a group of men huddled in the corner at a British Tourist Authority gathering. I have come to the conclusion that Woburn is a school for stately-home owners, for what we do one season will surely be copied elsewhere the next.

The big exception is our safari park, but then we did ask Henry Bath to open it on 19 May, 1970.

It was a splendid performance. Just as he was cutting the ribbon the baby elephant, who was slightly bored with the whole proceedings, trod on the Marquess's foot. His cry of 'Hell' was carried to the whole crowd, and set the tone for a happy, informal opening.

Whenever we are in England, every Thursday Ian and I just take off from Woburn. It is necessary simply so that we can see each other. Woburn consumes our attention and makes it almost impossible for us to find time for each other. Although I try to keep it as a family home, we are conscious all the time of living on the job or, to put it another way, living above the store.

Sometimes we stay in a London hotel and go to the theatre other times we drive to the country. One night we went to the theatre, then had dinner afterwards, arriving at the Carlton Tower Hotel—which was then new—well after midnight. I was tired, and flopped down on the banquette in the foyer while Ian went to see about our room.

The man at the reception desk looked up and said: 'The Duke of Bedford? Oh dear, we thought it was a joke when you telephoned, and we didn't keep the room.'

Ian was getting impatient: 'Well, do you have accommodation or not?'

'Oh yes, we have the London suite'—and then, looking across at me, the man asked: 'Is the lady with you?' We laughed.

We both fill many lecture engagements, and always try to arrange to take the following day off. In this way we cover much of the country, and can visit other stately homes.

On one of our Thursdays, we decided to go to Blenheim. We paid our 2s. 6d. entrance fee—the cost at the time—and met our guide, who did not recognise us. She went into her routine, opening the door of a room, herding her audience inside, closing the door, and offering a commentary on the room in question. As we were passing through the chapel, we heard whispering behind us, and realised that the other visitors had recognised Ian.

A man produced a Blenheim guidebook and asked Ian to sign it. At first Ian refused, as he thought that Bert Marlborough—who was then the Duke—would not approve, but almost before we knew what was happening, we were surrounded, and the guide looked at us in horror.

Once we were outside, Ian said: 'I suppose we are not in his house any more, so, all right, I'll do it.'

Then the imp in Ian took over. As people proffered their books for his autograph, he wrote in them: 'You should come to Woburn. It is better.' Everyone was highly amused. Next day, the story was in the William Hickey column of the *Daily Express*, and we had a good laugh. Bert Marlborough must have found out about it, because the following day, he made some sort of a reply to the effect that the Duke of Bedford was a cad!

The Marquess of Bath visits us regularly or sends someone over, and then we receive a little card, perhaps saying: 'Your tea is better than ours but your beer is flat.'

Lord Montagu of Beaulieu also visits us to see what is happening. He of course has a splendid motor museum, and my husband refers cattily to him and his collection of old cars as 'Edward and his garage'.

An extraordinary aspect of running a stately home is that much of its success depends not on how many Van Dycks you have, but on how many loos. No amount of beautiful objects can compensate a visitor who is kept queueing for hours in the cold outside a lavatory. They simply will not return, and we rely on our faithful visitors who come back year after year.

Each year we set aside £10,000 for renovating or building new loos. I have a terrible vision of waking up one day to find that the entire 3,000-acre park has become an immense field of lavatories.

I always remember sitting up until three in the morning with the Marquess of Hertford and his charming Belgian wife, telling them what souvenirs people preferred, how to compile an interesting guidebook, and the way of placing guides and stewards in strategic places throughout the house.

We also have visitors from France. The Comte de la Panouse came to Woburn about 20 times before opening his first game-reserve just south of Paris. The Marquis de Bréteuil and his wife spent three days with us so that we could give them the benefit of our advice and experience.

In June 1961, we had our first family wedding when my husband's eldest son Robin, the Marquess of Tavistock, married Henrietta.

I had known and liked Robin since Ian had taken me to visit him at Harvard while I was staying at Boston. He has a marvellous quality of honesty, integrity and tenacity. When his sons were born, I was pleased to see that my judgment of him was sound, for he raised those boys as a father should—with love and firm direction.

Andrew—Lord Howland—who will eventually be the 15th Duke—looks remarkably like Henrietta, and has her gentle manner and sweetness. He is very lovable, and we get along marvellously together. He is a very happy-go-lucky boy, always good-tempered, even when his brother teases him unmercifully.

Little Robin, called Robbie, is a true Russell—opiniated, tenacious, stubborn and very bright. I adore him because he is so much like my husband.

The children come to Woburn very often, and it is always a joy to have them. I love it when they say: 'Let's go and look at our ancestors,' and we go round the house and tell them stories —funny stories, sad stories—about their family.

Andrew is already knowledgeable about works of art, but Robbie prefers the park.

I came to the family loving my husband's sons unconditionally, especially the two eldest, whose mother was dead. Rudolf has become through the years, in spirit and affection, my son, and I have taken care of him more than of my own children.

His brother Robin has never liked me. I do not know why—maybe because I do not pronounce my aitches and he is so proper, or maybe because I am French and he is so traditionally English.

At first his father was opposed to Robin's marriage because the boy was so young. But my husband has now of course become reconciled, and they are such a wonderful united family.

Robin's wedding was one of the most highly organised events outside a royal marriage. Henrietta made an exceptionally beautiful bride in her Nina Ricci dress. She looked so pure and virginal as she entered St. Clement Danes—the Royal Air Force church in the Strand. Caterine, Anyes and Henrietta's best friend, the Countess Esterhazy, were bridesmaids, and when Caterine said that her turquoise silk dress looked like a lampshade, I did not entirely disagree. I still have the dresses; it is a pity that the girls never worn them again.

I wore a dress by Balmain which only arrived the night before, and I was absolutely livid when I noticed that the shocking-pink chiffon material of the coat was a shade yellower than the dress. The first thing Daphne, my sister-in-law, said when she saw me was: 'Your coat is not the same colour as your dress', which made me feel very uncomfortable. I later learnt that a girl in the workroom had burnt the original coat when she was pressing it, and they had ordered some more material and made another coat without checking that it was an exact match.

The reception was at Claridges, and Henrietta made a fabulous exit with everyone throwing roses as she disappeared. But it was only an exit, as they returned to Claridges, where we had prepared a suite for them—with amusing presents.

We were still asleep the morning after when Henrietta telephoned and invited us to breakfast with them. We thought this rather surprising but we dressed hurriedly and had a marvellous time discussing the previous day.

That summer was also the first to reveal some worthwhile

results of my gardening. Woburn has never been known for its gardens, as Chatsworth has, for instance. This is probably because our rolling parklands planted by Repton with thousands of trees that change colour with the seasons, and the ever-moving deer, have a beauty of their own.

I wanted a secret garden of my own, away from the public part of the Abbey, somewhere I could sunbathe in privacy. I created a circular rose-garden, which my friends say looks French. It is encircled with rambling-roses, and has a fountain of silver water in the centre.

I find contentment there, and whenever I have the chance, I spend an hour in peace. My husband never sets foot outside the house unless it is to be photographed or to get into his car. When he finally discovered my retreat, he was astonished and said, rather tersely: 'You are turning the whole place into a cottage,' a remark I found amusing when you consider that the cottage had 120 rooms!

I have also planted a long avenue of laburnum, trained in an arbour in the eighteenth-century French manner. Some of the trees died and had to be replaced last year, and it is very sad of course that I will never live to see them in their full glory.

At the opening of the Royal Academy Summer Exhibition that year, I was fascinated by an artist whose portraits were striking because of his technique of painting his subjects tall, slim and elegant in soft greyish colours.

As my husband always dressed in grey at the time, I asked the artist if he would come to Woburn to paint Ian's portrait. I was expecting a man just like his paintings, but instead Gerald Rose is about five feet two inches, with a shock of brilliant red hair. Perhaps his paintings reflected what his ideal man should look like—the exact opposite of himself.

Neither he nor I liked the first portrait he did of my husband. He repainted it, and I still did not like it—it did not have the elegance and willowy looks of his earlier work I had seen. The artist then said that we would try a sitting position, and the result was splendid. It was exhibited in the Academy, and received a great deal of comment. When you entered the room, its full impact hit you, and you were looking at a real human being on the canvas—moving, alive. The artist captured the two sides of my husband—his immense charm and his whimsical, slightly sarcastic smile.

When the portrait finally arrived at Woburn, it had been painted green. I was astonished, and asked Gerald Rose why he had done it. He simply answered: 'I think your husband has a green personality.'

That was also the year that my husband lost his driving licence. Ian has an eccentric way of driving and very little patience with people in front of him. As we drove on the M1 motorway every single day, and sometimes twice a day, he considered it almost like his own private road.

On this particular day he was driving alone, and as usual impatient of the car in front of him. He blew his horn several times but the man would not give way, so he just passed him on the inside lane. As Ian's number plate is 1 DOB, it was not difficult for the man to remember it and report the matter to the police.

Ian was summoned to appear in court, and elected to be tried by jury. The first jury failed to agree, and the case was tried a second time. This time the jury were out for three and a half hours. We were going to a dinner party in Paris, and as the jury were deliberating, we all sat around and kept looking at our watches. I was terrified that we were going to miss our plane.

Suddenly the jury returned, and the foreman, in a serious voice, announced that they found my husband guilty. I jumped up, turned to the man, and said 'Thank you so much.' The judge had hardly finished fining Ian £50 and banning him from driving for six months when I turned to Ian and said 'Give me the keys and let's go.' Everyone in the court was flabbergasted. I drove like a roaring March wind to the airport, and we just caught our plane. After that we engaged a chauffeur called Manning, and although my husband now drives occasionally, the jury will never know what a service they did for me—they lengthened my life by several years.

33   *Duchess duties*

UNFORTUNATELY I AM intolerant, and I do not suffer fools gladly. To make up a party for the weekend, one has to include brains, knowledge and a sense of humour. Good looks do no harm either. I would rather have an amusing, intelligent unknown every time, than a bore who might expect an invitation on account of his title or bank account.

From those early days, I was determined that we would never entertain bores as our personal guests at Woburn. To Ian's collection of friends, I would add my own from the world of the arts.

I always loved it when Nubar and Marie Gulbenkian came but of course there are always the giants, the great personalities that one loves to see in action.

Nubar and Marie were a truly remarkable couple. One never knew what to expect, but life was never dull when they were around. Marie was half French and half Irish, and had a temper accordingly. Nubar was just plain impossible—a lovely man to invite for lunch or dinner, but not, I should think, to live with. When he died, the London scene lost one of its most exotic characters.

I enjoyed Nubar because he made me laugh, and he was always so immaculate, his beard well trimmed and his daily orchid inevitably in his buttonhole, even when he was hunting.

One Sunday, Marie and Nubar, who lived near us, were expected for luncheon. Nubar arrived without Marie.

'Is Marie not coming?' I asked solicitously.

He laughed an enormous laugh, which came right from the depths of that plenteous stomach, and replied: 'I walked here.'

And I said: 'What do you mean, you walked?'

'Yes, Marie was driving on the M1, and I gave her directions, and she got fed up with me. Then she stopped the car and said: "If you would like to drive, you drive, but you must stop giving me directions. If you are not satisfied with my driving, you must get out of the car." '

Nubar was almost paralytic with laughter.

'So I left her and began walking. By chance I found a car that was coming in the right direction, and got a lift part of the way.'

By now Nubar could hardly speak: 'When the man dropped me, by some fantastic luck I found a taxi. Wait until Marie sees me here.'

A few minutes later Marie arrived. She was simply furious to find an exuberant Nubar, drink in hand, in his hour of triumph.

He was always keen on pretty girls, so whenever we invited him, I tried to arrange that he was surrounded by charming women who would amuse him.

At a dinner party one night, I took Nubar aside and asked him:

'Would you rather be seated according to protocol or next to a pretty girl?'

It was really a formality, as I already knew the answer. 'Pretty girl,' he said without hesitation, twinkling and shining like a Byzantine Father Christmas.

After dinner, Marie asked me: 'Why did you sit Nubar there at the end of the table?'

I just giggled and answered: 'Nubar knew about it,' thinking he would find a better explanation than I.

A Duchess has many duties besides giving dinner parties, of course. It was an extremely strange experience for me when I first appeared in public in England—in front of a vast television audience, in fact.

Ballroom-dancing does not exist in France in the organised way it does in Britain. All those dancing ladies with dresses made from hundreds of yards of tulle and thousands of sequins sewn on by their mothers or aunts; brothers and sisters who spend four nights a week touring with a ballroom-dancing team; suburban neighbours by day who become the Military Two Step champions of Great Britain by night; husbands and wives who have spent 40 years perfecting the Old-Fashioned Waltz—these are something so lovable and essentially English.

One evening I accompanied my husband to the Crystal Palace with Eric Morley, who runs the Miss World competition. Both the BBC and ITV cameras were covering the presentation of the Carl Allen Awards for dancing.

Just before the presentation of the awards, Eric Morley asked me to follow him, and before I knew it, I was in front of the cameras, being introduced to the world as the Duchess of Bedford.

The experience was still so new. I had been a television producer for many years, but always on the other side of the camera. Besides, I knew nothing about ballroom-dancing.

When the first couple came up, I felt like an absolute idiot. The only thing I could think of to say was: 'How do you store those dresses?'

The girl who won had in fact travelled by motorbike and stored her dress rolled tight and packed into a tube laced on the pillion seat.

By the time I left that evening, I knew more about ballroom-dancing than most people in England. I had been catapulted into one of the many facets of life that being a public figure in England entails. I felt very strange.

I soon discovered that being a Duchess meant being on show, and speaking in public. The first time was three months after we were married, just before Christmas, at the church in Eversholt —a small village on the edge of the estate.

I was so nervous. Ian had told me not to worry as there would only be 50 people there. In the end there were 500—I suppose they had never seen me before, so they wanted to have a look at me.

I began: 'First of all I have some good news and some bad news. The bad news is that I was burgled last night and my fur coat was stolen. The good news is that because I am now wearing such a thin coat and am absolutely freezing, I shall be very brief.'

It was the worst time for the Common Market, and many people were anti-French. I knew what they were thinking—that they were going to hate me. But when they discovered I was not the monster they expected, they all changed.

One of the many things I do outside my normal routine is to conduct parties of blind people around Woburn. This can be very difficult. You cannot just say that something is red or blue, or describe something as being transparent. You have to find another way.

Woburn on a summer's night with the calling of the deer, the sun setting red and purple beyond the lake, or in the white of winter with its Corot-like trees and the call of the wild duck, has a special kind of magic. To me it is so precious that I have commissioned a local artist called Peter Wagon to paint the view from my bedroom window. I want to take it with me wherever I go in the world, wherever I finally make my home.

But how can one adequately describe the view to someone who is blind? I remember a young girl of 18 who was extremely beautiful. She touched every statue and studied everything, and at one point she asked if I had a ring. I said 'Yes', and she said 'What is it?' 'A diamond solitaire,' I told her. 'Can I touch it?' she asked shyly. And of course I let her. She then put the ring to her lips, and I asked why.

'Because that is the most sensitive part of the individual, and I can feel it better that way,' she replied.

We have had special ramps built that can hurriedly be placed across the stairways at Woburn for the use of people in wheel-chairs. The guides are always especially helpful to blind or chair-ridden people, who are usually so much more attentive than the ordinary public, who often shuffle through room after room as if it were a duty.

One of my long-standing duchess duties has been the Berkeley Dress Show. Ten years ago, when I first undertook this assignment, I was distressed that young, sometimes awkward, girls were dressed in couture clothes by Dior and Balmain which were so obviously meant to be worn by chic, mature women who depended on their own personal style rather than on changes in fashion. Now the clothes are so much more suitable, being designed by young people like Sandra Rhodes, Gina Fratini, and Thea Porter.

My husband, who was compèring the show, once found himself short of a description, and to my horror I heard him describing an Empire-style dress with the words:

'This is a very lovely dress which is ideal when a girl goes dancing and afterwards when she is expecting.'

The model's mother was quite rightly incensed, and cornering Ian afterwards, said:

'My daughter is a virgin. How dare you suggest something as vulgar as that?'

Every year we have sorted out the girls who parade in the park—tall girls, awkward girls, stumpy girls, puppy-fat girls, skinny girls, happy girls, sad girls, with Ian in their midst. I have been only too pleased to assist, because the dress show was in connection with a charity to do with children, and anything to do with children commands my automatic help.

At Woburn our lives have always been organised one year in advance, and from Easter to Easter we always know what we are going to do. It is a peculiar feeling, as if you are a property and have no personal hand in your destiny.

For years the Easter Bonnet Parade has been an attraction for our visitors. In 1963 our interesting panel of judges included Lionel Bart, who wrote 'Oliver', and Marjorie Proops, the *Daily Mirror* columnist. Because it was snowing the judging was to be done on the top of the steps in the east front. We were all having lunch in the West Hall, and wondering what would happen to the competition in the awful weather, when suddenly the door from the outside of the west front opened and a girl in a bikini and large hat walked straight through the hall and out the east side. We watched her as she disappeared into the snow. As we say, 'Anything can happen at Woburn.'

We open many functions each year, and being a most punctual person myself, our travelling is always planned like a military operation.

One year I was asked to open the Antique Dealers' Fair at Solihull in the Midlands. The organisers sent a helicopter for us. I enjoyed the flight immensely; it was marvellous to fly all over Woburn and Bedfordshire, and to look down at some of the most beautiful countryside in England.

The idea was for us to travel in less modern style the short distance between our landing point and the hall where the fair was being held. Nobody had considered the problem however of a woman in a tight skirt getting out of a helicopter. There were no steps. I stood at the door, wondering what I was supposed to do. Finally two men came, and I put my arms on their shoulders and jumped, my dress slithering up alarmingly. Then, with great dignity, I entered a landau drawn by four white horses.

In the Sixties tight skirts were an enormous problem, and I for one was grateful when the more action-line fashions took over.

My husband was driving back from London one night at 3 a.m., when our car broke down. Once again I was wearing a skin-tight crystal-beaded dress in my favourite shade of turquoise blue. There was only one thing to do—hitch-hike. I collected my miniature Yorkshire terrier, Rembrandt, and we stood helplessly, and rather idiotically, in our evening clothes on the dark motor-way. Soon a lorry-driver stopped and offered to take us to the nearest service-station, where we could find a telephone to call home or a taxi. We were delighted, and as I handed Rembrandt to him, he said: 'What's this?'

He soon knew. Rembrandt bit him.

Then came the job of getting me into the lorry. There was only one thing to do, lift my dress to my waist. It must have been a strange sight to see the lorry-driver pulling furiously from the front and my husband pushing from behind, both trying to get me airborne!

Because we crowd our lives so exhaustively, both in our personal and public hours, changing our clothes is often a problem.

On the way to Glyndebourne, after a busy day in London, we decided to pull up at the side of the road to change behind some bushes. Manning stayed by the car while Ian and I went behind the bushes.

My husband is a peacock when it comes to fashion. I think it is a throwback to his frugal youth when as a young-man-about-town his father gave him an allowance of £92 a year. He was so terribly thin and cold one winter that Daphne Castlerosse took pity on him and bought him an overcoat.

Nowadays he tries out personally any new fashion that amuses him. His wardrobes are filled with a heterogeneous collection, ranging from Indian Raj coats to a full-length raccoon overcoat, which makes his conventional tailors blanch. But to Ian it is all fun, and because he is tall and elegant, he wears most clothes well.

At this particular time, he was passing through what the family called his 'dog-collar period'. With a clerical-cut dinner-jacket, he wore a white silk roll-neck shirt. The effect was starkly ecclesiastical.

I had already returned to the car. Women have only to unzip one thing and zip into another; it takes a man so much longer. As luck would have it, just as my husband came out of the bushes, clutching his London clothes, so three Sisters of Mercy passed by him. They stopped dead in their tracks, and in unison genuflected, saying:

'Good evening, Father.'

To our horror we found out that we had driven into the park of a convent.

We were invited by Conrad Hilton to the opening of the Hilton Hotel in London, but we first had to attend the opening of Parliament.

As I would have looked decidedly odd arriving for lunch in a long dress and tiara, I asked if we could change in a bedroom. A large suite at the top of the building was put at our disposal where there was a safe in which I could place my jewelry. The only problem was that there was no cold water; the taps ran scalding hot.

We did our usual quick-change act, and were led by a member of the staff down the back entrance, through the kitchens, to where the reception was being held. The first people we met were Reginald Maudling, his wife, Conrad Hilton and Charles Clore, who was a backer of the hotel.

Charles is a very old friend, and we are frequently at the same parties together. I had in fact seen him at a party the night before in the company of two women friends.

'How are you?' I said. 'It was a nice party last night, wasn't it? But you really mustn't be seen around with girls like that, as you'll never get your knighthood!'

A man in a pink coat came rushing towards me, flapping his hands:

'Your Grace, your Grace,' he said, 'the microphone is live. It is live. Everyone can hear what you say.'

Charles, dear Charles, laughed louder than anyone. He has a very good temper and always accepts me for what I am. And of course I was wrong—for he is now Sir Charles.

One of the most amusing affairs I remember was the Athenian Ball at the Savoy. I was sitting next to the late Prince Peter, a delightful man, and at the end of the evening the young ship-owners decided to dance the bazooki. They began by putting the bottles and glasses on the floor. After the dance is over, one is supposed to smash all the glass, which they did, much to the horror of the Savoy staff.

I was asked to draw the tombola prizes. Obviously there were many free cruises among the prizes, but one in particular intrigued everybody. It was a Mediterranean cruise on the *Romantica*, a ship belonging to our friends the Chandris brothers which had once been owned by King Farouk of Egypt. The winner of the first prize was to use King Farouk's very splendid cabin.

There was a roll of drums, and I drew out the first ticket. To my horror, it belonged to my husband. I naturally suggested that he should give it back, but all I got from him was a very firm 'no'. He fancied the cruise—and we went.

The year after, I was relieved that Princess Catherine of Greece was drawing the prizes, and I was able to sit back and sip cham-pagne in peace. But when it came to the big moment, I found, again to my horror, that we had won. It was terrible. I was convinced that people would say that the whole thing was rigged because I was the President of the Ball. The explanation may have been, of course, that Ian had shortened the odds by buying so many tickets—almost enough to pay for the cruise! So we went to Greece once more, and adored it.

Dances are very much part of our life and of the London season. Because there are now so many, I choose carefully, and only go to the ones I specially like.

I liked Charles Clore's daughter Vivienne, a girl with a bright mind, who was a friend of Anyes. On her 21st birthday, her father gave a party at the top of the London Hilton. There were two long tables at dinner—one for Charles's friends, and one for Vivienne's generation. After dinner, the dancing began.

I nudged Charles, and said 'You must go and dance with your daughter.'

He was just about to get up when a young man stepped in and whirled Vivienne away. Charles turned to me and said, 'There you are—she doesn't need me—come and dance with me yourself.'

I rose and went to dance with Charles, when suddenly an absolutely furious woman arrived and slapped me hard across the cheek. It was Charles's ex-wife, Francine, who thought I was a girl friend of his!

My husband, who had seen the whole incident, came towards us. Charles was also shaken, and apologised. We went back to our table, but I did not feel much like staying after that, so we left.

Paul Getty's 80th birthday was marked by a splendid party organised by Margaret, Duchess of Argyll. What on earth does one give to a man who can afford everything? Finlay had noticed that on Paul's frequent visits to Woburn, his suitcases were old and well used, so we bought him some Gucci luggage, which he seems to have used and enjoyed ever since.

At the dinner, dear Julian Melchett, who died suddenly soon after, was on my left, and Gordon Getty on my right. The cake was wheeled in, and Paul gave the first slice to Richard Nixon's daughter, Tricia Cox, who was sitting next to him. She was an attractive girl but rather naïve, and like one of those mechanical dolls you wind up at the back. She had a porcelain face, and beautiful ringlets, and she wore a pretty party dress. She bowed her head to the left and the right, always smiling. Maybe she was bored. It must have been very difficult to be the daughter of the President—even before the Watergate scandal—and I imagine she just adopted the attitude of smiling, smiling all the time. Luckily ex-King Umberto of Italy was there to entertain me and make me laugh.

It was at Paul Getty's house at Sutton Place that I had an amusing conversation with Queen Elizabeth the Queen Mother. It was a beautiful balmy evening. The doors and windows were open and the garden was looking its best. There was a dinner for about 30 people, followed by a concert, at which Yehudi Menuhin played. Afterwards, we returned to the drawing-room.

The Queen Mother sat in one part of the large room with Paul, and in the usual way people were brought to speak to her. I shall never know why she singled me out, but her opening remark was:

'I understand that you are very knowledgeable about eighteenth-century French works of art.'

'I am very interested in them,' I replied. 'I adore them, and Woburn is full of them.'

'Who do you think made those two wall-lights on each side of the fireplace?' she asked.

I looked up at the two beautiful lights, and said:
'Gouthières, of course.'

She called Paul over and asked him who had made them. I waited for his answer with a small prayer.

'Oh, they are Gouthières,' he confirmed. I could not help feeling rather pleased.

I like visiting other people's festivals to compare them with what we do at Woburn. We went to the English Bach Festival at Blenheim just after the death of the old Duke, so his son, the new Duke, was not present. It was a beautiful evening and the Bach sounded magnificent, but the occasion lacked the magic of an illuminated garden. Lord Campbell paid me the greatest compliment that evening when he said 'You do things so much better at Woburn.'

This was followed by another music festival at Weston Manor in Oxfordshire, and this was certainly one of the funniest evenings I have ever spent. We had taken the children, so there were about ten of us. We had a beautiful dinner, and at the end of it we could hear the musicians tuning up their instruments. I do not quite know why, but we all began getting up and changing places and moving about, speaking to friends.

Quite suddenly, there was a silence, and we saw five young men bowing from the gallery. Then I understood. There was so little organisation that what we had carelessly thought was tuning up had in fact been the concert! We had all been so busy talking that no one had listened.

I hope that by now those young musicians have forgiven us.

34   *Presence of mind*

MY FIRST EXPERIENCE of a State Opening of Parliament, was in 1961. I had a streaming cold.

We arrived at ten in the morning, and who should I see first but Martine de Courcel, wife of the French ambassador. We were discussing arrangements for going to the theatre later that week, when suddenly there was a kind of thundery noise behind me, and I turned to see a tall man with a gold-topped stick pointed at a forty-five-degree angle. In a deep voice, the gentleman-at-arms said:

'Your Grace, you are leading the procession.'

I felt my heart stop beating, because I simply had no idea what I was supposed to do. I had never even seen a State Opening of Parliament, and the ritual was totally new to me. My first thought was that if I did something wrong, all the other duchesses, marchionesses, countesses, viscountesses and baronesses would follow me, and this could so easily result in a comical fiasco.

I took a deep breath and called to God to guide my steps. I began walking behind the gentleman-at-arms, and suddenly the whole thing came back to me. I had seen a film on television, and my photographic memory recalled that in it one curtsied first to the mace and then to the throne—even if it was empty—as a mark of respect.

Everything went well until we entered the throne-room, and the gentleman-at-arms again thumped his stick on the floor.

There was I, in the centre of that great room, and I was suddenly aware of the millions of people watching throughout the country.

My head was full of that awful cold. I told myself not to panic, and for good measure I curtsied to the throne again. Like a sleepwalker, I began moving very slowly, desperately wondering what I was supposed to do. Suddenly I saw my name on the first seat of the third row. My eyes nearly jumped out of my head.

The first row is reserved for Royal Dukes and Earls, and the second is for the ladies of the Royal Family. With the crocodile following, I entered my own row. Panic again. I did not know whether to remain standing or to sit. Out of respect to the throne, and waiting to see what the next row would do, I kept standing. So did my crocodile.

Princess Margaret saw the panic in my eyes. She smiled at me and inclined her head. I then sat down, and a wave of tiaras did the same. The relief was tremendous.

To this day I still do not know whether in fact I did the right thing. I have since been to many State Openings, and often find myself in the lead because the oldest family takes precedence, and if there is any ducal family that precedes the Bedfords, they never seem to be there.

There is a wonderful feeling and sense of pageantry about a State Opening. Despite her small height the Queen is a very royal figure on the throne, glittering in her fabulous jewels. She has immense dignity. Prince Philip can sometimes look a trifle bored, but now that Prince Charles and Princess Anne take part, they are a most attractive and imposing group. It is easy to understand why they do so much for the prestige of Britain abroad and why they are so much loved at home.

Adaptability is part of the life of a duchess. For me it was especially difficult as I had not had the upbringing of a normal English girlhood to draw upon. I had not been to an English boarding school, I had never been to a village fête, I did not know or understand the bewildering complexities of English country-life.

In the beginning it was always a case of improvisation. I remember the fashion show at Malvern where I was supposed to sit on the stage and announce the clothes as the models came on. Unfortunately the cards I was given did not coincide with the order of the clothes. The result was that I was describing a beautiful beige coat when a pretty girl appeared in a bikini.

It was catastrophic. I was relieved when the time came for me to close the show with 'a few well chosen words'. Only then did I realise that the charity involved was not the National Society for the Prevention of Cruelty to Children but the Royal Society for the Prevention of Cruelty to Animals!

I had quickly to change my whole speech, and hope for the best. As I finished, a huge black labrador came towards me, carrying a bouquet of flowers in his teeth. This had obviously been so carefully and frequently rehearsed that the flowers had wilted.

I gave a little tug without success, then a pat on the head, then a really hard tug. Still he held on to the flowers. Obviously only his master could give the order, and from the side he called:

'Dead, dead.'

'And so are the flowers,' Ian was distinctly heard to say, as the dog let go.

I have never had much success with flower and vegetable shows. I am just not on the same wavelength as the judges. At the Bedfordshire Show I was being shown some monster marrows, huge cucumbers and giant-sized carrots, when I asked:

'What is the flavour like?'

There was complete silence. It is the size that matters. This seems a pity to me, for in France it is the small, succulent vegetables that are cherished and rewarded.

I have never been bored in my life. I am far too interested in everything going on around me. I find this useful when opening bazaars and handing out prizes. Besides, there is always the unexpected.

When I attended the opening of a swimming pool, for which I had helped raise money, the vicar and I were placed auspiciously in two wicker chairs, side by side, while the rest of the people sat around on the grass. Part of the festivities was a demonstration of life-saving.

A girl of 15, who had quite obviously not yet lost her puppy-fat, appeared in a shiny white bathing-suit, and jumped into the water, pretending to drown. The vicar and I watched attentively as a young man demonstrated life-saving techniques. He then raised himself out of the water and proceeded to hoist the supposedly unconscious girl onto the side of the pool.

To my horror I looked down and saw that her white bathing-suit had become completely transparent. My eyes met those of the vicar. I wondered whether I should grab a towel and cover her or, with typical Russell nonchalance, ignore the whole thing. I decided on the latter.

A duchess has to be prepared for the unexpected. I was once at the American Embassy when Evangeline Bruce, wife of the then ambassador, took my hand and said: 'Nicole, come quickly!'

I was on my feet immediately because I saw the urgency in her eyes. I followed her across the floor, which in itself is a great experience—she glides superbly like a stately frigate.

It appeared that George Brown, the Foreign Secretary, was quarrelling with Pamela Berry, now Lady Hartwell and wife of the proprietor of the *Daily Telegraph*. I was supposed to act as a tranquilliser and soothe the situation.

'But I don't know George Brown,' I protested.

'Never mind—just smile, be pleasant, and stop them arguing,' she said.

We arrived at the scene, and Evangeline said, with that suave smile of hers:

'Of course you know the Duchess of Bedford.'

Mr. Brown jumped to his feet, grabbed me to his plump paunch, and firmly put his arms around me. He then proceeded to kiss me smack on the mouth for what seemed like three whole minutes. Everyone around us was laughing, while I was just trying to breathe. The more I struggled, the tighter the embrace became—he is a very strong man.

Out of the corner of my eye, I saw Sophie Brown come over.

'George, let us go home,' she said quietly. Mrs. Brown turned around and George followed meekly.

Three days later we were at the première of a film, when I again saw Sophie and George Brown. Of course he would feel embarrassed. How could I spare his feelings?

Not at all. He had spotted me, and came rushing to shake my hand, saying 'How nice to see you again'. I was relieved to be spared the vacuum-cleaner kiss!

For years the incorrigible George kept London hostesses in suspense. What would he do next?

At a party at the French Embassy, he was seated between Madame Pompidou and Martine de Courcel.

He turned to the elegant Martine and said:

'And when are we going to make love?'

With superb presence of mind, she replied:

'Mr. Foreign Secretary, this is the first time in my life that I have been asked to make love before the potage.'

Lord George Brown, as he now is, is a warm, generous extrovert who adds colour wherever he is. I see him rather seldom, but—after my surprising introduction—I always enjoy his company.

London is filled with vivid and amusing people, which is one of the reasons that Ian and I like to circulate. It is more international than either Paris or Rome and is a crossroads for Americans.

At a luncheon in London one day I sat next to Lord Arran, a small, vivacious man, who turned to me and said:

'You are French, are you not?'

'Yes,' I said.

'I do not like the French.'

He then turned his back on me for the rest of the meal.

Some time later, I had my old friend Hervé Alphand and his wife as guests. Hervé was then in charge of French foreign affairs, and father of the Common Market. In the party were Geoffroy and Martine de Courcel, so I thought I would try to reconcile Lord Arran to France. He was completely charming, and some days later wrote in his column in the London *Evening News* something like:

'N***** and I** are not as bad as I thought. They are charming and amusing and not at all commercialised.'

'Boofy' Arran was totally forgiven, and we have been friends ever since.

The climate of Britain is good for breeding colourful men. They have their clubs, their exclusive rendezvous, their secrets. Women are never encouraged to bloom like they are in New York or Paris.

Careful as I am not to hurt people's feelings, I have made some terrible gaffes. I went to collect a friend before going on to a charity luncheon; she had a lovely baby who was brought in for me to admire by one of the most beautiful girls I have ever seen —tall, blond, with white teeth and a clear complexion. She handed me the baby, and went out. I turned to my friend and said: 'What a lovely nanny. I'm pleased you got rid of that dirty old gaga nanny you had before.' 'That was no nanny. That was my mother,' she said.

I nearly dropped the baby. I was white and I could not breathe.

The telephone rang and my friend went to answer it. When she came back, she said with perfect composure:

'You are right, she was gaga and dirty.'

The whole lunch was a nightmare, and I spent the time thinking how I could get out of this terrible situation.

I was still shaking when I met my husband at the Modigliani exhibition.

'What is the matter with you?' he asked.

When I told him, he began laughing until the tears rolled down his cheeks. He simply could not stop.

Now Modigliani is not exactly the funniest painter, and everyone at the private view was going round commenting how disgraceful it was that the Duke of Bedford was completely intoxicated.

My husband adores my gaffes. One of his favourites happened in Brisbane on a promotion trip when we arrived at our hotel to find flowers seemingly from everyone. I was reading the cards, and saw one saying 'To Ian and Nicole from John and Mary'. I said:

'Who the hell are John and Mary calling us Ian and Nicole? And what a nerve.'

Robert Haines, who was with us, gently said: 'They are Mr. & Mrs. **** and are here in the room. He is manager of the store you are visiting.'

I had to smile my way out of that one.

The messes into which I occasionally get are not always of my own making, however. I once received a telegram from Ruth Berle, saying 'Pierre Salinger is at Claridges. Please give dinner for him with the most super food and wine you can imagine, only beautiful women and brilliant, intelligent and prominent men.'

I read the telegram about ten times, saying to myself: 'Good luck, Nicole. What a task.'

I telephoned Mr. Salinger and asked what night he would like to come for dinner. To my dismay, he said his only free night was Monday. So I said 'Monday it will be, and I shall send our chauffeur and our car.'

I sat at my desk, totally crestfallen. He could not have chosen a worse night. Beautiful women and prominent men always spend the weekends somewhere, and their last desire is to go anywhere an hour from London on a Monday night.

I began my round of calls, blackmailing everybody on the basis of their friendship to me and their curiosity to meet Pierre Salinger. I arranged exactly what Ruth had requested—a dinner for seven beautiful women and six brilliant, prominent men, plus of course my guest of honour, my husband and myself.

On the Monday morning I telephoned to find out what time Mr. Salinger wanted the car, and to my consternation, heard him say: 'I was just going to telephone you as I am in bed with the 'flu and a temperature of 103.' I replied meekly: 'Never mind, do you want me to send you my doctor?'

I replaced the receiver and sat feeling as though I had fallen to the bottom of an abyss. What should I do? I decided to telephone each guest and say: 'Pierre Salinger is in bed with 'flu, but if you still want to come, you are welcome.'

Of course everybody would rather be at home on a Monday night. It was marvellous. We ended up, my husband and I, in bed with two trays full of delicacies, and the most delicious grouse I have ever had. We ate grouse and foie gras and drank 1947 Haut-Brion for a week.

35   *'Can I call you Nicky?'*

IN THE EARLY days of our marriage we spent two to four months every year selling Woburn to the world. As we have more visitors from America than any other overseas country, we naturally do a big promotion job over there, and besides, I love going to America where I have so many good friends.

It is extraordinary how American people are aware of tradition and works of art. They, more than any people, are ready to learn. They love to visit ancestral homes, and they have one very endearing quality—they do not mind saying: 'I do not know, please help me.'

We realised that, by doing half a dozen television shows, we could reach millions of people, instead of hopping madly from place to place speaking to audiences that varied from 50 to three or four thousand.

I am constantly amazed that people who may have seen me on a television show a long time ago seem to recognise my voice. They are always coming up to me and saying, 'I saw you on television', even though that was years ago.

In New York, especially, it is quite extraordinary. You may go on the 'Today' show, done by our friend Hugh Downs, which means getting to the studio at about 7.30 in the morning, and by the time you go shopping on Fifth Avenue at 11 a.m., you have probably been stopped already by at least 20 or 30 people. The power of these television shows is quite frightening, but marvellous from our point of view.

In their own gruelling way—and because both Ian and I like meeting people—our personal tours were always fun, particularly in America.

Whenever anyone mentions Allegheny Air Lines, I think of the time we flew in an appalling storm. The pilot had passed back a message that we could not land, but I thought of the 600 people who had spent $15 on their tickets in order to meet us.

I asked the air-hostess to tell the pilot of our predicament, and added: 'We must land, it is imperative.'

By this time we were already two hours late. When at last we landed, there were the usual ladies in their pale grey mink capes and hats with fruit and flowers and wisps of veiling. After the first frantic greetings, they rushed us into a car, and explained that, fortunately, the reception was to be held in the hotel where we were staying.

It was part of our routine on these trips to require two bathrooms, which can be a great help when you have to change quickly. This time our bathrooms were separated by a sitting-room in between.

Ian ran his bath, but because one of his suitcases had been put into my room, he dashed in for it. Just as he reached the sitting-room door, the president of the club walked in; doubtless she had knocked, but with both baths running we did not hear her. She stood at the door, surveying the whole situation, and said: 'You are late, you know.' Then, as Ian stood there absolutely naked, she looked him up and down, and told me with a smile: 'Your husband is built just like mine.'

When we arrived downstairs—Ian still a little shaken by this naked appraisal, and I still in hysterics—we had to stand, shaking hands with the long line of people who had come to see us. It is part of the attraction of these lectures to be able to say afterwards: 'We shook hands with the Duke and Duchess.'

In the middle of the proceedings, there was a power-cut due to the storm, so someone rushed and placed a candle in front of us. This meant that we could be seen, but found ourselves shaking a lot of faceless hands. I turned to get my handbag, which I had placed behind me on a table. In the dark, I plonked my hand straight into a bowl of shrimp-mayonnaise dip. With nothing to wipe it on, as my handkerchief was still in my handbag, I could only lick it clean and carry on shaking with a sticky hand.

Eventually they managed a few more candles, and then we had to visit what they called an antique show. The earliest of these antiques dated from about 1920. Our own Antique Centre at Woburn enjoys a world-wide reputation, as we are the only centre that has a weekly vetting committee to reject anything not fitting the date, or which has been repaired. We guarantee the description on the ticket—a very rare, if not unique, safeguard.

After the handshaking, we were supposed to give a lecture with slides, which is far from easy without electricity. On this occasion, our task was made even more difficult because most of the people present were conscious of the power-cut and the effect it was having on their deep-freezes. There was a great deal of restlessness and chattering, as one by one they slipped out. In the end, we were left with an audience of 12 ladies who obviously did not own deep-freezes.

American audiences varied a great deal, but we always expected them to have some connection with, or interest in, art. But the questions afterwards always flabbergasted me. I remember one time we had been talking for an hour and a half about Woburn's priceless heirlooms, and then came the usual question-time. Up stood a man who just asked:

'Do you wear seamless stockings?'

We became unwitting experts on Jacqueline Kennedy and Aristotle Onassis, as we were lecturing at the time of their romance. Onassis we knew slightly, but we had never met Jackie Kennedy in our lives.

'Don't you think it is revolting that a beautiful woman like Jacqueline Kennedy should marry an old man like Onassis?' someone asked.

I was absolutely infuriated by this irrelevant question, so I replied:

'In fact she is an extremely lucky woman, because although Mr. Onassis is older than she, he is an intelligent and most amusing man—a man with great compassion, with warmth and charisma, and a man who can give her all the things she needs both in the material sense and in terms of background.' I added: 'I would not mind having him for myself.'

I felt sorry for Jacqueline Kennedy, who had been made into a kind of Joan of Arc. The Americans seemed to have involved themselves personally in her private life. The fact that she had human qualities and wanted to marry again was her business.

In Detroit, our lecture was organised by one of the most powerful, forceful and enchanting women I have ever encountered. On arrival we were met by a motor cavalcade with six outriders, and whenever we came to an intersection, the way would be cleared for us. It was one of the few occasions on which I appreciated the advantage of being somebody politically important.

It was also in Detroit that I was asked about the Royal Family. 'Does Liz fight with Philip?'

'By Liz, I expect you mean Her Majesty the Queen?' I began.

Ian laughed very much afterwards. He said it was the first time he had ever seen me in the rôle of royalist.

One day in San Diego a woman asked: 'What is it like to live in a circus like Woburn?' It is the sort of question to which I have become accustomed, and it is usually asked by someone who has not seen the magnificent grounds with their 3,000 acres of trees and lakes, and who does not realise that we live on the south side, where we are very secluded from noise and crowds.

When I get angry, I become very quiet, very calm, just like my grandmother. I took a deep breath, and very slowly, hardly audible, I answered:

'What do you see from your window? Do you see another window?'

'Yes, I can see across the street.'

'When I awake,' I said, 'I can see acres and acres of green land with 300-year-old trees, three lakes and herds of deer grazing peacefully. As for a circus, I do not know what you mean.'

When I was raised in my convent, familiarity did not exist. We used the French formal 'Vous' (You) instead of the friendly 'Tu' (Thou), and called each other Mademoiselle (Miss). Today still, even with long-standing friends, I remain very formal. I dislike familiarity and sloppiness of behaviour, and I am a firm believer that 'Familiarity breeds contempt'. I address my children as 'Tu', but they reply respectfully, using 'Vous'. I suppose that is why I had such a problem in America responding to the usual habit of calling you by your first name almost as soon as you met.

In Kansas City we were asked to speak to a group of chic, elegant, rich people. They were charming, and received us very well. At one point in the evening, the wife of a prominent man turned to my husband and said: 'What is your wife called?'

My husband of course said 'Nicole'.

'Can I call her Nicky?'

'You can try,' he replied.

Suddenly I heard a woman's voice call, 'Hey, Nicky.'

I ignored her.

'Hey, Duchess, can I call you Nicky?'

This time I turned to her and replied, smiling:

'That is what the basset hound at Woburn is called.' It was, in fact, true.

That night was going to be a strange one anyway. In the early morning, I was suddenly awakened by my bed rocking, as if at sea. I sat up and watched the pictures on the wall balancing left to right, and the furniture sliding across the floor.

I looked towards my husband's bed and saw that it was empty.

I called out in panic: 'Darling, where are you? We are having an earthquake.'

From the other side of the apartment, came the reply: 'On the loo.' I burst into laughter, shouting: 'That is no fitting place to die.'

Our lectures are usually split up into periods of about twelve minutes, during which Ian and I take it in turns to speak. My husband normally starts the proceedings, explaining how he became the 13th Duke of Bedford and inherited the property, and then he talks about the family and how they came from Bordeaux in 1410. He then calls for darkness, and the first slide is shown. It is an aerial view of Woburn.

'And this is our little pad,' he says, which always brings a laugh.

He then speaks about the park, the 3,000 acres, the 13 miles of walls, and the 3,000 deer of 11 varieties.

I then join in and talk about the more interesting duchesses. Ian does the first three Dukes, but the 4th, who was an ambassador in Paris, and his wife, are left to me, as are the objets d'art, furniture, paintings and porcelain. My husband takes over from the 5th Duke to the 13th—himself, of course—and I wind up by explaining the running of Woburn. If the audience consists mainly of women, I tell them stories about the household and the children; if they are mostly men, I am more serious and give facts and figures.

It is awfully easy to become bored giving the same lecture every night, so on occasions we switch over; I do Ian's part and he does mine.

Experience has taught us to gauge the type of question we shall be asked. If there are more men in the audience, the questions will concern the financial side of running a stately home. Occasionally we encounter specialist groups, who want to know details about the porcelain, for example, but mostly our audiences consist of friendly people with a genuine curiosity about us.

In St. Louis, we were walking up the stairs after dinner to the lecture-room. I heard one of two elderly gentlemen ahead of us say to the other:

'What I like about these talks with slides is that they are in the dark, so you can have a good snooze.' That was very encouraging!

In Oakland there was chaos. All the slides were mysteriously put in upside down, so that all my husband's ancestors looked like Yoga-addicted dukes or sleeping duchesses. It was hilarious.

When I said: 'And now the 4th Duke,' a deer appeared on the screen; and when I spoke of Queen Victoria, a Sèvres soup-tureen was projected. By then the entire audience was in hysterics and the organiser near to fainting.

Both Ian and I are critical of each other's television performances. We have to be. In the ducal world, one tends to be surrounded by sycophants, so we have to keep a realistic and healthy check on ourselves.

In Australia once, Ian was appearing on television, and I was watching with friends at their house. I suddenly realised that he was uncharacteristically boring.

I considered rapidly how to liven the show. We had just arrived from New York, where Drue Heinz, the wife of my dear Jack—Mr. 57 Varieties—had taken us to the Peppermint Lounge. It had been a fantastic evening. She had taken all our jewelry, bags and money, and locked them up at home. When we arrived, we were greeted by a mob of people trying to gain admission. Drue knew her way, and we entered through a side door to find ourselves in a most garish neon-lit hall. We were assailed by a new sound of blaring music—'the twist'. Everyone was on his own. A sailor grabbed me, gyrating, rocking his body and flapping his arms. I imitated him, receiving my first lesson in what was soon to become a craze throughout the world.

Australia had not yet seen it, so my astonished hosts were amazed when I rushed to the telephone to speak to the television studio.

'Will you tell my husband to do the twist?' I said.

Ian, with his elegant long body, was an accomplished twister. Within minutes, the interviewer had received the message through his ear-plug from the studio producer, and stopped Ian in mid-sentence.

'Your wife says you are to do the twist,' he said, in that direct way I like so much about Australians.

And Ian, dear Ian, without more ado, began to twist furiously. He was absolutely splendid and every newspaper next day carried stories and photographs of the twisting Duke.

We were invited to Texas to take part in the British week at Neiman Marcus, that superb store in Dallas. Our friend, Stanley Marcus, asked us to go into every department and speak about the quality of British goods. His brother Sidney asked us to demonstrate the quality of British bicycles, so we both rode through the store—much to the joy of the customers.

I seldom care about where we speak, and at Lancaster, Penn sylvania, we found ourselves at the Opera House. What I did mind was that, during the entire lecture, a woman in the front row sat knitting. I do not know of anything more distracting when you are lecturing. All through the lecture I was torn

Entry into the Common Market at Woburn, with Clement Freud, and the French and German Ambassadors

Whit Monday Highland Gathering. 17 regiments of pipers through the West Hall—the house trembled, my husband fled

The Japanese grand master

Two beautiful human beings. How can I be their mother?

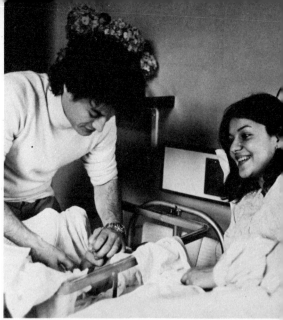

Caterine, Mati, Serafine

Gilles, Galaad (one day old), Manuella

With the grandchildren Andrew and Robbie

La belle Anyes

Persepolis festivities. What was I saying to the Shah's beautiful wife?

And what was ex-King Umberto of Italy saying to me? I look so attentive

Two very good friends in Sydney, Australia—Lady Fairfax (the ebullient Mary) and thoughtful Charles Lloyd Jones

The superbly beautiful Begum covered in turquoises, the Duchess dripping in heirloom diamonds. The tiara was made for Queen Caroline, the sister of Napoleon

Paul Getty learning the twist from Regine

Duchess at the Zoo party as a flamboyant ostrich

St. Trinian's in Paris. Ian as the headmistress

St. Trinian's pupils—Nicole, Twiggy, Mary Quant

The private drawing-room at Woburn, under the Rembrandts. A tender look from the 13th Duke to Nicole Nobody between the woman counting her stitches and Mrs. Stinman, the Grand Lady of Lancaster. She wore a marvellous long evening dress in black satin, embroidered with birds, by Paul Poiret. The body of one bird came up on her stomach, and the long neck swirled across one bosom with the reddish head and long beak disappearing into her corsage. I was so fascinated by the superb dress, which I should love to have possessed, that I kept staring at it all evening.

In Vancouver, our plane having been delayed, we were rushed to the studio and put straight onto a television programme without a first warm-up talk with the interviewer, and with no time to comb my hair. I was breathless when I heard the most impertinent question: 'Don't you think that the Queen spends too much money?'

'I am French, so I do not think it is for me to answer that question,' I replied.

'Do you enjoy being a Duchess?' I became very annoyed with the dreary voice of the interviewer. 'Only a trivial mind could ask such a trivial question,' I snapped back.

Each question struck me as more stupid than the last, until I brought the proceedings to a halt by saying: 'I shall not answer any more of your inadequate questions.'

When I returned to the hotel, I was inundated with flowers from the television audience, who thought I had been mistreated.

When we were in New York we often spent the weekends with Barbara and Stanley Mortimer in the peace and beauty o their estate in Lichfield, Connecticut, away from the noise and pollution. Barbara is a brilliant sculptress and has many talented friends. She is marvellous at organising parties and dinners with well-chosen guests who stimulate the brain. I loved Alex and Tatiana Liberman of American Vogue, and Arthur Miller, who is incapable of dreary small talk.

Before lunch one weekend, *Time* magazine telephoned to ask if they could take a photograph of my beautiful Caterine, against a background of autumn leaves, for a colour page of young fashion. Knowing we were four hours' drive from the city, I said: 'The photographers will arrive after dark!'

My words were drowned by a great noise as a helicopter landed among the sheep, and a cameraman jumped out.

It was during the same weekend that I saw an advertisement in the very respectable *New York Times*. It read: 'David, by Michelangelo. This durastone reproduction of world-famous sculpture, finished in antique bronze or white marble. *Also available with fig leaf.*'

America, you will always astound me!

36   *In haste as usual*

TRAVELLING HAS BEEN a part of my life since I began working in 1946, so I have become an expert at making myself comfortable. We stay constantly in different hotels, sleeping in strange beds, eating unfamiliar food. After several years of discomfort, I decided to take my own equipment with me.

It has become a joke with my family and staff when I prepare for a trip. They talk about my 'travelling paraphernalia'. I have a special room off my dressing-room where I begin collecting the clothes and belongings I shall need for my next journey. It was once a guest-room, and has one of the loveliest Gainsboroughs in the house. It is the last picture I look at before I leave.

First there is my basic 'field equipment'. I carry my own pillow and pillowcases but have abandoned the habit of sending sheets ahead.

After a day's hot sightseeing in India or Bali, I enjoyed slipping into cool 1904 Woburn starched linen sheets, but now, despite jet travel, the provision of sheets has really become too complicated.

Naturally I carry my own medicine chest to cover every emergency. My children call me 'Mother Earth', because no matter where I am, if someone is ill they gravitate towards me and I have the remedy. We can be in the South African veldt or the Iranian desert, but someone always crops up who can make use of my medicine chest. As I am an exceedingly healthy person, I rarely need it myself.

Because Ian and I are constant tea-drinkers, we have perfected a routine whereby my maid makes up little gauze bags of Earl Grey or Lapsang Souchong, which she then rolls in silver paper and puts in a plastic bag. This means that wherever and whenever we arrive, all we need do is to ask for a pot of boiling water.

Strange food can be upsetting, so we invariably begin the day with the same breakfast that we have at home. We take a supply of Bircher-Benner Muesli to which we add our own honey, hazel-nuts, raisins, almonds, walnuts and fresh fruit. We even take our own grinder.

On the hardware side, I carry a couple of 100-watt bulbs, which I immediately screw into our reading-lamps. Most hotel lights are far too dim. My Carmen rollers are fitted with plugs to meet every possible electrical system. By the way, these rollers were created by a friend of one of my hairdressers in London. I was given one of the first sets to try, and have used them ever since.

Of course like any other woman I carry all my face necessities and bath-oil.

We have our own writing-paper specially designed for travelling, with 'Woburn Abbey' and 'En Voyage' and a space left for the name of the hotel. My family and friends know my letters, which invariably begin 'In haste as usual'. This phrase is now such a joke around Woburn that I may even have it engraved on my tombstone.

On long trips, I try to keep a cryptic diary of all our activities and the people we meet. This is then sent to Woburn, duplicated by my secretary, and distributed among our large immediate family and a few friends across the world.

On our first trip to Russia, in 1965, we travelled on our own, and had a superb time. But the Customs were in for a shock when they insisted on inspecting my luggage. The Customs lady, a bleached blond, spotted the tapestry bag I had bought in New York, and decided to search it thoroughly.

Everyone gives you advice when you go to Russia, and back in 1963 I ended up with quantities of nylon tights, lipsticks, felt pens, chocolate bars, lemons, a bath plug, lavatory paper and a wig. I was also carrying several books, including 'My Life with Picasso' written by his mistress Françoise Gillot. It was the most amazing sight as the Customs officer took everything out and placed the contents on a large table in front of her so that everyone from the plane had a good view. There must have been at least 70 pairs of eyes riveted on my belongings.

'Why so many tights?' she began. I had two dozen pairs.

'Well, they are not very good quality and they run easily,' I answered lamely.

She picked up the box of lipsticks, which I had bought at a chain chemists. There must have been 50 in all different shades. Her eyes took on a very steely glaze as she demanded:

'And why so many lipsticks?'

'Oh I am very vain,' I replied, entering into the spirit of the game. 'I use them only once and then throw them away.'

Seventy mouths dropped open.

Picking up each lemon and turning it round in her pudgy fingers with slow deliberation, the lady's eyes narrowed a trifle.

'The lemons?' she barked.

'I am very delicate. I am anaemic, and I need a lemon a day,' I answered feebly.

When she grabbed the wig, giggles exploded all around me. She took it, turned it inside out and pulled the hair in clumps. She had obviously never seen a wig in her life. It was then too that she pounced on the book by Françoise Gillot. This was too much for her, and she promptly disappeared.

Ian turned to me and said: 'You know where you'll be sleeping tonight, in the Lubianka gaol!'

She was gone for what seemed a long time, during which my 70 new friends buzzed condolences round my head like wasps on a summer's day. By now I had remembered that in my bag were all the British Sunday newspapers, one of which contained a pungent interview with Brezhnev.

The Customs lady returned. She solemnly handed me first the book and then the wig. Not one word, smile or twinkle passed between us.

As anyone who has ever been to Russia knows, one's whole state of happiness in one's hotel is controlled by the woman concierge on each floor. She sits there, 200 pounds of solid flesh, always smiling, rarely speaking. You cannot go to your room, you cannot take the lift, you cannot do anything, without first passing 'the woman with the key'.

I quickly made friends with mine by giving her two lemons and a pair of tights. Gratitude glowed from her eyes, and from then on we were just two women who understood each other. The lines of communication had been established.

The chambermaid was fascinated with my nylon underwear. The women's underwear we saw in the shops was made of coarse cotton, and could have stood up by itself like mediaeval armour. When she saw my empty plastic bottle of shampoo, she asked if she could keep it, as it was the first she had seen.

Instead of boots, many people had made their own snow-shoes from pieces of rubber tyres tied up with string. And I remember one morning, when it was raining, walking out of the hotel and suddenly seeing an entire population of women all wearing the same blue raincoat. I am pleased to report that I noticed a vast difference on our next trip in 1972, when everyone had good boots and young girls were very elegant.

I liked the ordinary Russians we met. They are nice people, jolly people if you get the chance to communicate with them. It was simply fascinating to see the Russian public—mothers, fathers and children—who can have seen very few foreigners before. They came and touched my boots and the gilt chain on my Chanel suit. It was clear that they were very excited.

'What are they saying?' I asked our guide.

'They are telling each other that to get a pair of boots like that would cost about £60—several months' wages. They are amazed to see you wearing them when there is no snow.'

As private individuals, we received better treatment than if we had belonged to a group. In the restaurants in a group, it took two and a half hours to get one course, as we discovered on our second visit.

Our days were spent in wondrous sightseeing. The restoration in Russia is fantastic. It makes one wonder why for so many years the British Government has left the care of historic properties to individuals. At Woburn we have never had a penny in the way of a grant, so it is no wonder that we need our visitors. Of course the National Trust does admirable work, but the system under which they operate means that the family concerned loses the intimate association that private ownership inspires.

My husband has preferred to keep Woburn in the family, despite the enormous responsibility this has entailed. One only hopes that his children and grandchildren will take the same view. For all its fairground and animal parks, Woburn still has the proud stamp of a home belonging to a family, and this is what visitors seem to enjoy.

I was totally enamoured with Pavlovsk. It is such a beautiful palace of human proportions. There is the central building and two round wings that are pure eighteenth century. All the ceilings have been repainted, craftsmen from Italy were brought in to teach the Russians how to paint those large blowsy ladies who float in the sky in chariots drawn by cherubs.

The silk wall-hangings have been expertly restored. The Russians are so meticulous that they not only grew the mulberry trees to feed the silkworms, but found the original dyes that had been used by grinding malachite and lapis lazuli as well as the strain from vegetables and plants. After the silk was dyed, it was woven on hand-looms. It is an extraordinary achievement.

The curator was an enchanting man called Mr. Kutchoumov. I took an enormous liking to him because he is so dedicated and knowledgeable. As a young boy in Pavlovsk, he had been an apprentice electrician, and knew the place well. During the war, the entire contents were taken back to Germany, and Mr. Kutchoumov later spent ten years tracing every single piece of furniture and all the objets d'art that he remembered as a young boy.

I had always wanted to go to the Tobogan, a palace of Catherine the Great which is extremely beautiful and built in the Palladian style, and has a most complete collection of Meissen figures by Kandler. Our Intourist guide was adamant that it was not open—I remember him now, standing there in a raincoat with a grey hat that he never removed, a cigarette hanging from the corner of his mouth.

'You ask us what we want to do, and when I tell you, you say we cannot. So forget it,' I said. 'And do not be so cocky about everything. If you are frightened that I will photograph the Fortress of Kronstad, I shall leave my camera at the hotel. All I want to see are the Meissen Kandler porcelain-figures.'

Finally he said, 'I will tell you tomorrow.'

In the morning he appeared and said that we could visit the palace. At first the woman curator was clearly not amused, but on reading our letter of introduction, she took us round, albeit sullenly. We also visited the magnificent Hermitage. It is so vast that it requires at least a week to see it properly.

One of the joys of that first trip was meeting Christabel Aberconway. She is a dream of a woman—a wonderful person. To be with Christabel is like surf-riding in Australia, which can be exciting, heady, exhausting, stimulating. She is endlessly amusing. And she is over 90.

It was about ten in the morning, and the curator of a museum was showing us round and explaining everything in delightfully florid eighteenth-century French, which I was interpreting for the group. Suddenly, looking at a wobbly Christabel tapping her cane, he said to me:

'It is so sad about that lady being blind.'

I replied: 'She's "blind" all right.'

No one enjoyed the joke more than Christabel.

I loved the Tolstoi house and rambling garden, which took me right back to Ronquerolles with its wooden shutters and large sunny rooms. In the main salon was a centre table, and you could just imagine Tolstoi and his wife sitting there with all their children and grandchildren tumbling in from the garden.

We went to a restaurant with the Belgian ambassador, Jean van der Bosch and his wife Hélène, and Rosy d'Avigdor-Goldsmid, and noticed a family bridal party entering an adjacent room. The bride was in white with a crown of flowers, and the bridegroom wore the conventional carnation in his buttonhole, just as at any village wedding in France or England.

Everyone looked so happy, and we enjoyed watching, when unexpectedly out of the crowd came a young man who asked me to dance. I looked at my husband, who indicated that I should accept as it would have been churlish to refuse.

It was not dancing. He whizzed me round the floor as if he were competing in the 5,000 metres. The music does not stop in Russia—new partners cut in all the time. The experience was exhausting but I enjoyed it tremendously.

There was thick fog at the airport on the morning of our departure, and faces were gloomy. Christabel Aberconway, however, was as bright-eyed as a sparrow, even at six in the morning. She appeared with jars of caviar, so Ian went to buy some vodka. Since it was sold at the airport only in packs of three bottles, a party was soon born.

At the next table a group of Finns were waiting. In Finland it is the custom to drink only when you are eating, and they had come to Moscow for a day's drinking. Christabel wanted to add to their happiness, and bought three more bottles. They needed little encouragement.

By the time our plane was announced, there was Christabel, this tiny aged English dowager with huge blue eyes, perched on top of the Finns' table, proposing a toast to the women of Finland.

It was Christabel who later dared to explain to Paul Getty one of the subtleties of English country-house visiting. They were leaving Woburn together on one occasion when she asked him what he did with his envelope. Paul looked completely mystified, and said 'What envelope?' 'The envelope for the staff,' she answered.

Paul, one of the richest men in the world, and quite one of the nicest, did not know it was the custom to leave an envelope with money for the staff. Next day, however, he sent a handsome cheque, and has always remembered his envelope ever since. He wrote me the best 'thank you' letter I have ever received. It simply said: 'Five miles before I arrived at your house I started feeling happy.'

One of the joys of having money in past centuries was that it allowed people to become eccentrics, like many of my husband's ancestors. My husband prefers the freedom it gives one to travel, and together we have enjoyed visiting all the corners of the world. Living in the eighteenth-century surroundings of Woburn, we like to see how the ancient countries have adapted their culture to the technology and pace of the twentieth century.

Russia fascinates me. So much has changed in even the short period between our two visits. The difference was enormous— from the suspicious atmosphere of 1964 to the more relaxed ambience of 1972. It gives one so much hope for the future.

All the girls can now have their hair well done, and I had mine set quite as well as in London or Paris. The presents I took on our second visit were also more sophisticated. I took tights again, but also pretty scarves in brilliant colours, and cigarette lighters.

Israel is another country that inspired me. We visited it in the early 1960s to study the tourist industry.

We were greeted by the Press and movie and television cameras. My husband was asked the purpose of our visit, and he said it was to enquire about tourism for 'goys'—which is Yiddish for Gentiles.

I said that I was interested to see a kibbutz, which offered perhaps the nearest thing to an ideal life, except that I thought it was bad to take children away from their parents. In all I visited 54 kibbutzim—English, French, American, old and new.

I disagreed in principle with the way young children slept the night at their nursery school. A mother did not always have enough time with her children, which is wrong. The personal relationship between parents and children, as formed in those early years, is desperately important. I know, when I compare my own unfulfilled childhood with that of my children.

We lunched in a French kibbutz where, to my astonishment, I looked at my plate and tasted a delicious roast pork, so I turned to the leader of the camp and said: 'Is it what I think it is?' He smiled and replied: 'Yes, we call it the unknown animal.'

When we returned from a visit to Jordan, Ian caused a furore when he was asked by reporters what he thought of the country and described it as filthy, and full of dirty Arabs.

The remark was broadcast on radio and television, and the newspapers made headlines out of it. The morning after, we found that we were the centre of a diplomatic incident.

The Jordanian Prime Minister, through the British ambassador, demanded a letter of apology from Ian who, quite naturally, as a member of the House of Lords, was regarded as an eminent representative of England. And naturally he should not have made such a remark, even if he thought it to be true. Personally, I totally disagreed with him. Their King is very brave.

The incident was forgotten until later, back in London, Lady Rowlandson asked Ian if he would stand with her at her daughter's coming-out party as her husband was confined to a wheelchair. Ian was only too pleased to oblige, and as they were greeting the distinguished guests at the top of the stairs, with her husband and I sitting nearby, a group of people arrived together.

The toastmaster called out: 'His Excellency the Jordanian Ambassador.'

When the ambassador was introduced to me, he heard my name, and reacted as if he had been shot. 'The Duchess of Bedford?' he said, thunderstruck.

He turned on his heel, collected all the Arab diplomats who were there, and departed. It was a terrible drama, as Lady Rowlandson had gone to a great deal of trouble to observe all the proper protocol. For a moment I could not understand what I had done. Lady Rowlandson was naturally in a great state, and asked me what on earth had happened. Then it suddenly struck me.

'Ian,' I said. 'Do you not remember saying that Jordan was a filthy country, full of dirty Arabs?'

To this day I wonder what Lady Rowlandson thought. Certainly she could be forgiven for thinking that we were a disaster. The dinner went on, of course, but I shall never forget that huge table with those empty spaces around it.

It made me realise how inflammable the Middle East situation really is, and one wonders whether it will ever really be solved.

Perhaps because of my education, I have always been drawn to the classical countries of the Middle East. So when our friend Aleko Papamarkou invited us to Persepolis for the Bal des Petits Lits Blancs—which was to take place a few days after the grand official opening—I jumped with joy. I was so excited not only about seeing Persepolis and the festive camp, but also of course about visiting that beautiful country, Iran. We have many friends in Teheran, including Miriam and Terry Massoudi and my sweet, dashing 'Don Juan', Ardeshir Zahedy, the son-in-law of the Shah and Ambassador to Washington.

We arrived in the city on the way back from the Far East. At our hotel, I met a group of French friends, led by Baronne Sellière, who were arranging the ball. They told me that there had been endless difficulties, and that they were bored and ready to cancel the ball. I laughed and said 'It's always that way. I am dead tired and am going to bed. Tomorrow will be another day.'

La Baronne Sellière is a remarkable woman who could have been the sister of 'The Flying Duchess'. She is petite, always smiling, always pleasant, and underneath has the iron personality of Napoleon leading the army to victory. Thanks to her, the ball did take place. Two full planes arrived from Paris with the gayest, most 'beautiful people'.

We visited Isfahan, one of the most beautiful cities in the Middle East, with the smell of jasmine and roses everywhere. We then flew to Shiraz, and drove by car to Persepolis.

The Darius Hotel had been reserved entirely for our party. It had marble fountains, grass—in the middle of nowhere—and everything was visually beautiful. Functionally, however, it was a disaster. I asked for a dress to be pressed, but there was no iron, and the air-conditioning was faulty.

The staff consisted of peasants who had been taken out of the fields and dressed up for the day. They were entirely unable to cope. As for the restaurant, the Duke of Bedford turned out to be the best waiter. There was total chaos. There were not enough plates, so we ate out of aluminium serving-dishes. Ian was running in and out of the kitchens, taking the ham out of the refrigerators and cutting slices. Luckily everybody knew everybody, so it was all done with a great deal of laughter.

When we arrived at the famous camp, we were given half an hour to tour it. It was an extraordinary place, rather like Las Vegas. You drove through miles and miles of sand, and suddenly there was a splendid oasis of green and freshness.

The great evening arrived when we were to be received by the

Empress. Hairdressers had arrived specially from Paris, and I went to Jean d'Estré. For the party, I wore a long purple chiffon dress, with bracelet, necklace, ring, and brooch—all amethyst and diamonds—and a tiara. The amethysts on the bracelet are so large that I call them my brake-lights.

A moustached gentleman informed us that we were to sit with the Empress's party. That was lucky because it meant that dinner would be served to us, while the rest of the party had to fight to help themselves at the buffet. I actually saw waiters being bribed, and tins of caviar disappearing under the tables!

I was ashamed of the behaviour of the Western world.

At the end of dinner a friend from my youth, Dr. Mehdy Bouchery, who had married Princess Ashraf, the beautiful sister of the Shah, came over to me, bowed with great dignity, and led me to sit next to the Empress for a conversation. I was amazed to learn that she knew a lot about Woburn, including details of our organisation for visitors. We laughed a great deal when I started to outline plans for turning the famous camp into a tourist attraction!

The whole camp was straight out of a fairytale, but the room that most enchanted me was the anteroom, a very large circular room with red velvet walls and a magnificent chandelier. I commented on the chandelier, and Her Imperial Highness said, with her throaty laugh: 'I have a secret for you. It is all made of plastic.'

The Empress is a charming, intelligent and educated woman, but for me her main quality is the total peace and serenity that emanate from her. She has large brown, expressive eyes, with a glint of humour, beautiful bone structure and a wide generous smile. She is, of course, far too thin.

When we returned to Teheran, I noticed that all the Iranian women used eye-shadow below their eyes as well as on top. One morning I was busy with my turquoise stick, and said to my husband:

'Should I do it like the Iranian women and paint the underneath of my eyes?'

He retorted with a smile: 'What do you want? Painted bags?'

I laughed. Thank God I am not vain.

[291]

37   *No time for embarrassment*

SOME DAY WHEN the last will and testament of the 13th Duke of
Bedford is read, there will be some raising of eyebrows.

The will was signed at Bora Bora, a small island in the Pacific,
near Tahiti.

To arrive at Bora Bora, you have to take a plane from Papeete
to Raiatea, and then a boat. From there you can travel by motor-
car across the island, and finally by speedboat to the Bora Bora
Hotel.

It is not something that you do for a weekend, but once you
are there, it is one of the most beautiful places on earth. The hotel
consists of a series of bungalows that stand over the water on
stilts. The sea is a lucid aquamarine colour.

Every morning six croissants would arrive for breakfast which
I promptly took to the water's edge. From deep down, the fish
came swimming up through the clear water—thousands and
thousands of them, small, large, flat, round, pink, blue, orange,
and that strange tropical variety with black or transparent faces.
They were so tame that they came to the surface to suck your
fingers. When we tired of this, we lay on our tummies and gazed
down through goggles into a fantasy world of coral.

This, then, was Bora Bora, our paradise. In our private bungalow, away from everyone, Ian and I were absolutely happy.
There was only one telephone, and that was by radio to the
mainland.

For some reason that is still a mystery to me, Ian had to sign his will at that very time. He could not hear the man in London over the radio telephone, so his solicitor decided to come out to Bora Bora.

He arrived a few days later, complete with Briggs umbrella and wearing a dark City suit.

'Come and have some lunch,' I suggested, but he firmly refused, saying there was something that had to be altered and he would first get on with his work.

When we returned to the bungalow after lunch, we needed an English witness. Ian was scanning the horizon, looking for an Englishman, when suddenly we heard a voice in the nearby water.

'Are you British?' Ian called. A man's head popped up, revealing a wet, sunburnt face with a wide smile.

'Yes,' came the reply, so Ian asked the man to swim to the bungalow. He hauled himself out and came up our steps, dripping wet.

'Do you mind witnessing my signature?' my husband asked.

As if it were a perfectly everyday occurrence, the man replied 'With pleasure.' He signed, and dived back into the water. The man from London picked up his umbrella and went straight back home the same day!

I have always thought how peculiar it will be for everyone who goes through the family papers a century hence to discover that the last will of the 13th Duke was signed at Bora Bora.

Ian and I love the Pacific. We like the climate, and the friendliness of the people. Maybe human beings need extremes of temperature to get along together. Perhaps the inner warmth and charm of the Russians, in a cold climate, is due to their need physically and mentally to huddle together to keep warm.

People in temperate climates do not make the effort, and remain aloof and distant.

It is easy, of course, to be happy in the sun. I often think of the marvellous marble house that friends of mine, Charlotte and Henry Kimelman, have built on the top of the hill in St. Thomas, among the luscious green palm-trees, flowers and tropical vegetation.

It is an open-plan house of the highest comfort, and we love to go there for a rest, particularly after a tiring visit to Australia. Henry, who is a yoga addict, tried to teach my husband to stand on his head, but it was always by the swimming pool, and Ian invariably ended up in the water.

Three months after the birth of my granddaughter Serafine in Santa Fé, New Mexico, Caterine and the baby came to stay with us in St. Thomas. It was one of the most blissful moments of my life, having my husband, the sun, that beautifully organised house with delicious Caribbean food, and a new baby.

Caterine used to take the baby to the swimming pool, and I am proud to report that now, at the age of two, Serafine not only swims perfectly, but when we were in Meribel last winter, she amazed everyone by following me down the mountain on her tiny skis, turning and stopping with ease.

Bali is our favourite place in the world. While the Western world has developed a civilisation based on refrigeraters and television, and a change of car every two years, theirs is still centred round the family and life in the compound.

In Bali we like to stay at the Tang Jung Sari at Sanur Beach, where we always have bungalow number one with its thatched roof, and where a family of coconut Monkeys live. The whole of the interior of the bungalow is decorated with Balinese paintings and drawings.

On our last trip, I woke the first morning at 5 o'clock to find my husband's bed empty, so I went out for a swim. Even at that hour, the light is as bright there as on the Côte d'Azur at midday. When I reached the beach with its white sand, I saw a lone figure in the distance, running towards me. It was Ian—Ian who never goes out of the house except to get into a car, who never breathes a breath of fresh air. There he was, jogging along. I joined him every morning after that.

When the tide goes out, the high sea disappears, leaving behind thousands of shells. Like an excited little girl, I used to join the hundreds of people who collect the delicate shells and lumps of coral. I have now arranged my collection on the centre table in my private sitting-room at Woburn, along with my other treasures.

One morning I heard the sound of a guitar that did not belong to Bali, but to the London scene. I poked my head out and saw, sitting all alone on the steps of a bungalow just behind ours, Mick Jagger of The Rolling Stones. I could hardly believe my eyes.

Ian, who had seen him on television, had told me that Mick Jagger was very intelligent. We invited him to join us to see a ketjack, which is a trance-dance in which the dancers walk on the hot ashes of coconuts, in time to the non-stop beating of drums.

I was delighted to find Mick Jagger so charming. He is a sensible, articulate man, and all that nonsense when he performs is just a very clever act. He enjoyed the ritual of the dance as seen through the easy smoke of his cigarette. He looked very happy.

I love watching the elaborate Balinese weddings. They marry en masse, and in the midst of a group of 200 people, you can often see a middle-aged couple surrounded by their children. They have waited perhaps 40 years before they can afford to get married.

Bangkok is another place where we enjoy behaving like tourists. There is a different festival every night, and in the morning you get up early and go to the floating market. It is almost incredible to see people brushing their teeth, while below them in the water are dead dogs and rotten coconuts, and beside them are people nonchalantly peeing while they greet one another.

Australia is now like a second home to us. All the Australians I know are highly sophisticated—and in no way uncouth, as many people wrongly suppose. They have beautiful houses and superb art collections, and the country has also produced some very fine painters like Sidney Nolan, Donald Friend, Ian Fairweather and Arthur Boyd.

When we arrived in Australia the first time, I was not sure that I would get on well with Lady Lloyd Jones, who seemed to want to organise me. There are those who consider her the uncrowned queen of Australia.

Thinking of her now, one of our first dinners in Sydney was at the house of Warwick Fairfax, the enchanting Australian newspaper owner. The Fairfax name in Australia is comparable to that of Hearst in America, Thomson in Britain, and Springer in Germany. Dinner was delightful. The only thing I did not like was that, after dinner, the men stayed with their cigars in the dining-room while the ladies were told to go and freshen themselves—which none of us wanted to do! I became very bored. Lady Lloyd Jones was arguing with another woman about whether smoked salmon was better in Australia or in Scotland; another lady was on the telephone to her lover. I thought I had better take a promenade.

A delicate little kitten came to play with me as I sat by the pool, which was surrounded by jasmine. When I returned to the house Lady Lloyd Jones and friend were still talking about smoked salmon; and the other woman was still on the telephone.

Quite consciously, I decided that I did not want to hang around while the men pleased themselves in the other room, so I simply marched through the garden to the front of the house, found my chauffeur, and said to him: 'Please drive me home. You can come back for His Grace.'

Before going, I wrote a note for Ian, saying that as he looked like being a long time with the men and the port, it was goodbye for now and I was going to bed.

My behaviour caused a scandal. Lady Lloyd Jones was courageous enough to telephone me, and rather like a mother, said: 'What you did was too rude. Warwick is very upset indeed.'

We ourselves entertain thousands of Australian visitors every year at Woburn. We like their friendliness and directness, which spring from a nation that has not only found prosperity and security but is supremely confident of its future. They have managed to turn the best of both worlds—America and England—into a mixture truly Australian.

Warwick and Mary Fairfax brought their six-year-old son, also called Warwick, to lunch at Woburn one day. It was a day I shall never forget. After luncheon, when I was pouring coffee in the drawing-room, I noticed that Ian and the child had disappeared. I could only assume that they had gone to try the roundabouts.

Big Warwick suddenly became very worried, and said: 'Where is my child? Please find out where he went.'

Of course, I ordered an immediate search and alerted Security, who promised that they would scour the grounds. As I thought, Ian and the child returned some minutes later. Exactly as I thought, they had been on the roundabouts. Warwick senior was immensely relieved:

The following day Ian had gone to London, and the watchman came and said that Master Warwick Fairfax was in the West Hall.

'You must be wrong,' I said. 'He was here yesterday.'

'Yes, I know,' he replied. 'But he is here again today.'

I asked my secretary, Mrs. Bain, to investigate, and sure enough young Warwick was there, asking to be taken to the miniature trains again. I went to see him for myself.

'Your mother and father have not telephoned,' I said, hoping for an explanation.

'I know,' he said coolly. 'My mother and father have gone out this morning, so I came here to go and look at the model railways, where I was yesterday.'

The huge model railway had obviously captivated this child-who-had-everything.

'Please will you tell the people not to make me pay,' he added endearingly, if somewhat precociously. 'And do you think I could have lunch here?'

If this astonishing child was self-assured, I certainly was not. When I asked where his parents were, he said:

'They left early, so I told Nanny to go and do an errand. While she was doing it, I ordered the Rolls, and told the chauffeur to go to Woburn Abbey. I have told him to go to the village, have his lunch and be back here at 5 o'clock.'

I could hardly believe my ears, and was terrified of the re-sponsibility of looking after the child in view of his father's concern the day before, particularly as I had an engagement in London. I summoned Ann, one of our young secretaries, and said:

'See that child. Never let him out of your sight. You are totally responsible for him. You must lunch with him, wait outside the lavatory for him, and if he asks you to go on an errand, in no circumstances go. Return him to the West Hall at 5 p.m., and make sure you see them driving away. You are entirely responsible for him.'

I was so terrified that something might happen that I even made arrangements for him to lunch with Ann at Finlay's table in the pantry, where the chef David and Finlay could also keep an eye on him.

David prepared what he thought was suitable for a child of that age—melon, chicken with mashed potatoes, and ice cream.

When lunchtime came, Ann took young Warwick to the pantry, as instructed. Warwick took one look round the room, and said:

'This is not where I had lunch yesterday.'

Finlay replied: 'No, we thought that you would be too lonely up there alone.'

And young Warwick sternly replied:

'I had lunch in the Canaletto room yesterday. I shall have lunch there today.'

Such presence of mind at the age of six surely guarantees him a successful future.

My husband, of course, is very English in his attitude to meeting overseas guests. He tends mischievously to plead poverty, by saying such things as: 'How nice it would be to have money.'

He is, of course, too astute to try this on our English guests, who through the newspapers are kept au fait with every move in the Bedford fortunes.

Lady Lloyd Jones must have had all this nonsense in her mind when she came to spend her first weekend at Woburn. She had heard Ian talking endlessly about his ruin, about the roof falling down on our heads, the dry rot, and the crumbling walls.

In Australia she had been so charming and hospitable to us that we wanted to give her a good party and ensure for her a memorable stay at Woburn.

It was very sweet of her to dress down for her weekend in the country. She came to dinner in a little understated number by Givenchy and one row of pearls. We felt slightly uncomfortable when the first couple arrived, the wife covered in jewelry. Then the second couple, the third and fourth arrived, each more resplendent than the last. Then finally came the pièce de résistance, a little breathless and bursting into the room like the aurora borealis.

This was the romantic novelist, Barbara Cartland, looking so much larger than life.

Barbara is terrific. She is immense fun, has a heart of pure gold, and is the best public relations officer for Barbara Cartland who ever existed.

Her arrival was the most spectacular thing about the evening. With a décolletage that plunged like a great white glacier, and absolutely dripping with diamonds, she stepped out of a white Rolls-Royce. A large necklace hung from her throat down to her great quivering bosom. From her ears drooped chandeliers of diamonds, surrounding aquamarines the size of cherries. Her face was dead white, her hair a froth of moonlight blond, and her mouth a gash of glistening, brilliant scarlet. Six layers of mascara hung from each eyelash. Barbara was at her best, incredible and marvellous.

All Miss Cartland's friends enjoy her entry into a room. She does not walk, but by some strange mechanism comes running in on her toes in little steps, calling in a high shrill voice:

'Nicole, darling, darling, where are you?'

Of course, I am standing right in front of her, but nothing must spoil Barbara's little bit of social 'business'.

Identifying our Australian guest, she enveloped her:

'Oh, Lady Lloyd Jones, I've heard how kind you were to Nicole and Ian when they were in Australia. What a sweet person you must be.'

Surrounded by women lit up like Fifth Avenue Christmas trees, all Lady Lloyd Jones could say was something about what a pity Nicole had not told her what a magnificent party it was to be, because she had thought she was spending a quiet weekend in the country and she had left all her jewelry in London.

New Zealand is quite different from Australia. It is a country of farmers. They are not sophisticated, but down to earth. I have such marvellous memories of one of our trips there some years ago on what we call an 'official tour'. I was assigned Mrs. Goot as a kind of lady-in-waiting. She could be hilarious. How I enjoyed her commentary as she walked a foot behind me, whispering in my ear: 'Oh, that is Mr. So-and-so. Here is his wife, but they don't live together. He has a mistress.'

At Rotorua, where we met the famous guide Rangi, who is now dead, I heard her say: 'Don't believe a word she says. You cannot trust her.'

She had such a wonderful sense of humour, and must have delighted many official visitors.

In Auckland we were received by the mayor, and we listened as Gounod's 'Ave Maria' was sung in French in my honour. Then a man brought a basket in which a kiwi nestled, but as kiwis are essentially nocturnal, the bird did not want to budge.

The mayor began his speech by saying: 'I am going to give you a few biological details about the Duke of Bedford.'

Out of the corner of my eye I saw Ian's eyebrows rise.

'I mean biographical,' the mayor corrected himself.

Whenever we go abroad, I prefer, instead of going to an international-style hotel, where you find the same people, the same food, the same furniture, to go to one typical of the country. In this way you have a chance to see people in their own sur-roundings.

So in Japan we live Japanese, and love every minute of it—except for the raw fish. One of my favourite places in Japan is the guest-house at Tsuruga. It is truly charming. You enter by crossing a river dotted with rushes, flowers, lilies and small, fat pink and white ducks that float like children's ducks in a bath.

You walk on large flat stones, automatically stepping from the twentieth century into the seventeenth. The hotel garden is a typical Japanese garden of peace, which is made from rock, green lichen, moss and perhaps some beautifully shaped plants.

You enter, as usual in Japan, through an anteroom, where you remove your shoes which are then taken away, cleaned and stored in a cupboard by the door. In the 'welcome room' it is customary to sit on your knees, yoga fashion, and drink green tea, which is served with small squares of something that tastes like chewing-gum but in actual fact is raw fish dipped in soy sauce.

The 13th Duke endures the ritual with patience and good grace, but he does look comical as he retracts his long legs under him like the undercarriage on an aeroplane.

There is no such thing as a private bathroom in a Japanese inn. All the family, adults and children, are packed tight into a tall, square wooden tub, sometimes four or five foot deep.

Before getting into the bath, the great cleaning takes place. Everyone is given a small stool, like one used for milking. There you sit, feeling extraordinarily silly, while a strong Japanese girl gets to work on you. With a large brush, like one used for paper-hanging, she lathers you all over and then begins scrubbing, far from gently—indeed, as if she were on her knees scrubbing the floor.

There is no time for embarrassment. You cling to your seat as she bashes on ruthlessly, until every part of your body is clean. Whereupon several buckets of hot water are tipped over you so that the soapy, dirty water can float away in the slats beneath your feet. You begin to feel like a new-born babe.

You are then led to the edge of the tub and you descend into the water. It is so hot that I have to lower myself by inches. And there you are like sardines in a can, everyone kindly, everyone smiling.

We once indicated that we would like a massage. That was an experience. Two extremely pretty Japanese girls in pink bikinis took charge of us. They did not speak a word of English, and everything was done in sign language.

There we stood naked and unlovely. They showed us to a table and then began discussing us between themselves like a couple of chattering budgerigars. They were in hysterics as they picked up my husband's vital part and bent their heads over my nipples like a scientist over his microscope.

Ian was asked to turn over and lie on his tummy—not before time. He had just got settled when up jumped little Madam Butterfly who, giggling herself silly, began walking up and down his spine.

Japanese have small chubby feet and you seem to feel their toes wiggling each of your vertebræ back into place. This is a highly skilled art. Great damage could be done but they are so trained that they are as light and graceful as the Russian gymnast, Olga Korbut. You feel marvellous afterwards.

I was not a great success at a Geisha party. As I do not like playing parlour games in England, why should I enjoy them in Japan? But even I, who am strong willed, found myself trapped into taking part in one of their innocent games—with a man and four giggling Japanese baby-geishas, as the young girls are called. While music played, the man made all kinds of gestures, such as jumping on one leg, waving his arms, nodding his head, clicking his tongue, closing and opening his eyes. The idea was to re-member the sequence.

I do not know if the Japanese were especially polite in letting me win or if I was especially clever in remembering the idiotic sequence, but I concentrated like mad, and in the end won a fan.

Ian was laughing outrageously at me until it came to his turn. With his usual vagueness, he got everything mixed up. The 50 people present, including the geishas, had tears running down their faces as this beanstalk of a man flapped about like a crazy windmill.

We had organised our trip for April so that we would be there in cherry-blossom time, but in 1972 the weather was so cold that there was still snow everywhere. Instead of pink buds bursting, they remained brown and firmly shut.

Were the resourceful Japanese dismayed that the country was filled with disappointed tourists? Not at all. Their faces filled with smiles, they covered the trees with plastic cherry-blossom.

I remembered this little face-saving trick myself, and once adopted it at Woburn when we were to be photograped in the garden with bulbs that had not opened. That was truly an occasion of travel broadening the mind.

In Kyoto, like all good tourists, we took endless photographs. Our guide was very thorough. Cold or not, he insisted that Their Graces be exposed to Japanese culture. He took us to a frozen waterfall of remarkable beauty. The ice froze in different coloured layers, green at the bottom, then blue and, through every shade of the rainbow, until at the top it was a delicate iridescent pink.

As we stood in wonder, our guide lapsed into what we were told was a 20-page poem all about a young man of 19 who, desperate from unrequited love, jumped into the waterfall and committed suicide.

My husband, who hates cold, himself almost changed through the various colours of the ice. When the poem was finished, he positively sprinted all the way back to huddle over a hot stove.

In the evening he was still so cold and miserable that I suggested he have a massage. The girl at the desk indicated the number 10, which I took to mean 10 o'clock in the morning. After dinner we went to bed to thaw out after our day of endurance, Ian promptly fell asleep.

I was reading when suddenly the door opened and in stepped a giant of a woman. She was almost as round as she was tall—and she must have been about six foot four! Her head was enormous, and in the centre of her face was one large tooth.

In the semi-darkness of a Japanese room, this huge creature looked as if she had walked straight out of a horror film. I was fascinated as she took off her coat to reveal a white smock underneath. I looked at my watch. It was just 10 p.m. So this was the masseuse.

She came towards me, but I hurriedly indicated the sleeping form at my side. Ian is so tall that if he sleeps under the normal eiderdown in a Japanese inn, his feet and his chest remain uncovered, so we always ask for two eiderdowns, which I then ioin together with safety-pins.

She slowly removed the bedclothes, and giggled at Ian's naked sleeping form. I was too mesmerised to move. With remarkable agility, she put herself astride on top of him, and began pummelling.

Ian awoke and looked up at this grinning gargoyle. He screamed in terror. I shall never forget his face, filled with horror and agony, as those arms like huge bolsters kneaded and pounded him. When she had finished, he nearly passed out.

That was the end of massage, Japanese-style, on that trip!

Some Japanese hotels are filled with droll notices in English which have been too literally translated from the Japanese.

'Do not go to the dining-room in your underwear,' was one of the funniest. But it had a perfectly logical explanation. The Japanese are scrupulously clean, and each day on your bed a set of white cotton underclothes is laid out which you put on after your bath, and wear in your private apartment. On top, again only in your room, you wear an elegantly patterned cotton kimono. It shocks the Japanese tremendously when foreigners baking in these over-heated hotels, go to the dining-room wearing these clothes.

Another notice I loved was: 'Keep your screaming children out of the corridors.' By 'screaming', they mean 'crying'.

My husband was highly amused by: 'If you are drunk, do not swim in the pool because we will not save you.'

During our stay we were invited by the Minister of Tourism to a Japanese luncheon. One begins with sweet things and finishes with raw fish in vinegar.

The whole time was spent in exchanging niceties. Everyone spoke to each other with a nice smile and said nice things. We would say how beautiful Japan was. Everyone would smile and nod slightly. Then they would say how beautiful England was. And we would nod.

We planned to have a Japanese flower-arranging exhibition at Woburn, and wanted to invite one of the most celebrated masters from Japan for the occasion. We sought the help of the Minister's wife, who was supposed to be the grand lady of flower-arrangement.

When we first met her, she had been dressed in a kimono. Subdued and acquiescent to her husband, she was the traditional Japanese wife. When she arrived by appointment at our hotel in Tokyo, she was totally transformed. She was now an exacting and efficient business executive. She wore a Chanel-type suit and very smart boots.

Her whole manner has changed. She went straight to the point, and asked about the fee, the conditions, and the number of people we could guarantee. The transformation was incredible.

Many months later the flower-arranging exhibition took place at Woburn, in aid of the Church of England, in front of 300 specially invited guests.

Even that occasion was not without its drama. We had arranged that the Japanese master would arrive at Woburn in good time before the actual demonstration took place in the evening. When he had not turned up by 4 p.m., we telephoned London but got no answer.

I was desperate. Had our expert been involved in a crash on the motorway? We telephoned the police, who told us that there had been no crash, but that there had been an accident of sorts. The master had put all his flowers and branches in boxes on the roof of the car, and the piece of plastic holding the boxes had broken, scattering their contents over the Bedfordshire countryside. The police had been called in and were at that moment searching for each precious piece alongside the motorway.

The party finally arrived at 5.30, with the master in a terrible, terrible temper. He said he must see the room at once where the demonstration would take place.

There was a long, pregnant pause as the small Japanese gentleman inspected the room. We all held our breath.

'It will do,' he announced solemnly, turning to his two English hand-maidens, who by now were red in the face, their beautiful coiffures having been dishevelled by the wind on the motorway.

He asked them to cover all the tables with white linen, to put the remains of his flowers in buckets, and to telephone to the nearest town for more flowers.

A request had earlier been made that he be given a room where he could meditate. I had chosen the yellow bedroom because I thought it might put him in a happy mood. We supplied him with some China tea, and oddly enough he had brought his own water.

The exhibition was due to start at 7 o'clock, but in Bedfordshire people always seem to arrive early. Great droves began arriving at 6.30. The Japanese Ambassador and his wife, who were spending the night at Woburn, were with us. We waited. We waited. And we waited.

I went to ask our administrator what was happening. It appears that the little master had arrived in the demonstration room after his meditation. He had taken six buckets of water and thrown them on the floor, until the room was like a lake. He said this was to purify it. There was water everywhere, and we had to call in the catering staff to mop it up.

By now the master was pacing up and down, and I decided that this was no time for me to get into a state! I asked him to join us and the Ambassador in the next room while the floor was being dried. Apparently that was quite the wrong thing to have said. He insisted on standing by the door, saying that he was the master and it was the Ambassador's duty to come to him.

I enjoy Japan, but I doubt that I will ever understand its people, no matter how often we go there. I had great difficulty in coping with this particular Japanese occasion, but fortunately all ended well. As far as the public was concerned, it was a most enjoyable exhibition which brought many people to Woburn.

I AM NO longer averse to advertising, because it helps to provide
revenue for the restoration fund I started.

The Abbey fund looks after the utilitarian projects, such as day-
to-day repairs, but I am more concerned with preserving and
improving the beauty of Woburn. I am like the mother who puts
a pretty dress on the child before the party.

The daily visitors to Woburn bring in the much-needed upkeep money. With my special fund, I can do things that have no
priority in my husband's eyes, such as lighting the pictures and
building the pavilions for the Sèvres porcelain.

One morning my husband announced excitedly that the manufacturers of a hair product wanted me for their advertising. I was
not at all keen. I hate being photographed. I always look like a
mashed potato. In any case, the idea of seeing my face in newspapers and magazines did not appeal to me.

Maybe I was still sensitive to the remark of a woman who
accosted me in Covent Garden and said:

'Are you the Duchess of Bedford?' 'Yes, I am,' I replied. 'Oh,
you don't look as bad as your photographs.'

Of course she meant that as a compliment, and over the years
I have learnt not to be self-conscious about such remarks.

I was slightly indignant at my husband's report, but I agreed
to see the manufacturers' representative. When he arrived, I
entered the room in a furious mood, only to be met by a
charming, cosy man who turned out to be Nigel Burgess,

brother of Guy Burgess of the famous Burgess–Maclean spy drama.

When he offered me £200, I replied rather crossly:

'If I have to prostitute myself, it will cost you £2,000.'

To my amazement, he agreed immediately. My husband was livid as he had been offered—and accepted—£500 for a similar advertisement, which only proves my point that one should never underestimate oneself.

Eventually, both my daughters took part in the advertisement, which became a family act. The photography went smoothly, and I was pleased to endorse a worthwhile product.

I was then asked to do a hand-cream commercial for television, and I have been using the product ever since. It is an inexpensive hand-cream, which I apply all over my body after each bath. I buy several bottles at a time, and put the cream in an empty spray-bottle. I add a few drops of Floris's 127 or of lime, to give the cream the scent I like. It costs very little and keeps my skin like that of a newborn baby.

The next television commercial I did was for chocolate biscuits. Actually there were three different commercials—one involving me alone, one my husband, and one the two of us together in our office, with the secretary bringing us morning coffee.

Mine went well. I said and did the right thing and did not fluff my words, as I had felt sure I would. Then came my husband, who had to eat a chocolate biscuit with an orange filling.

At the first rehearsal, he took a bite and spat the biscuit out, saying: 'Filthy, disgusting stuff.' The man in charge was in such a state that he made Ian sign a declaration that he would not say anything derogatory about the biscuit in public.

I was not a chocolate biscuit eater, but the biscuit I ate was so delicious that I was converted, and still eat that particular variety. Made from layers of caramel, it is simply smothered with chocolate.

When my husband was asked to do a commercial for detergent, I was fascinated, and decided to watch him. I am not a woman who glibly accepts what I am told; I want to find out for myself, and I abhor untruths of any kind.

This advertisement seemed to me dishonest. Our perfectly polished, unblemished floor was specially dirtied, either side of a clean strip. Just before the scene was shot, clean water was poured over the floor, and the camera tracked down a broom the exact width of the clean strip. I was astonished and appalled.

Every day our mail includes letters from charities, 'begging letters', normal business letters, letters from friends—and letters from people offering some form of promotion.

Our great, sweeping lawns were once sprinkled with daisies. I found them enchanting, but my husband thought it untidy. He was delighted and intrigued therefore when we were approached by a weed-killing manufacturer with an amusing idea. It was proposed to draw huge profiles of our faces on the lawns, either side of the east entrance. These were then to be filled in with weed-killer, leaving them pure and green in contrast to the crazy-daisy background.

It was fascinating to watch the artist at work. He arrived armed with ropes and wooden pegs, and skilfully drew in the silhouette, which was then sprayed with a blue powder. This would kill the weeds once it had been watered in with rain.

Everybody in the house was sceptical of the results. My husband said:

'My ancestors were painted in oils and I am painted in weed-killer.'

Three weeks later, when it rained, the result was quite amazing. There was not a flower to be seen on our faces, while the rest of the lawn was thick with little white daisies. We went up on the roof, with a photographer who had come from one of the national newspapers, to look down on ourselves.

I remember commenting: 'Look, look, I've got a double chin' —which was probably true enough. Next day a man arrived with a little extra powder to trim my chin, and everyone in the family laughed at me for days, as I deserved.

People think that I like—and seek—publicity. This is quite untrue. I am a very private person by nature, and even now, after so many years, I find I have to make a mental effort each time I appear at a public function.

That I do so at all is only acceptable because it is part of my duty to, and love for, Woburn.

Both Ian and I have become experts in public relations, simply because we have had considerable practice at it. From experience we know that to keep Woburn in the news, we ourselves must always be in the public eye.

A man I admire tremendously for doing just that is Liberace. He is the true perfectionist and professional. He is also a kind man —and kindness does not always go with success.

For his visit to Woburn on a quiet Sunday afternoon, he wore a brocade waistcoat embossed with flowers. Of course everyone recognised him, just as he had intended.

When we visited him in his house in the middle of the desert outside Las Vegas, the lawns were emerald green—a highly expensive achievement in that debilitating heat. In front of his house, instead of a carriage lamp or lantern, he has giant candelabra which he has made his leitmotif.

Liberace realised that, far from being envious, ordinary people like to look at extravagance. They enjoy peering in at a way of life they can never have. It is a form of escapism.

That is one reason why stately homes have been able to flourish in a changing Britain.

Another source of revenue for my restoration fund was one of my husband's bright ideas. When he first suggested taking in paying guests, I was aghast. I did not want people intruding on my privacy, which I guard jealously, but he then suggested that the money could be earmarked for lighting the paintings properly.

What is the use of having £9,000,000-worth of art treasures on the walls if nobody can see them? I decided to use the money to light each picture individually by a special beam system.

On a visit to the museum in Toledo, Ohio, I noticed an eighteenth-century painting of the French school, probably by Watteau or Fragonard—I do not remember exactly. It was on an easel.

It looked translucent and jumped out at you, screaming to you to pay attention to its beauty. I turned and twisted and bent until

I discovered the secret—a small beam of light directed exactly onto the painting from the ceiling.

The curator informed me that the lighting was the work of Dr. Uher of Vienna. I wrote at once to him saying:

'When you come to England, can you come to Woburn Abbey and ask to see the Canaletto room? Then will you please send me an estimate for the lighting of the Canalettos?'

I forgot all about it, and months went by. One day Ian and I were lunching in the Canaletto room with Anyes, who was going on a skiing holiday to Zermatt. There was a cholera scare at the time.

'If you go to Zermatt, you must have a booster to your cholera shot', I said.

'No,' Anyes replied, 'I don't want an injection.'

'Anyes, don't be ridiculous. If you go to a place where there's been a cholera outbreak, you must protect yourself.'

Anyes, who was then just a young girl, was not keen on injections, and finally after five minutes' discussion, I said: 'Well, that's that. After lunch I shall call the doctor and he will come and give you the injection this afternoon.'

I had to leave for one of my usual Saturday afternoon charity functions. While I was out, at about three o'clock, the doorbell rang and a very respectable grey-haired gentleman, followed by a younger man who carried a briefcase, asked to speak to me. As I was out, my husband was called. Hearing the word 'doctor', Ian said: 'It is for Miss Anyes,' so someone telephoned Anyes to say that the doctor was on his way. The two men were escorted to the bedroom where Anyes had removed her blue jeans in preparation. When the men entered her room, she looked up and said: 'You are not the doctor from the village.'

'No, I am from Vienna.'

'Have you come for my cholera shot?' Anyes asked, a little puzzled.

'No, I have come for the lighting of the Canalettos,' said Dr. Uher, petrified.

He has returned several times to Woburn and never fails to ask after Anyes.

Dr. Uher's technique involves an intricate operation, because the floor has to be taken up in the rooms above. A complicated mathematical calculation reveals the precise place at which holes must be bored through the ceiling so that the beams of light will be directed to the exact spot inside the frames, thus illuminating the paintings to best advantage.

The lighting in the Canaletto room turned out to be a great success. The room contains 24 pictures, however, and we face an enormous lighting bill, so I dared not begin to think what it would cost to light the rest of the house in the same manner. Hence my reason for agreeing to paying guests.

We first announced our decision during a television interview and we always mentioned it in our travels. The idea was to deal with potential guests as far as possible on a personal basis, by word of mouth, enabling me to form a judgment of the people concerned. I could not allow just anybody to stay with us, and I required not only bank references but character references as well. I always asked the guests to write about their interests and hobbies, as it helped me to understand them and choose suitable people to meet them.

The first time we received a paying guest, the whole house was in an uproar. Everybody was determined that the venture should succeed.

Our great house, which regularly has 20 to 30 guests for a weekend, was dressed in its best, with glorious flowers everywhere. When the guest-room was ready, I made my last-minute inspection.

Our guests always find fruit and flowers, biscuits, champagne and a decanter of whisky in their room, and I like to choose the books and magazines myself. If the guests are on a grand tour of Europe, I choose art and travel books relating to the countries they are going to visit. On the sofa-table we place the latest international magazines. Chess-players find a set in their rooms, and bridge players find cards.

Our overnight guests are invited to arrive at 4 p.m. They are met by a butler and taken to their rooms, where a maid and valet unpack.

After tea my husband takes them round the safari park and shows them the superb collection of animals, the trees and the lakes. They always enjoy the rare herds of deer—particularly the famous Père David herd.

Then they are taken to their rooms, where a bath has been run for them and their evening clothes laid out.

Before dinner we serve champagne in the drawing-room, and then comes one of the great moments of their stay when we go into the Canaletto room for dinner. I have experienced the scene once, and witnessed it a hundred times. I think it is the most beautiful dining-room in the world, and banal as it sounds, everyone gasps when they see it for the first time. On the table is superb silver by Paul de Lamerie and Paul Storr; the flowers blend with the red of the damask on the walls; and the Canaletto paintings themselves are unbelievably beautiful. In the summer, the sunset can be seen through the Venetian window that my husband unblocked when he came to Woburn; before then, another huge Canaletto and two small ones hung on the west wall, and these are now in our bedroom.

When my husband asked one of our guests what she thought of the Canalettos, she replied: 'Oh, I love them, especially with cheese.'

An Egyptian dinner-guest was spellbound. He stood perfectly quiet for some time, before remarking: 'I have never seen such good colour transparencies.'

After dinner we have coffee and liqueurs, and then we begin the grand tour. The whole house is lit by candles and chandeliers—which it takes two men an hour to light. By the time our guests return to the drawing-room, it is nearly midnight, and they are too mentally satiated with all they have seen to do anything except go to bed.

Next morning they have breakfast in their room and leave. They invariably write to thank us, as if they were old friends, and many send flowers or presents. Over the years I have learnt a lot through our paying guests, because they are invariably connoisseurs of porcelain, furniture and works of art, and not once in all the years have we ever had an unpleasant experience with one of them.

The first paying guest we had was an American chess-player. There are two games of which I know nothing—cricket, and chess. All through dinner and the tour of the house, he spoke about nothing but chess and great chess-players. For me, it was a nightmare of kings and queens and pawns.

The next guests were a Swiss banker and his two charming daughters, so we had more in common. Then came an American lady who brought her grandson, a pernickety 14-year-old who demanded piping-hot toast for breakfast in such a manner that John, the butler, decided that the boy would get his toast so hot that it would burn his precocious fingers. A toaster was taken to his room, and while he sat up in bed, John made toast; as soon as one slice disappeared, another was put into the toaster. At least we had no complaints about the service.

A party of paying guests can often be fun. Sometimes they behave strangely. One German visitor got a little tipsy, and as he left the dinner table, took a large handful of sugared almonds and put them into his pocket.

Some charming young men from Austria came twice, first with their parents and next with their girlfriends and a movie camera to make a film of the grounds. They brought me three wigs as a gift, which I thought was a very practical idea.

I was very moved by the father who was taking his son on a world tour in which Woburn was one of the highlights. The boy was dying of leukaemia, and the father was filling the last months of his son's life with beauty. I hope he found it at Woburn.

Probably the strangest of all our guests was the 17-year-old scion of one of America's most exclusive families. He was not only a very rich young man, but had a brilliant brain. He had taken degrees in both law and fine arts.

On his first visit, he asked my husband's advice about choosing a complete wardrobe of clothes suitable for a gentleman. Ian, of course, was in his element, and told him exactly what to order from his own tailor, Poole's.

On his second visit some months later—with a magnificent wardrobe—a spirited argument took place at the dinner table with Ian's sister as to whether the Duchess of Windsor was entitled to use the prefix Her Royal Highness. The American brought all his legal guns into action, but he had not bargained for Ian's sister, with her Russell stubbornness and over 400 years of tradition of reverence for the Establishment. My children were also there and were riveted by the spirited battle. But this was nothing compared to what came later.

On that particular evening the young American had arrived at dinner in white tie with a sweeping evening cloak lined with royal purple silk, above which his elongated neck bobbed like a puppet. In his hand he carried a malacca cane.

Precisely at ten o'clock he jumped up, looked at his watch and pronounced in solemn tones: 'I am sorry, but from this minute I have come of age. You will all now have to address me as "Your Grace".'

I dared not look at the children. But our guest was completely serious. He had delved back into his family tree and resurrected a dormant Austrian title. From then on we gave him the full treatment, with as many 'Your Graces' as we could possibly slip into the conversation.

He was a fascinating, if somewhat eccentric young man, and we kept in touch for several years. I thought of him as a whimsical wayward son, and was distressed when I heard some years later that he had taken his own life.

As part of our effort to make Woburn attractive to visitors, we are always organising events. We once had a music festival for the 'flower children'. Both my husband and I are very keen on good jazz, and we selected the other side of the park, where the animal kingdom is now, as the location.

The festival began on a Friday, but we did not visit it until the Saturday evening. We drove over with the children, and as I left the car, a girl ran to me and offered me some flowers. I was very touched.

The music was deafening, as young people seem to like it nowadays. It was a beautiful evening, and we sat on the grass and watched the fireworks. Everything was peaceful. It might have been a huge rally for Girl Guides and Boy Scouts had it not been for the weird clothes and the faces painted with flowers and butterflies.

I returned at dusk on the Sunday, and everything was still peaceful. Nobody had fought, nobody had misbehaved. The youngsters were preparing to leave, so I went to the microphone, thanked them all for coming, and said I hoped they had enjoyed themselves. I then added that I would like them to help me by collecting everything plastic within reach, because plastic or polythene would be fatal to the deer when they moved back into the area. In half an hour, the place was clear.

What we did not know was that there was a strike of railway workers, and our visitors could not return home, so they slept rough in the village, antagonising some of the villagers. In the morning, they drank all the pints of milk on the door-steps.

Next day I was told that a reporter from a German magazine wanted to speak to me. He said: 'I have been to the festival site, and I cannot find an empty bottle of spirits.'

I replied: 'No indeed, they drank milk.

The man then said: 'What I'll do is to go down to the village collect a sack full of empties, throw the bottles and some rubbish on the lawn, and take a photograph of you looking at the scene with repulsion.'

I was furious. 'Certainly not,' I said, 'Why should I do such a thing? They were very nice young people.'

He then had the nerve to suggest: 'If you do the photograph, I will give you £20.'

Every Whitsun Bank Holiday we have the annual Scottish show when as many as 12 entire regimental bands march through the hall at lunchtime between our tables and the buffet, playing bagpipes and drums. It is a beautiful, magnificently noisy and exhilarating experience, and all the guests stand and applaud as the Abbey seems to shake—except for my husband who cannot stand bagpipes.

One year I noticed that the music had attracted a huge crowd to the front door, so I told the Head Security Officer to let them through the house instead of making them walk the long way round. So thousands of people walked through, making remarks about our lunch.

One day, Eric Morley telephoned to ask if he might hold the Miss World Competition at Woburn. Everybody thought it was a marvellous idea. In fact it was a major operation, and I ended up organising it like a military campaign, with the pantry as headquarters.

My idea was that each contestant should have as an escort an attractive bachelor from her own country. This in itself took me three months to arrange, I had to telephone my friends all over the world to find the right people.

To add extra spice, I invited all the men I knew who liked pretty girls—age being no barrier. I had Bob Boothby, Nubar Gulbenkian, Paul Getty, and Bertrand Russell, who happened to be making one of his infrequent visits to us. He was a cousin of my husband's, and was holding an exhibition at Woburn in aid of his peace project, for which I organised a separate luncheon.

The house was filled with people, 30 of whom were to sit down to lunch at round tables in the Canaletto room, and another 50 in the hall—including all the artists who had donated works to the exhibition.

We were assembled in the drawing-room for drinks when lunch was announced. I had, naturally, placed Bertrand on my right, but he had disappeared. 'Where is Bertrand?' I kept asking.

'He is always popping off somewhere. He'll pop back,' his wife Edith said, philosophically.

I finally sent Finlay to find him, who returned, smiling:

'His Lordship says that he would prefer to lunch in the hall.' Indeed he spent the rest of the afternoon with Miss Surinam, who he said was very comely.

Bertrand was 93, I think, at that time!

It was on the same day when I heard cousin Bertrand make a priceless remark to Professor Freddie Ayer:

'I have come to the conclusion that philosophy is a very silly subject.'

The week was to conclude with an Elizabethan banquet—not quite the thing for an eighteenth-century house. It was one of the most exhausting things I have ever arranged at Woburn. We removed all the furniture from the Long Gallery and made one long table—in itself quite a feat. Our forestry department made carved wooden plates and bowls to add authenticity. This caused one of the beauty queens from Africa to remark:

'I am amazed that people living in a big house like this should have such backward plates. We eat off china at home.'

The seating at the table was an enormous problem because I had to mix ambassadors from all the countries with movie stars we had asked and of course the Miss Worlds and all those beautiful men. With ambassadors, there is a strict rule of protocol, so you cannot go wrong; but people from the film world can be extraordinarily temperamental, and they can get very fidgety if they think that insufficient attention is being paid to them. As some people did not know until the last minute whether they could attend, I decided to break my rule about planning well in advance, and to do the placings an hour before the guests arrived. Right up to the final minute our telephone switchboard was almost jammed with calls.

At last the plan was complete, the Elizabethan serving wenches were lined up, the sickly mead was ready to be served, the barons of beef were sizzling, and the candles were lit.

I had made my usual five-minute change into a long dress, and was standing in the ante-library receiving guests, when I saw Rex Harrison and his wife at the time, Rachel Roberts. They had apparently sent a letter of non-acceptance and then changed their minds without advising us. As we talked and smiled politely, my mind switched to the table-plan, and I realised that you simply cannot squeeze Rex Harrison in at the end of the table. He is not that kind of a person.

There was nothing for it but to start again. Poor Miss Hughes, our patient secretary, stood behind me whispering suggestions as I carried on receiving the guests. There was also another problem: Nubar Gulbenkian, more resplendent than ever with his monocle and the most flamboyant orchid I have ever seen in his buttonhole, idled up to me and said:

'Nicole, I am not very keen on my Miss Turkey. I would

rather sit between Miss England and Miss Australia.' They had the largest bosoms in the business, and Nubar was radiant.

When Nubar requested something, it was impossible to refuse him. So off Miss Hughes went to type the list yet again.

It was an enchanting, extraordinary, unforgettable evening. I do not know whether it was the good food, the plentitude of beauty or the abundance of wine, but the evening took on a most exotic air.

In the middle of dinner, Bob Boothby, in expansive mood, suddenly decided to ask Miss Egypt, who was sitting next to him, to do a belly dance. And of course she obliged.

I watched horrified as Bob and Miss Egypt climbed up onto the table and began gyrating. Miss Egypt looked fine as her trim little belly circled round and round, but I heard a crunching of crockery and glass as dear Bob tried it. Soon the whole table began to belly-dance. It was infectious. Even the minstrels in the gallery, who were supposed to be playing seventeenth-century music, switched to something more appropriate for the occasion!

I had planned a traditional Elizabethan night with Woburn lit by candlelight and seduced by soft music, but something quite different happened. The breakfast-room, which I had converted into a discotheque, became the centre of the party. We had installed a juke-box and an ingenious apparatus called a Scopitone, which shows a dance on film, so that everybody can copy the experts.

You can imagine the fun with the beautiful lithesome Miss Worlds and my enthusiastic middle-aged men guests as they shed their cares—and years!

Just when the party was really going, the head chaperone announced that it was time her girls went to bed to get their beauty sleep. I was amused that even the modern Cinderella had to be in bed by midnight—or, to be more exact, 3 a.m.

As the girls were leaving, there was a commotion in the State Saloon. It appeared that Rex Harrison wanted to punch an Italian on the nose because he considered the man had been trying to dance too closely with his wife Rachel.

Fortunately my son Didier, who is a strong boy, restrained the

Italian, and someone else grabbed Rex. The next day Rex sent me two dozen red roses with a card. It read: 'It was an Elizabethan banquet so I brought my Elizabethan manners. Do forgive me.' What a charming note!

I received a telegram from Roger Moore, who had left early in the morning: 'I spent a few glorious hours with you in your house, more unglorious hours in the fog in your park. Got lost and could not get out. Shall be your ghost forever.'

Woburn suits pretty girls and pretty girls suit Woburn. For ten years the Dairy Princess of Great Britain finals were held there.

The Dairy Princesses were quite different from our usual sophisticated beauties. They had been chosen because of their white teeth, glowing skin, clear eyes and shining hair. They had all pledged that they did not smoke, and that they drank three pints of milk a day.

Ironically, I remember pouring tea one day and saying: 'Milk or lemon?' 'Lemon, please,' one girl piped up. 'I hate milk.' Which only goes to show that you cannot even trust a Dairy Princess.

39   *'Your Disgrace'*

THE LATE MADAME Helena Rubinstein wrote in her memoirs that she 'hated being touched'. Being touched is unfortunately one of the prices that everyone in the public eye has to pay.

I dislike it intensely. I simply detest it when strangers mob me and try to grab hold of me. It is like giving away something that belongs to my family.

A visitor to Woburn once rushed up to me and enveloped my hand in his two huge paws. The flesh was damp and spongy.

'Hi ya, duchess,' he began.

I jumped back in horror. I like to choose whom I want to touch me. It is perhaps strange that I do not like familiarity. The same also applies to people calling me by my Christian name. It probably stems from my infancy when I was never cuddled or loved.

We have, of course, thousands of charming visitors at Woburn and some of my friendliest days 'on duty' have been spent at The Flying Duchess' buffet when we have had staff shortages over holiday periods.

I talk to our visitors and ask them what they enjoy seeing most. Almost invariably, I end up autographing their guidebooks or being photographed with their families.

I prefer English visitors because they are more reserved. Many of them, too, come back year after year and take a genuine interest in any improvements we have made.

Our most constant visitor is Mrs. Doreen Farmer. To date

she has visited us close on 300 times, until now she has a permanent pass that enables her to come whenever she wishes.

Mrs. Farmer is a little chaffinch of a woman who works as a machinist in a trouser factory in the East End of London. She has a husband, a son and a daughter.

She came to Woburn the first year it was opened to the public, and returned the following year. This was touchingly loyal of her because in those days we did not have a bus service between Woburn and the train, so she walked the 15 miles.

When she first began her visits, she used to plant herself in front of my husband and just stare up at him. She followed him around the whole day, mesmerised. Before leaving for the long walk back, she always pressed a pound note into his hand. At first he was very embarrassed, and did not want to take it, but Mrs. Farmer was insistent.

'You must take it,' she said, 'because you are my joy, and coming to Woburn is like coming to my own private home. I want to be part of the whole restoration of Woburn. I look at the roof, and when I see that a new tile has been replaced, then I think that it is mine. It gives me great happiness.'

So my husband took Mrs. Farmer's money and invested it each time in premium bonds. Imagine our joy when one of them won a prize, and he was able to give her the prize money.

Every Christmas, my husband's long present list includes a gift for Mrs. Farmer. She gives him sock suspenders. As she is also devoted to Maria Callas, he has given her many of the singer's records. One of his strangest gifts, and the one that has probably delighted Mrs. Farmer most, was her first flight.

She had never been in an aeroplane, and longed to go up in the sky, so Ian arranged for her to fly in a jet, circle London and have dinner served in her seat. The only snag was that, as it was at night, the beautiful sky was pitch black, and once she was up above the clouds Mrs. Farmer saw nothing.

But it did not matter to her. She had been up in an aeroplane, and that was what mattered.

Mrs. Farmer dressed specially for her hundredth visit. Sadly, Ian had quite obviously forgotten the occasion, and was in London.

I was told by the staff that Mrs. Farmer was in tears. We would not—we could not—hurt Mrs. Farmer knowingly. How could anyone be unkind to such a devoted Woburn fan who takes the trouble after every visit to write and comment if we have moved even the smallest object, which she requests us to replace where it belonged?

When I heard the news of her arrival, I invited Mrs. Farmer into our big office and explained that the Duke was away. Meanwhile the chef had whipped up a cake—with 100 iced on it—for Mrs. Farmer to take home. We had a pleasant, easy time together, discussing all the new improvements and our plans for the future.

Now when Mrs. Farmer arrives, the chauffeur always takes her back to the station in the car. She has become part of the rich human tapestry of Woburn Abbey.

When I was in the London Clinic for an operation on my foot, I had a notice put on my door that I did not wish to see visitors—and the whole family was advised accordingly. I was so exhausted after the season that all I wanted to do was read and sleep.

While I was lying on my bed one hot August day, the door opened very slowly, inch by inch. In the chink of space, there first appeared a bouquet, and then Mrs. Farmer's little pinched face.

She had been to Woburn and had somehow prised out of a member of the staff where I was. 'I just had to come, dear, and see for myself how you are,' she said.

Such consistent loyalty constantly amazes me.

I had a letter from an American lady once who wrote:

'I was in your house recently and meeting you and shaking your hand made my trip. The treasury for our Civic Beautification Project is never very large so I would like you to know that you are contributing indirectly as I charge a fee to shake the hand which shook the hand of the Duchess of Bedford.'

But she did not tell me if hers was a golden handshake or a copper one!

Not all our guests enchant us. My husband received a letter from one woman who wrote on pink, scented paper:

'Your Grace, I was sitting on the Via Veneto facing you and I opened my legs. I know you looked, so I am prepared to be your mistress. I will be at the —— Hotel in London waiting for you, lying naked on my bed.'

The secretary who opened the letter showed it to us and, of course, we all had a good laugh.

Some time later Ian received another pink love letter:

'I think it is about time we met and I quite realise that you have been busy. I have bought myself a pink hat and I want you to take me to Ascot.'

The third letter was rather more insistent:

'I notice that you have not got rid of Nicole yet, so I will come and get rid of her myself.'

I did not think that was so funny, because I always move among the crowds and am, therefore, vulnerable to attack.

My husband teasingly said:

'Hide yourself. Don't go in the garden. Find a big cupboard and stay there.'

Then one afternoon, as I was walking through the West Hall, I was amazed to see Ian running. He was as white as a sheet, and I rushed up to him and asked what was the matter.

He had encountered the mad woman. She had entered the kiosk where he was selling souvenirs, put a vice-like arm around him, and with the other arm had tried to undo his trousers. The poor creature had apparently suffered brain damage in a motor crash. Ian had to call the police to take her away. She returned however with such regularity that finally she was committed to a mental home in Scotland.

We had another strange visitor from Scotland one day. Neither Ian nor I was at home when Mr. Miller's taxi drove up and deposited a woman aged about 70. Mr. Miller, one of our local taxi-drivers, is a living encyclopedia on Woburn. From her pocket the lady took a handful of silver, which she threw among the pebbles on the drive, announcing to Mr. Miller: 'This is for you, my good man.' Mr. Miller was not exactly pleased at such feudal behaviour but he helped her with her suitcase.

The doorman was surprised to see a visitor because we were

not at home and were not expecting any guests, so he called Finlay.

'Take my case to my bedroom,' the woman ordered him.

'I am terribly sorry but Their Graces are not here,' Finlay replied.

'Don't you know who I am?' she continued.

'Well, I am terribly sorry, but maybe my memory is not so good.' Finlay is very polite, and a born diplomat.

'I am the Duchess of Bedford. Now take my suitcase to my room immediately,' she commanded.

Finlay knew he had a lunatic on his hands, and thought quickly.

'Of course, madam. While your room is being prepared, do you mind sitting here, and we will bring you some tea.'

While the secretary was ringing the police, my son Gilles and a friend entered the hall. He was about 18 at the time and in tennis shorts, and did not give a second glance to the skinny old lady, but she jumped up and rushed at the boys:

'Oh, you darlings, I shall take you both out to dinner tonight.' Saying which, she took off her coat.

She was stark naked underneath. Poor Gilles still remembers the occasion with horror.

One day my husband received a letter from a woman saying that she wanted to record an interview on tape to raise money for blind babies in Canada.

She turned out to be a neat woman in a navy blue suit and white gloves, a white collar and small hat perched on the top of her head. The interview was not complete by lunchtime, so out of courtesy I asked her to stay.

I showed her to the cloakroom before lunch, and she turned to me and said:

'Do you know, when I knew that I was going to see Him, I had three baths.'

I began to suspect something, and after lunch—which went off quite normally—I reported her remark to my husband, but he dismissed it lightly.

Some weeks afterwards, he received a letter from the woman, thanking him for the interview. Then three days later came another letter, thanking him for a delicious luncheon. Thereafter the letters started to arrive every few days. She progressed from 'Your Grace' to 'Dear Duke' to 'Darling' and to 'My love' in no time at all. Suddenly Ian was receiving twenty pages three times a day. Then the telegrams began. On one occasion 50 arrived on a single day, each three pages long.

Naturally, I became really concerned, and I rang the head of the police in the town from which the telegrams were despatched. I told him the story, and suggested that the local post-office be alerted not to accept telegrams from the woman.

Before anything could be done the poor lady tried to take her life. Her husband wrote an apologetic note to us, explaining that she had been admitted to a mental hospital. Some months later we were most surprised to receive a letter from the woman herself. It was an extremely courteous letter in which she apologised for her earlier behaviour, saying that she was now quite back to normal.

No wonder a friend of mine called the private apartment at Woburn 'the padded wing'!

Some of our correspondence is far from complimentary. When I was doing a column for the *Daily Sketch*, I received a letter written on Dorchester Hotel writing paper, It read: 'Your Disgrace, They call you on both sides of the Atlantic, and there never was a more apt title for anyone. It is well known that your husband would do anything for a fast quid but the English dukedom is still something very idealistic. You have ridiculed that image with this idiotic picture where you look like a drunken tart at a fancy dress ball. As for the sparkling duchess, you are as sparkling as the cheapest pop drink in a railway canteen . . .'

We receive many critical letters and I usually answer when an address is given, but what can you do when the writer is anonymous?

Souvenir hunters also plague our life. They became so troublesome at one time that we had to cover the curtains with lengths of netting to stop people from cutting away the tassels and swatches of the original silk.

Our personal friends are often amused by our visitors. We

were giving a birthday luncheon for a very dear and loved friend of mine, Jules Buck. There were about 20 people round the table, and because we had started lunch late that day, we were still eating well past the time when we normally open the Canaletto room to visitors.

Finlay had been told three times that some visitors had come specially from Canada to look at the pictures, and as they had a plane to catch, they wanted to know what time the room would be available. Finally, he whispered this information in my ear. Everyone at the table was merry. We were drinking champagne and had still to eat a large birthday cake.

On the spur of the moment, I told Finlay to put up the ropes and let the Canadians in, but before we knew it all the Sunday visitors streamed through the room. We were like the figures in 'The Last Supper' on exhibition!

It was terribly funny to see the people's reaction. Some of them were horrified at interrupting our meal, and looked up towards the ceiling in embarrassment before they dashed out of the room. as quickly as their dignity would allow.

Two Lancashire women, however, stood there, holding the ropes and discussing us:

'Oh look, they are eating chocolate cake. It looks good. The one with grey hair must be the Duke, and the marmalade one must be the Duchess.'

One group of visitors who amused me consisted of 80 American ladies. Tea was laid out in the Long Gallery in the traditional English way, with cucumber sandwiches, hot muffins, and chocolate fruit cakes.

Seeing the large quantity of food, one of the women felt genuinely sorry for me, and leant across to me, saying:

'Poor little lady. You must have worked all night!'

Another one came up to me and said:

'Your plastic camellias are so beautiful, may I take one?'

'Take them all,' I replied, 'we have hundreds growing in the greenhouse.'

There was another visitor I could well have done without. We were awakened by a fantastic screaming and I thought an intruder must be trying to kill the watchman. Ian jumped out of bed and ran down the corridor without any clothes. I followed, throwing him a dressing-gown. He kept calling to me: 'Ring the police, ring the police.'

I remembered all the scenes on television and knew I had to dial 9 to get an outside line and then a further 999. Trying very hard to remain calm, I said: 'I am terribly sorry to disturb you at this early hour of the morning. This is the Duchess of Bedford speaking.'

Before I could continue, the officer said: 'Yes, we know, you have a madman in your house—a patrol car is on its way.'

I went quietly downstairs to see what was happening. I could hear a tremendous banging noise, and I came into the hall to find Scott, the night-watchman, who used to be chauffeur to my husband's grandfather.

Scott was shouting: 'He is crackers, he is crackers.'

There in the West Hall stood an attractive young man who was trying to smash everything within reach with a cricket bat.

'What on earth does he want?' I said.

'He wants Your Grace,' came Scott's reply.

The young man saw me, and cried: 'Duchess, duchess, I must speak to you.'

I thought it might calm him if I spoke to him, so I said: 'Yes—I am the Duchess of Bedford.'

He stopped and turned to me:

'Your father is in danger,' he said.

My father had of course been dead for some time.

In anguish, he continued: 'Yes, yes, they are taking him to the Wash.'

It transpired that he thought we were in the thirteenth century and that I was the daughter of King John. By this time it was 6 a.m., and the patrol car had arrived. By an extraordinary coincidence, Mr. King, our milkman, arrived at the same time, and our intruder heard someone say to him 'Good morning, King.'

The young man at once took up the cry:

'Ah the king, the king. You are being taken to the Wash.'

How fine is the line between normality and mental instability.

We learnt later that the young man had been studying for the priesthood and had worked too hard for his theological examinations. The strain had been too much.

Woburn is certainly a powerful house that has an extraordinary effect on many people.

40   'Nine ghosts in your bathroom'

IT IS FAR into the deep of the night, long after the last house guest has gone to bed, that I have time to appreciate and love the peace and beauty of Woburn. I like to wander through this dignified, mellowed house. I pass from room to room, looking up at the portraits of the ancestors. Woburn is primarily a private house that through 400 years has belonged to one family—the Russells—and to one family of ghosts.

Several rooms at Woburn have been permanently haunted, and to these was added the State Salon last year. The new poltergeist was discovered by the grandchildren, who were sleeping in the room directly above.

All through the night they could hear what sounded like someone rummaging in the room below. The workmen, who had been taking down the faded blue silk embossed with gold which had hung there for over 60 years, had long gone home. The silk was being replaced with modern murals that my husband had commissioned.

Next morning we found the rolls of silk tossed about on the floor as though someone had been examining them.

Now we wonder whether, in fact, it was the Flying Duchess, who may have been furious that the room she had personally decorated was now being in her view desecrated.

On the whole our ghosts are amiable, docile creatures who are inquisitive rather than malicious, pathetic rather than vindictive.

Our close friend Paul Getty must by now have slept in every bedroom at Woburn. One morning at ten, I was walking along the East Corridor when I saw Paul jumping up and down like a yo-yo. Now Paul is no youngster, but there he was bouncing away on the crimson carpet on the second floor, where our main guest-bedrooms are situated.

'What are you doing, Paul?' I asked in complete amazement.

'Something very strange happened in the night,' he explained, and then went on to tell me that Penelope Kitson, who was then designing the interiors of his various houses and was staying with us at the time, had complained that the doors of her bedroom opened again and again during the night and that she had felt a cold draught—a chilling experience.

Her bedroom has two doors, one the anteroom door and the other the bathroom door, and she had finally got up and closed them, shaking each one to make sure it was firmly secured.

It made no difference—the doors still opened.

'It just occurred to me,' said Paul, 'that perhaps the weight of the night-watchman on these floorboards made enough movement to cause the doors to open, and I was just putting that theory to the test.'

Paul Getty is a very practical man, and his theory seemed quite convincing. After all, how else could one explain this strange incident?

The strange thing about the spectral phenomenon in this part of the house is that the bedrooms there are fairly recent additions to the house. Ian's father demolished so much of the house that, when we married with seven children between us, we were actually short of bedrooms, so these extra rooms were built.

They were located in the space along the corridor where there had been extensive cupboards for keeping various items, including all the fancy clothes for masquerades and balls.

In the time of the 7th Duke a manservant was murdered in the masquerade room. The poor man did not die immediately, so he was hidden in the cupboard until his body could be disposed of that night.

The sordid, shameful story continued when late that dark

night his murderers pushed his body out of the window and dragged it to the lake, where it sank.

It is this manservant who is supposed to haunt that corridor.

The children accept the ghosts with the same nonchalance as they accept the Canalettos, and they constantly startle guests by their mundane approach to the supernatural.

When Stephen Hastings, M.P. for Bedfordshire, came to lunch my younger daughter Anyes fixed her huge blue eyes on him and very seriously told her own personal ghost story.

'He kept opening the door when I was in bed with influenza and so I said: 'Ghost, go away, because I just can't keep on getting out of bed to close the door all the time.' So he did not come any more.'

Mr. Hastings laughed, probably putting the story down to the romantic inclinations of a young girl.

'Well, come to my room and I will show you,' Anyes said.

Up they went to the second floor, and she asked him to close both doors firmly himself. She stood back, and then said:

'Ghost, come out,' and both doors opened. Stephen Hastings went as white as a ghost himself.

On one occasion I had returned from London at 3 a.m. and was really thirsty. I wanted something cool, and as my refrigerator on the second floor contained only champagne, I decided to go down to the first floor, where the drinks are kept and have an ice-cool beer.

We have pilot lights everywhere, so I did not bother to switch on the main lights. The dogs were following me down the corridor, and being more sensitive to ghosts than human beings are, they were the first to react. They suddenly planted themselves against the wall with their tails tucked between their legs, and howled—terrible, pitiful howls.

'The ghosts are about tonight,' I told myself. It was a strange feeling that I was suddenly in contact with another dimension, another shadowy world that I was unable to reach. I stopped dead in my track and thought:

'Do ghosts take the lift?'

I was so furious with this thought that I forced myself to go down in the lift and, of course, nothing happened.

'Nine ghosts in your bathroom'

In the north wing there is a room in the staff quarters that is supposed to be haunted. Nobody would sleep in this room, so I decided to use it for storing things I had brought from France.

I had one of those huge laundry-baskets filled with letters and memorabilia, and I was sitting sorting them one day, because the room was to be decorated while we were away in Australia. I had become so absorbed that I had completely forgotten the time, and was amazed to find that it was 3 a.m. It was at that moment that the dogs began howling and trembling with fear.

The door opened, but I paid no attention because I had just come across the letter that Michel had thrown from the lorry for me as he was being taken to the concentration camp—a truly brave letter, so filled with love and tenderness.

I began to cry at the remembrance of all those people from our group who had died. I cried for the sheer futility of those war years. Only one of our small group, George, was alive, and I had not heard of him in 23 years.

I found myself saying to that empty room:

'Ghost, instead of coming here and frightening me, why do you not go and find George?'

Two mornings later, a letter arrived which began:

'Dear Bricole', the name by which I was known in the Resistance movement, and continued:

'You appeared at the foot of my bed last night, no longer a blond but a redhead. You were wearing a blue dress and you were crying and saying: "George, George, where are you?"

'I know where you are because I read about you in the newspapers. I write to tell you that I am still at the same address and one day I would like to visit you.'

Was it a supernatural experience or just coincidence? As I am neither religious nor superstitious, I believe that it was probably the latter, but I wonder:

Some months later, when I went to Paris, I rang George's doorbell, and when he opened the door we simply fell into each other's arms.

George had made a museum for the Resistance movement in the attic of his home. He had become an authority on those years, and had all kinds of grim mementos, including photographs and a piece of bread from a concentration camp, which he kept under glass.

When we were digging under the Abbey for the exit staircase for visitors, we began clearing the rooms nearby, which were full of rubbish. The curator, several of our cleaning women, Finlay and I began sorting out what we wanted to keep, what was to be repaired and what was to be burnt.

One evening we all left rather late and I asked one of the cleaning women to sweep the floor so that we could begin afresh the next morning. She remained there alone, and ten minutes later came out screaming, saying that a monk was walking about.

We laughed and sent the watchman to lock up. Two minutes later he returned, white and shaken, saying that indeed there was a monk down there.

This may well have been true as we were digging the monk's burial ground and had moved their ancient bones about.

Not once, but several times, we have had our staff and visitors in the Antique Centre meet a gentleman with a top-hat. He is always in the same place on the second floor. It is interesting because the last shop, which is where he seems to live, was a walled room, and was only revealed when the Centre was opened.

It is unfortunate that no one seems to know the full story about the room, but it was once occupied by the head groom, and maybe the top-hat was part of his uniform.

Another mysterious ghost walks about in the Sculpture Gallery, Some years ago, after the restaurants, buffet and pubs had been established, I talked to David, the chef, and Ray Beardow, our partner in the catering business, and we decided to cater for functions. The Sculpture Gallery, built by Holland and Wyatville. is very beautiful as it overlooks the private rose garden, and it seemed a great pity not to use it. Claude Serre from Paris was with us at the time, and helped us to rehouse the statues in the private rooms so that we could have the joy of looking at them every day.

I covered the central Roman mosaic with a specially built

suspended dance-floor so that the mosaic would not be damaged The Gallery was then ready for weddings, seminars, dances and parties.

The first time a woman turned round to slap the face of the man behind her, we thought she must have good reason for it. By the tenth time we knew that we had another ghost. He would caress the naked backs of women in evening dresses in a permissive way. So far he has not materialised, however, so we have no idea what this charming roué looks like.

Ian never goes into the Wood Library without feeling another presence. He finds himself totally unable to concentrate there.

A venerable professor from Cambridge University came to the Abbey one day, rang the front door bell and said:

'I've come to investigate your ghost.'

I took him round the house, and we spoke to all the women guides who had seen a ghost. One of the women claimed to be able to see a ghost in a painting. How much more of a snob can you be than to have not only your own ancestors on the walls, but your own ghosts?

Most visitors to Woburn delight in our ghosts and beg us never to have them exorcised. However, one day I was sunbathing with my cousin in my private rose-garden. As I have a secret way of going back to my apartment—which means that I do not meet visitors, friends or staff—I did not bother to put on my bathing-robe.

Up to the second floor I went. I was just about to enter my small, intimate bathroom when I was confronted by a very skinny lady with frizzy hair.

'I'm the president of the Ghost Society, and we've just found nine ghosts in your bathroom,' she piped up cheerfully.

Every time now that I have a bath, I have visions of ghostly vapours disappearing down the plughole like Aladdin's lamp in reverse.

41 'I hear you've offered Harold Wilson a job'

THE FIRST TIME I went to Downing Street was when Mr. Harold Wilson was Prime Minister. When we were invited Ian had immediately said in his Russell way, 'I am not going', but I wanted to go because I was curious about the inside of Number 10, and besides I thought Mr. Wilson had beautiful blue eyes, and I wanted to see them close to.

And so we arrived. The only thing that I really dislike at formal occasions is having my name screamed out by a man in a red coat, with everyone turning round looking at you. I always give idiotic names like Joan of Arc or Virginia Woolf. I have several times been announced as Mrs. Virginia Woolf, much to everyone's astonishment.

At Downing Street, of course, I was serious. I have a great sense of occasion. So as I arrived I said to the toast-master, 'Please do not announce me.'

As I reached the top of the stairs, Mrs. Wilson was standing there—a pretty, uncomplicated woman with twinkling blue eyes. In my normal tone of voice I said, 'I am the Duchess of Bedford.'

The minute she heard my name, she grabbed my hand, would not let it go, and called, 'Harold, Harold, she is here.'

When the Prime Minister arrived, it was clear that he was not going to leave me for the whole evening. He took me round, and made me visit the entire house, I was surprised to find how much he knew about works of art. He has incredible charm, a charisma that has nothing to do with his pipe-smoking television image. We laughed all the time. When we came to the room downstairs where the Cabinet Meetings are held, I noticed that on the side table was Vittel water and Vichy, but no Malvern and I remarked: 'That is not very good for the English Market.' The Prime Minister threw back his head and chuckled.

When we had finished the tour I told him:

'Well, when you are out of a job, you can always come to Woburn Abbey and I can employ you as a guide.'

The day afterwards a friend called me from Westminster and said: 'I hear you've offered Harold Wilson a job as a guide.'— which proves of course that all politicians are merely school boys grown tall.

On my next visit to Downing Street Edward Heath was Prime Minister. When I arrived he kissed my hand with touching gallantry. I had not expected such old-world courtesy, but I thought it rather nice and very French. We spoke French the entire evening, and I enjoyed Mr. Heath's French. It has an old-fashioned textbook flavour and, like the man himself, is highly professional and full of kindness.

My husband always thought I should be in politics because of my ability to be comfortable wherever I am, and to speak in public without shyness, and also because of my strong views about the welfare of other people. Personally I do not think I could be in politics because I am far too sincere and truthful. I can excuse most behaviour, but I cannot tolerate a person who is dishonest, a cheat, or a fake. Once I have given my word I never break it, and in politics that would not do.

I suppose it is because I am French that I love English pageantry so much, and ceremonial dinners. A dinner at the Mansion House is a must, and I have been to many. I recall three in particular—one because as we were announced by the master of ceremonies, and as I began moving towards the Lady Mayoress, steadying my tiara, one of the guards in armour fell flat on his face in front of me. What do do you when that happens? Pick him up, jump over him or make a detour?

Another time, the dinner was for a charity occasion. We had been asked to come in Georgian costume, and we went with a group of friends, including Charlotte and Henry Kimelman.

Charlotte and I had spent the afternoon at the hairdresser, and when we set off for the ball we had many laughs because our crinolines took up most of the back seat of the motor-car.

I was disappointed to see that our hostess had not dressed as she had demanded of her guests but, I was even more horrified when I discovered that we were expected to have dinner in our laps sitting on the staircase.

I collected my party immediately and departed for Annabel's, where we made a rather noticeable entrance in our eighteenth-century costumes.

The third time was when we went to Lord Kenilworth's dinner when he was John Siddeley. I was placed between the Marquess of Bristol and the Bishop of Southwark.

I spoke first to the Marquess. We chatted about stately homes, of course, as he owns Ickworth. Then I turned to the other side, filled with pleasant anticipation of the refined conversation I was going to have with Mervyn Stockwood. I have heard him speak many times at the House of Lords, a beautiful tall, figure with wavy grey hair and a profile as on a Roman coin, making great gestures with his lace sleeves. I am always fascinated by his impeccable English and grand voice.

As I began to speak, he interrupted me by looking at his watch, saying: 'We are running late.'

I replied, 'Are you in a hurry?'

'I have to go home to get the joint out of the freezer,' he replied.

Dumbfounded I said: 'Do you have to do that yourself?' He then proceeded unknowingly to weary me with all his household staff problems, a conversation I always refuse to have with another woman.

The following night we were having dinner at the Danish Embassy. As usual the dinner was delicious, as Mrs. Christiansen is a superb hostess. I was seated next to the Danish Ambassador, and on the other side I had one of London's most colourful ambassadors, who said: 'I saw you last night at the Mansion House. You must have had a marvellous highbrow evening, sitting next to the Bishop of Southwark.'

I replied rather forcibly: 'If you must know, it was the dullest conversation possible. He told me he had to go home to get the joint out of the freezer.'

The ambassador turned to me with a whimsical look, and said: 'I could have told him what to do with his joint.'

It was inevitable that Woburn should get involved in Britain's entry into the Common Market. But it was not exactly as I had planned it. At the annual general meeting of the London Tourist Board, Lord Mancroft turned to me and said: 'What are you going to do at Woburn about the Common Market?'

'Nothing,' I replied.

'But you must do something,' he insisted. 'I'll give you the finance, the people to run it, and all the help you want.'

'Absolutely not,' I replied. 'Everybody is exhausted at the end of the year, and besides, I'm always in my little retreat in the mountains at that time, getting back my red cells for next year.'

'I don't want to hear about it,' Mancroft said. 'You are the leader of the stately homes, and you must do something,'

Either because he had misunderstood me, or did not take my refusal seriously, he announced in front of 300 newspapermen—all the tourist Press—that: 'I have just had a word with the Duchess of Bedford, and she tells me that Woburn is going to lead the way, as always where stately homes are concerned, and that she is willing to hold there the opening of the festivities into the Common Market.'

I was absolutely stunned. Before I could even catch my breath he added: 'And she is going to tell you about it herself.' He sat down. Hundreds of eyes were riveted on me as I rose, not knowing what to say.

'Well, it is very nice of Lord Mancroft, but at the end of the year we are tired.'

Behind me I could hear Lord Mancroft muttering: 'We'll give you the staff.'

'And we're busy preparing for next year.'

'We will also help you financially,' the voice continued.

I was completely trapped, of course. Perhaps Lord Mancroft thought I had wanted to be!

Back at the Abbey we called the 'Woburn family' together, and I explained the whole situation.

'It is not a yes or no any longer,' I told them all. 'We are getting help and finance from the Tourist Board, so please think of something.'

David, the chef, was the first one. He suggested that he prepare a menu with nine dishes from the nine countries of the Common Market. Peter Bennett, the catering manager, came up with the idea of a special drink made with ingredients from each country (the result incidentally was the most potent drink you have ever tasted!). Mrs. Enid Barratt, who is in charge of the arts and crafts and the Exhibition Hall, promised to call all the commercial attachés and arrange a crafts exhibition.

In the Exhibition Hall we decided to hold an exhibition of works of art from the nine countries, and we would also arrange in each room of the Abbey a display representing the nine countries. Woburn is so rich in art from all over the world that it was not difficult—except that we have very little from Norway. When I read the news that Norway had dropped out of the Common Market, I was profoundly grateful. We had plenty of Royal Copenhagen porcelain, Irish glass, Dutch paintings, German Meissen and French furniture and Sèvres, and naturally Italy was made easy by the Canalettos.

As always happens at Woburn, we all became fascinated with our various jobs. I went round the house putting little flags from the nine countries on the works of art.

Everybody worked incredibly hard to put on an exhibition of some kind. In the Antique Centre the dealers labelled all their antiques with little flags, and there was a prize for the best window.

We opened the exhibition with a superb luncheon on December 17, 1972. The ambassadors from the various countries were invited, and nearly all accepted. On the morning I received a letter from Lord Mancroft, who had begun the whole thing and was to represent Britain, saying, 'Dear Duchess, alas, alas, I will not be with you on that famous day but I am delegating our good friend Clement Freud who I am sure will do the job as well as I.'

I was so livid that poor Clement Freud, who has been a friend of ours for many years, but is, after all, the grandson of a German psychiatrist, should represent this country that I decided my husband would do so instead, and Clem could represent the Tourist Board.

The whole thing was a wonderful success, and thousands of people came from all over the country, and on New Year's Eve we had a superb fireworks display.

In connection with the affair, we worked closely with the Foreign Office, and we were invited to the dinner party given by the Queen following the gala celebrations at Covent Garden.

The earlier part of the evening was badly organised and boring. Even the Queen, who usually conceals her feelings, looked unhappy as she and the Prime Minister got out of their cars and were pelted with nasty little balls, and there was a crowd chanting anti-Common Market slogans.

As later we walked into the entrance of the Palace for the Queen's party, I felt the elastic of my panties falling down around my hips. There was only one thing to do—wiggle and let them drop on my foot, then kick up my foot, catch them, and push them into my husband's pocket. He was furious with me, but what could I do? Leave them like a cluster of rose petals in the courtyard?

It is a far cry from dining with the Queen to attending the Eddie Barclay ball in Paris. It is, however, a big event in its own way, and one year the theme was England. We had to dress up as something traditionally English, and Ian had an inspiration. He would go as the headmistress of that delicious fictitious girls' school, St. Trinian's, and I would go as one of the girls. I invited Mary Quant and Twiggy to join me, and Alexander Plunkett-Green, who dressed as a Boy Scout. All the girls had bloomers and satchels and pigtails, and we looked a frightfully superb dotty mess.

Such costume would have been entirely out of place at the party in his Paris house given by Karim, the Aga Khan, who is my husband's nephew. He is a charming serious young man with an excessive responsibility on his young shoulders. I have known him since his years at Harvard and always respected his determination to do things as they should be done.

The house was built by the architect Pouillon for himself before he fled to Algeria. Karim bought it when it was still almost mediaeval in style, but I was happy to see that his wife has broken down its austerity and made it into a home.

It is just across the Seine from my own flat on the Ile St. Louis, and as it was a beautiful night, Ian and I decided to walk there. I was wearing an orange chiffon dress that flowed out behind me like the lady on the Rolls-Royce radiator-top. The dress looked pretty in the bluish evening light. I was also wearing the family diamonds, and I had no coat. Quite a few heads turned as I crossed the bridge. It was good to know that you can still walk through the streets of Paris unafraid.

At first I sat with Saõ Schlumberger, who told me that she was worried about her husband's health. A million people seemed to be there, including Bettina, looking like a ripe apricot, beautifully reposed, and smelling of tuberose, which I had thought was my monopoly.

Later I sat with Florence van der Kemp, the wife of that brilliant curator of the Château de Versailles. She began to tell me about everybody's new face, new bust, even new bottom. She told me about her neck, too, looking at mine, so I got the message.

Facing us, my husband was sitting with the Duchess of Windsor an enchanting, bright, and attractive woman, but above all amusing. She was, as always, extremely elegant, and looking specially well that night. Ian was bringing her dishes from the buffet. First she had him bring her roast beef and salad, but she took one look at it and said:

'That beef's been dead a long time.'

My husband went back to the buffet and returned with a *chaud froid de volaille*—cold chicken covered with a cream sauce and glazed with aspic, with a truffle in the centre.

The Duchess took a look at that, and said: 'What have they covered that chicken with—library paste?'

As I said, she is an amusing woman.

42 'You are wearing your chandelier'

DURING THE FOURTEEN years I have been at Woburn I have worked for one ideal—to make Woburn more beautiful, to leave Woburn more enriched, more lovely, more enduring than the day when I arrived. If I have succeeded in this, I shall go well contented.

For years I had nurtured an idea—a crazy, wilful, marvellous idea—of turning the Tenants Hall of the Crypt into a place where visitors to Woburn could see some of our most precious possessions—to create a beautiful 'heirloom vault'.

My chance came when Ian broke his leg in four places in a skiing accident in France. Dr. Lecroart, a remarkable surgeon in the next city, inserted four screws and a plate, Ian was flown back to Woburn in a plaster cast that reached from the top of his hip down to his feet.

He was immobilised, trapped a prisoner in his bed on the second floor.

Was this fate? By an extraordinary chance of circumstances, our administrator—who would have been there to tell me not to spend the money—was on a month's holiday.

Now was my chance. I called into our big office all the carpenters, gilders and painters, and told them of my project. We have extremely devoted people at Woburn, and as Mr. Cable, the security officer, once said:

'We don't live at Woburn. It is a way of living.'

The staff were intrigued, and all offered to help me. I knew that without their enthusiasm and co-operation the job was impossible. Of course the trustees had to be asked, but I made light of the whole thing, and everyone agreed.

Until then we had called the Tenants Hall 'the Garbage Hall'. It was stacked high with broken tables and chairs, torn or cracked paintings, mattresses bursting at the seams, old frying pans, cracked china, copper pans, pieces of carpet, discarded ornaments, forgotten treasures. In fact, the place was a serious fire hazard.

The mess was unbelievable. There were hundreds of years of mess. Thanks largely to the help of the curator and of Finlay, who is almost as knowledgeable about works of art, we made four separate piles, and tagged every object with a coloured label —green, pink, red or blue, according to which pile it belonged to. There was a pile of books (we found several Redouté books of roses), letters and prints; one for objets d'art and for household things we wanted to keep; one for broken furniture and moth, eaten old carpets to be burnt; and one for articles that were precious enough to put on show immediately so that the public could enjoy them.

Time and hours did not matter. Day flowed into evening, and into late night. By the end of the day we were black with dirt. The staff worked endlessly, sorting and sifting all through the winter. When spirits flagged, we made a party with drinks and food.

Whenever my husband asked: 'What are you doing downstairs?' I would shrug and say: 'Oh, there is so much to do in the office.'

My secretary joined in the conspiracy, and shielded me from the heaps of daily correspondence. She wrote to everyone: 'In Her Grace's absence, I am acknowledging . . .', thus leaving me free to proceed with the project.

I had nightmares for about three weeks because we had to dig under the early part of the Abbey, the north side built in 1626. We had an excavating contraption that took the earth from underneath and scooped it out to be shovelled into lorries for dumping.

Every night I went to bed knowing that a vast seventeenth-century inglenook and seventeenth-century walls were hanging over emptiness, and fearing one morning there would be a crash and I would become known, not as the Flying Duchess but as the Demolition Duchess.

Every day I would go to the workmen in an acute state of anxiety and say: 'For God's sake, you know, hurry up and put all the beams and planks to support the floor so that the whole edifice will not collapse.'

This particular part of the Abbey had been a Cistercian Monastery in the twelfth century, and a burial ground for the monks. We dug up skulls and bones, and one of our guides, Mrs. Aspinwall, was in a terrible state because I kept some of them on my desk, which she said was very unlucky.

We even began to see monks floating about in the gloom. When one of the cleaners said she had heard a monk singing in the corridor, I thought it was time to call in the parish Catholic priest. We reburied the bones with proper ceremony so that the monks could sleep eternally.

On the walls I should like one day to draw an impression of what a Cistercian Monastery looked like in the twelfth century. It would be lovely to have a form of Evensong there daily to which visitors to Woburn would be welcome.

Some evenings when the last of the crowds had gone, Ian would say:

'I think I can hear hammering all the time. What do you think it is?'

'Nothing, darling. Just your imagination,' I would reply blandly.

The first rooms when one turns right in the corridor are the Silver Room and the Silver Gilt Room. For security reasons, we had to have strong doors like the ones used in a bank. They looked so forbidding, and ugly that I had them painted with trompe l'oeil. Everyone now thinks they are Georgian panelled wood doors, but in fact they are steel—as strong as the Bank of England.

In the Silver Room we painted the walls and floor black, and lit the cases round the wall and in the centre with brilliant light, which gives the silver another exciting dimension.

In the centre cases I arranged all the Paul de Lamerie pieces. Like many men at the time of the religious wars in the eighteenth century, he changed his style. The work he did in France was austere and stark. When he came to England, he began doing very beautiful and involved chiselled rococo work. The Woburn collection is mostly dated 1737.

From my point of view, the most interesting items in that room are the two travelling cases designed by John Schofield and used by the 4th Duke and Duchess when they went by coach, and the bread baskets of Paul de Lamerie.

One travelling case is for making tea, and contains six elegant porcelain cups with a tea caddy and a kettle and the spirit lamp to make it boil. The other contains a picnic set for eight people—plates, knives and forks, and covered dishes for the vegetables.

What style they had in those days, and how differently we do things nowadays! When Ian and I travelled the 40 miles to London I was always asking him to stop so that I could have a quick cup of tea in a transport café. He hated the idea and would not get out of the car, so Manning, our chauffeur, went in with me. He disliked it just as much.

Now we have a machine in the back of the latest Rolls-Royce where I can make the tea as we drive along. Of course, I did not think to ask for an estimate and was horrified when I heard that my capricious whim had cost £600. I could have had a lot of café cups of tea for that!

I have a horror of picnics and buffet meals. It must be something decadent in me. When I eat food, I like to enjoy it sitting down at a table. I am definitely not as sporting as the former Duchesses when it comes to impromptu eating and picnicking.

My grandmother had the right idea about picnics. Hers were elaborate affairs, and she took chairs and tables, silver and china. While the chauffeur and Madelaine, the maid, set up the picnic luncheon, we children would be sent to pick flowers.

On one occasion, Charles Clore—who gives marvellous parties —invited us to a dance at Claridges, and I was disappointed to find that when it came to dinner, there was a buffet. Even Paul Getty ate his food sitting on the floor, but I was in a white satin evening dress and said to Ian:

'You had better take me into the restaurant and give me dinner there.'

Charles came running after us, obviously distressed, but I said:

'Charles, my dear, how do you expect me to sit on the floor in this dress?'

When Ian went to pay the bill in the restaurant, he discovered that Charles had already paid—the wonderfully typical gesture of a very generous man.

For the Gold Room at Woburn, I chose a rich purple backing to show off the James I standing salt and cover with rock-crystal stem, the Queen Anne sugar castors and the set of four William and Mary candlesticks.

In the next showcase there are two travelling cases, one each for a man and a woman, in gold. I was amused to see that the man's contained pots for the pomade for his moustache and beard. Eighteenth-century man was no less vain than the twentieth-century variety.

The woman's case in gold and turquoise was made for an aunt of my husband's called Ermyntrude Mallet. Her husband was very much in love with her, and decided to take her to the south of France where he had bought a beautiful place near Juan les Pins called Château Mallet. The considerate man went ahead to prepare it for her, but as a parting gift gave her the travelling case. It contains a button hook, two kinds of delicate scissors, fine little combs and brushes for her eyebrows and eyelashes, a double-headed spoon, and even a thermometer.

When the château was ready, Ermyntrude and her lady companion set off on their trip. They arrived at Boulogne, got out of the train and saw two Senegalese walking on the platform. Ermyntrude put her hand to her heart and said: 'Good lord, the French are black.'

At once she stepped back on the train and returned to England. Nothing would make her change her mind.

The château was eventually sold to Theo Rossi of the famous apéritif family. Theo is a very good friend of ours now. He still lives there and always teases us: 'Come and see your family property and all the lovely things done by your great-granduncle.'

It is all very sad. We would have a lovely house there today if old Ermyntrude had not been so stupid.

There is also a collection of 200 miniatures in the Gold Room. In the centre showcase I placed rings and seals belonging to my husband's ancestors. The seals are made of cornelian and agate and bear the coats of arms of the various Dukes and Duchesses, and many of the rings are mourning ones.

We found that we needed a passage for the public to visit Major Rowe's collection of model soldiers. After that visitors would go through a vast corridor with three large alcoves and showcases.

The first alcove contains virtually a small museum of toys, partly discovered in the house and partly bought in the course of our travels. I brought back from Moscow a child's service belonging to the Czar Nicholas II which we found in a pawn shop. Ian fell in love with an antique rocking horse, which we bought at Christie's to add to our collection.

Queen Victoria and Prince Albert stayed several times at Woburn, the first time soon after their marriage, in 1841. The bedroom where she slept and Prince Albert's dressing-room are open to visitors, with everything arranged just as it was for their visit.

But I decided to make a more personal memento of the Queen in the second showcase. I covered the whole of the back wall with an enlargement from an old print of Windsor Castle. In front of it is a make-believe window. I furnished the showcase with the stuffed Victorian chairs and table that Victoria had used on her visit.

From various people I collected articles from the Queen's own wardrobe. There is a nightgown with its demure black ribbon at the throat because she was then a widow. Her stockings are incredibly elegant. They are in fine black silk, but the tops and heels and toes are woven in white silk. The initials V.R. and the Imperial Crown are woven at the top.

I think it is rather chic to have one's initials and crown displayed thus, in contrast to the Marks and Sparks tights that I wear.

John Morley, director of the Brighton Pavilion, had a death-mask of Queen Victoria which he had used in an exhibition about her. He generously told me he was prepared to give it to me for Woburn. I was of course thrilled, and sent Manning down to collect it.

The mask was on a big pole with a stand, and Manning tied it to the seat next to his, nearly causing several accidents on the way back as motorists stared through the window at the dead Victoria's image lying back on the cushions.

I then began to dress the Queen in clothes that had belonged to her. To give her the necessary curves, I squeezed several little cushions into shape. It was after midnight when I applied the final touches, combing her hair and putting a little shawl softly on her head.

I then studied the result of my handiwork, and decided that the death-mask face needed more life, so I went to my handbag and took out my lipstick. I smudged her cheeks, which were hard and cold to touch, until they had a faint glow, and I finished off by smoothing her lips with a little colour.

As I preened her, all alone in the silence of the Crypt, I had the strangest feeling that somehow she was present. I do not know whether she was disapproving, or on the contrary approving, but I definitely had a feeling that she was telling me to comb her hair more forward and not to use so much rouge.

It was a very peculiar sensation.

In one corner of the alcove I tucked the sprig of orange blossom that Duchess Anna Maria, wife of the 7th Duke, had received from the Queen's bridal bouquet when she had been in attendance at her wedding. There is also the gift given her by the Queen—a golden bracelet with a cameo of the Queen surrounded by pearls.

We organised candlelight tours of the Crypt, because in candlelight it is particularly beautiful, as in a fairytale. Six months after the Crypt was completed, Amy Pilgrim went in to sweep up after our visitors, in preparation for one of these tours. Suddenly she screamed and rushed to the night-watchman.

'Queen Victoria is moving. I tell you she's moving.'

Everybody rushed down to the Crypt. Amy Pilgrim was indeed under no delusion. Queen Victoria was moving. Her bustle was quivering. We opened the glass window and found that the cushions I had placed to puff up her fashionable bustle were filled with little dancing mice.

The third showcase is for the family robes. I find them so totally out of keeping with modern life, but our guests seem to like them—and that is all that matters. There are the robes for the coronation, for receiving the Order of the Garter, and a robe for each time we attend the Opening of Parliament.

In the showcases for porcelain I was most careful in choosing the colours of the silk to line the cases—turquoise pleated taffeta for the Sèvres figures, pale pink vieux rose for the Meissen and the Dresden, for example.

For the famous Sévres dinner-service—there are only three left in the world—I created a glass pavilion in the manner of Versailles. From a sun symbol in the sky, I hung hundreds of yards of pleated taffeta. The low walls were covered with mirror-glass so that the table would reflect from every angle. The table was set in the authentic manner of a banquet at the time of Louis XV, with its white silk tablecloth to match the beautiful white chairs, decorated with gold.

On the two side tables I placed Dom Perignon, which I thought appropriate for the period. Constance Spry did the flowers, and from Trousellier in Paris, who made my orange-blossom wedding crown, I bought the imitation fruits, because they are better than anywhere else in the world.

Whenever I feel homesick for the elegance of the France I love so much, I go down to this little pavilion in the late hours of the night. Perhaps it is this pavilion for which I would most like to be remembered.

When Ian inherited Woburn Abbey the lawyers solemnly took him to the vault where the family jewelry was kept. It was like the hold of a Spanish galleon. There were stacked, all over the place, all the jewels that the Russells had collected down the ages.

At that time my husband only saw them as an added liability to the problem of death duties. There seemed little hope that anything could be saved to be worn again.

In my personal life I seldom wear jewelry, except for my engagement ring, which never leaves my hand. But when I play my rôle as a duchess, Ian not only discusses what I will wear but chooses the jewelry that he would like me to wear.

I first wore the great Bedford tiara three months before we were married. It was in June 1960 for Caterine's coming-out party at Versailles.

I had ordered a dress of white lace flowers, edged with silver, from Ted Lapidus, and Caterine had chosen masses and masses of virginal white tulle from Balmain.

'Would you like to wear a tiara?' Ian had asked me.

Now the one time that a woman wants to look her best is at her daughter's début. Besides, Caterine was wearing the traditional débutante coronet of pearls. Both Ian, to whom I was by then officially engaged, and his son Robin, the Marquess of Tavistock, were coming over for the occasion.

Caterine and I were waiting in my Paris flat when Ian arrived. He dumped a brown carrier-bag into my lap, which he had brought over in the plane like a bag of apples, and said:

'There you are. I am sure you will look lovely.'

I opened the bag and there lay the beautiful Bedford tiara. The thistles, roses and wheat, which are mounted on springs, quivered gently, and the evening sun caught the facets of light. It shimmered and shone, so delicate, so beautiful. This type of tiara is called a tremblant. It was made in the eighteenth century, and this particular example once belonged to Queen Caroline of Naples, the sister of Napoleon. It is still the tiara I love best.

Today, when I wear any of the Bedford jewels, I feel extra special. You do not have to be pretty on the night you wear a magnificent tiara. All eyes will be on the diamonds, and not on the face. Even if you are tired and not looking your best, a tiara makes you stand erect. If you walk 'tall', you can feel it shimmering on your head, attracting all eyes.

When you are young, you have a fresh attractive face and do not need jewels; in middle age, your face goes, but you can attract the eye away from it by wearing good jewelry.

I grew up when children were forced to sit on a stool at meals so that their back would be straight. This, combined with my strict ballet training has ensured one thing at least—I can wear a tiara with aplomb.

On the great day, we were thrown into confusion when we learnt that the hairdresser who was supposed to come from London to fix our hair was unavoidably detained, so Caterine and I decided to do our own hair. It was my first experience of the tiara technique. I was wearing a chignon, so I attached this first, and then began the business of fixing the tiara with small strands of hair wound round the edge, and dozens of long hairpins. It became heavier and heavier. No wonder that every time I wear a tiara, I have a headache after the first hour.

That night I also wore the great diamond necklace that hangs in three strands. Each diamond would make the most fantastic engagement ring. The necklace and the tiara are considered of national importance, and each time I take them out of the country, I have to get permission from the Treasury.

Since then I have worn the Bedford jewels many times. I never thought of them as important, but rather as something beautiful, until one day in an aeroplane I read the copy of authorisation to export the jewels temporarily, and saw the value that was placed on them by Her Majesty's Treasury!

I was so flabbergasted that now I never wear the tiara without thinking that some thief is going to snatch it off my head. It terrifies me to think that something as unique and lovely as Queen Caroline's tiara should be broken up and the design lost.

I shall never forget crossing the courtyard in Versailles at Caterine's coming-out. All the big spotlights were trained on us. My head was like the sky in a clear summer night, with dazzling stars shining gaily. As Diane Beatty told me one night: 'Oh, you are wearing your chandelier.'

At a dance at Luton Hoo, home of Sir Harold and Lady Wernher, which was attended by all the members of the Royal Family, I noticed that I was wearing a bigger and better tiara than the Queen. I was so embarrassed and kept avoiding her, but she noticed it and came closer to have a look—not at my face but at the tiara.

Among the important family jewelry, there is also a most

impressive amethyst and diamond set of tiara, necklace, bracelet, brooch, and earrings.

When we first opened the Antique Centre, we had a special display of the Bedford jewelry. We had, of course, to make fantastic security precautions. First the jewelry had to be brought in five different cars from the vault by five different routes. When it arrived, it was allocated to five models to wear. The idea was for each girl to wear a complete set of jewelry and a period costume to match. They posed together in period settings, while the public filed by.

Flanking the girls was a man with a gun concealed under his coat, and another armed guard stood opposite them under the window. Every time one of the girls needed to go to the cloak-room, a female security guard had to accompany her. Our security chief, Mr. Cable, had the James Bond idea of stretching a net inside the loo, at the bottom of the pan, in case a diamond slipped down by mistake!

That one cannot be too security conscious where jewelry is concerned is illustrated by the experience of Collingwood's, the Royal Family jewellers and also the Bedford family jewellers for generations, who had taken a shop on the first floor of the Antiques Centre. On the day of the opening Barry Wieland was coming down with his assistants and a case of jewelry for display. He was late, and we were getting really worried, when we had a telephone call to say that he had been attacked on the motorway at exit 13, had been coshed over the head and that his jewelry had been stolen. There were a lot of reporters about, and I told them the story.

I was only met with 'Ha ha, another of your publicity stunts!'

I insisted that the story was true, but they did not believe me until poor Barry Wieland arrived, head bleeding, and black and blue all over. Immediately all the reporters dived for any available telephone.

I have twice personally been robbed of jewelry. As every woman knows, it can be the most heart-rending experience because no money can replace the sentimental value.

Maybe my favourite piece of jewelry was a flat platinum watch surrounded by diamonds. It had been left to me by my grand-mother—the woman who had meant so much to me. I think of my grandmother wearing it, and to me it was more precious than the largest diamond. I also lost the first piece of jewelry that my husband gave me—a brooch with a turquoise spray.

It is of course a great responsibility to wear heirloom jewelry, but I hope that the day will never come when it will be locked up in a museum and no longer adorn the dances and dinners and balls for which it was designed.

When Ian chooses what jewelry I should wear, he is often in-fluenced by the period of the house we are visiting. If it is a Georgian house, then I wear the Georgian tiara; if it is a Regency house, he selects something of a later date. I doubt if anyone notices or even cares, but it is a charming idea.

Not only does my husband choose my jewelry, but over the years he has bought nearly all my wardrobe.

Ian is known to almost every salesgirl in London, from Picca-dilly to the King's Road. Whenever they have something special that would suit me, they ring him up and he goes to inspect it.

Clothes do not impress me. I treat them as decorative covering and if something goes wrong, I never bother.

I once arrived in London in a little pink wool dress, carrying a formal black one for a very important dinner party. I bathed and, as usual, was in a rush. I got into the black dress and asked my husband to zip me up. He broke the fastener and caught it in my hair at the same time. I struggled out of the black dress and had to wear the pink one after all. I had felt so tired before the incident but suddenly I felt alive. We laughed, and I felt marvellous and had a wonderful night.

To me, the greatest luxury would be to have no possessions, or very few—not to be tied down to anything. In life the moment you get attached to something, you suffer, because you live in fear that it may be snatched away from you.

43   *I'm there*

ON JUNE 29, 1970, I reached the age of fifty. I was very pleased to be fifty. I stopped and looked back at my life. I liked what I saw, and I decided that I could stop running and fighting and begin to enjoy my life and what I had achieved in it.

When the war ended I bought a beautiful fast sports car called a Delahaye, turquoise blue outside, red crimson leather inside. I used to speed up and pass limousines, looking at them with contempt and curiosity. I asked myself who could wish to drive in such mausoleums. Now I know who sits in such a car. It is a woman of 50—me!

We live a hectic life of fast jet-travel, back and forth to the airport, and every day on the motorway, Woburn–London–London–Woburn, what I call the yo-yo life—too much work, too large a house, too much mail, too many friends.

When my birthday approached, I said to my husband: 'I want an ambulance to travel in comfort,' so I have it, the DOB 1 Phantom 6, of such comfort it is almost sinful, brown astrakhan in colour to suit my hair.

I never understand why women lie about their age. Either you look less than your real age, in which case everybody says, 'You'd never believe she was as old as . . .' or you look more than your age, and then people say, 'Is she only . . .? I thought she was more.' Either way you cannot lose.

Unfortunately, or rather fortunately, it takes two to make love. When you are 20 there is no problem, so you make love all the time. When you are 50 there is a problem, so you settle for creamy chocolate and hot croissants. Actually it is about the same —hot and crusty, sweet and gooey. It is very comforting.

One of the great satisfactions I get on my birthday is to see it announced in the birthday column of the Court Circular. It gives me the strange feeling that if *The Times* says so, I must indeed be alive.

Fortunately I have never been pretty, for prettiness can fade with age. So I have to have a good head, and as at 50 it is the only thing I have left, I had better not lose it.

Once I was in Paris for the opening of the Hilton, and I was sitting next to Charles Clore, who said: 'And now where are you going, Nicole?'

I replied: 'Nowhere, Charles, I'm there.'

When I went from 29 to 30, I hated it, and I thought life was over. I really did. I remember walking alone in the flea-market in Paris, looking at the stalls and feeling despondent and lost. I was hungry, so I went into Louisette, the flea-market restaurant. Louisette is a truculent personality, but she has hundreds of friends, as she is so friendly herself.

She had not seen me for months, maybe years, but she greeted me with a warmth that I needed badly. I sat by myself at a table near the window, and I was eating my solitary lunch of steak and frites when a gypsy came in. She tore off a corner of the paper tablecloth, put some salt in it, closed her eyes and recited some mumbo-jumbo in Romany.

She opened my left hand, put the little packet of salt in it and said: 'I have brought a little parcel of happiness to the sad-faced lady.'

It made me laugh. I knew of course that the whole thing was a fake, but the gesture was enough to take me out of my gloom, go home, change, make myself attractive and join some friends for dinner.

Forty I do not remember, but 50 I loved. My husband wanted to give a dance for me, and I replied: 'No, thank you very much, I will have to invite all kinds of people I do not like. It will cost a lot of money and I will end up being tired and unhappy.'

I said to Ian, 'I would like a trip to our honeymoon hotel, the Cipriani in Venice, with all the children—yours and mine, a fireworks display, and a dinner for us and the children in the Canaletto room, and a dinner for the Woburn family of employees n the Sculpture Gallery.' He generously decided to give me, instead of the ball, a little country retreat; he has not done so yet, but I am certain that it will come one day.

I had told everybody that this was the one day of my life when I wanted to live in complete peace and tranquility. I did not want to know who had been invited, what the menu was, or about the organising of bedrooms for guests. I had a leisurely morning in bed, reading the papers and six months' back numbers of magazines, which I never have time to read. I had lunch with the children, who were all very excited and mysterious.

In the afternoon I drove myself in the grounds, unhurriedly looking at the deer, the lions, the trees, the lakes. In the evening I returned, had a long bath, read and prepared myself for a marvellous dinner.

For one day I wanted to shed responsibility and I did.

What I did not know was that there had been a crisis in the kitchen because the duty chef, in David's absence, was taken suddenly ill.

I was still floating on my cloud of irresponsibility, but meanwhile everyone else was saying: 'What about dinner?' Of course they all turned to Didier, who has been to catering school, and he and a friend, Daniel Durand, who is now the owner of Noel's restaurant in Beauchamp Place, rolled up their sleeves and prepared a superb meal, and then unrolled them to help eat it.

After dinner, family and staff joined us on the terrace for the fireworks. There were gilt armchairs for my husband and me, and at the end of the display, when it said in the sky 'Happy Birthday, Nicole', a little donkey came with a present from the staff on his saddle, a 'signature book', bound in red Morocco leather, from Asprey, and a travelling desk set, a most useful present because I always write and sign my mail in the car on the M1.

I always enjoy birthdays and try to make them special days for the people concerned. They mean much more to me than

Christmas, when I think presents should be given only to children. Most of us end up by getting a whole lot of things we do not like or want, and it takes me a year to recover financially from my Christmas list.

For my husband's fiftieth birthday, I wanted something very special. I decided to organise a series of parties, beginning on Monday and carrying on for three days.

I invited about 30 close friends to rendezvous with us at the Eros statue in Piccadilly Circus. Suddenly, as if on wings, a table and champagne emerged from the Criterion Theatre, carried by two waiters. Sharp at 8 p.m. on the huge screen that carries election results and important news flashes, there appeared 'Happy birthday, my love, have another lovely 50 years'. Then we all drank to Ian. I had rented the newscaster as a surprise.

People wandering about, looking at the big screen and hearing the laughter, smiled shyly, and went about their business. English people are not uncurious, but they have a reserved way of not wanting to become involved. In Italy or France the same events would have caused total confusion.

From there we went up onto the roof of the Criterion for a party given by Lord Thomson for Ian.

I wanted a second party in our house in Chester Terrace, which had become too large for just Ian and me. Once it had been filled with the children, with their noise, their bustle, their exuberance.

I remember it as one of the happiest houses in my life. It lived for the present and the future, and not in the past. But now Didier was married, Caterine was in America, Rudolf had taken an apartment, Gilles was in Paris, and Anyes had decided she wanted her own little house in London.

So there we were, Ian and I, in a four-storey house that was obviously too big for us. As we travelled constantly, we did not need a house that required a minimum staff of three.

I loved that house and thought that one day I might retire to live there as a dowager duchess! We had acquired it in a very strange way. I said to my husband in the car once: 'We must have a house that is between where we always are—Claridges, the

Connaught, Michaeljohn my hairdresser, Asprey, Cartier and Savile Row—a house that is between Mayfair and Swiss Cottage, which is on the way out to Woburn.'

Then driving in Regent's Park, we saw this house, white as an iced cake, cool in the green shadows of big trees, facing south with an attractive garden behind.

My husband said it had belonged to Pamela Churchill. I knew instinctively that this was where I wanted to live.

We stopped the car and I went to speak to some workmen who were putting up scaffolding. The garden was like a giant mud-pack. Branches had been broken off the trees, there was not a blade of grass left—but with my vivid imagination and un-tarnishable optimism, I could see roses, prunus and hydrangeas. One thing that enchanted me was a mulberry tree.

'There is no point in searching any more,' I told my husband. 'This is the house where we should live.'

We bought the house, planted the garden, and moved the children in. But now, alas, it had outgrown its purpose.

Because I loved the house, I did not want it to disappear from my life, so I suggested to my husband that we find some friends who would like to have it in exchange for using their house, perhaps in the south of France or America.

One day we met a charming man called Mr. Fortinberry—he was head of *Time-Life*—who was looking for just such a house. They brought their pictures and furniture and they moved in.

When Mrs. Fortinberry first saw the dining-room she said:

'Of course I won't need that furniture, because that's where I shall put my rocks.'

Fascinated, I said: 'Your rocks? How many rocks?' Rocks to me—having lived in America—suggested big diamond rings.

'Everywhere we go,' she said, 'you know my husband is always moving from country to country, I just stop the car and get pieces of rock from the side of the road. I have crates and crates of them. They are coming from Tokyo.'

That had been a year before my husband's birthday. Now I wanted to have a party in London so that all our friends could come and have drinks with us, and I had the bright idea to

telephone **Mr.** Fortinberry and ask if he would mind letting me
have my house back for one evening.

He was most charming, and generously agreed. I told him that
we would put up a marquee in the garden and that it would be
necessary to remove the furniture from the dining-room.

As the party had to be a surprise, and my husband and I lived
like Siamese twins and were never apart, my secretary had to
organise the whole thing—which she did superbly. She and I
used to meet hurriedly in the garden, and she would show me
patterns of various colours for the sides of the tent—I decided on
blue, turquoise and white—and we discussed the food for 300 or
400 guests.

I wanted to invite a cross-section of people because my husband,
as well as being the Duke of Bedford with the connections that his
title implies, is tremendously interested in the theatre, cinema and
fashion industries.

I remember that we sent an invitation to Miss Lesley Hornby,
and back came a request from a secretary that all correspondence
should be addressed to just Twiggy. I thought that rather sweet.
Twiggy was enchanted to meet the peers at the party, and they
were enchanted to meet her. She kept coming up to me and
saying:

'You know, I've met three dukes and four earls.'

After a family lunch, I told Ian that we were expected for a
drink with Mr. Fortinberry at 6 p.m. When we arrived, innocent
Ian said in his wry way; 'Oh, it's a big do. I've never seen a tent
in the garden before.'

We entered the hall and went upstairs to the first floor.
Absolutely nobody was there except the Fortinberrys.

We had a drink with them and then my husband looked at his
watch and said, 'I think it's time we went now—it was nice to
have seen you.' Mr. Fortinberry led us downstairs and straight to
the tent. As we entered there was a chorus of 'Happy Birthday,
Ian', from the early guests, who had been hiding themselves and
waiting for our arrival. It turned out to be a very good party
indeed.

Six days afterwards, still in a very happy mood, we went off to join Dosia and Terence Young, who had rented a large boat for a cruise.

The first leg of the trip was a flight to Istanbul, where all the Youngs' guests stayed on the top floor of the Hilton hotel, next to one another.

Also in the party were Yul and Doris Brynner, Mel Ferrer, Richard Johnson, Anne Orr-Lewis and Fleur and Tom Montaigne Meyer.

At every harbour we visited, some of us disembarked and others joined us, bringing fresh blood to the party. From Istanbul we passed through the Dardanelles to Greece and then on to Italy and France.

It was an absolute dream, but having Yul Brynner on board was quite a problem. Everywhere we went people wanted to touch him. One of his films had just been released in Istanbul, and the hotel was besieged. It was the same everywhere, that extraordinary human desire to touch someone famous or whom you admire. Wherever we went, people appeared to be hypnotised by him, and even stood for hours chanting his name.

I like Yul Brynner very much. Someone had given me a simply delicious box of chocolates, stuffed with figs. One evening we were playing cards, and I was eating my chocolates, when he took the box and threw it through the porthole, saying:

'You don't need that, you're fat enough.'

I suppose he was right.

44   *What of the future?*

WRITING YOUR AUTOBIOGRAPHY is joyful and at the same time painful. Memories flash back at you. Long-forgotten tenderness engulfs you. The closed wounds of despair over loved ones are reopened. Your ears become filled with the sound of childhood, your nose reminds you of the smells of the war, like the scent of exploded ripe tomatoes under hot shrapnel, your arms search for the innocent feeling of the first embrace, your eyes close to recall the beauty and sadness of all your memories. The trouble about writing about yourself is that you have the terrible feeling of being smug and complacent.

I wrote this book so that the facts, good or bad, would be recorded for my children, grandchildren, my two families and my friends. I am proud of my life. I have not been always clever. I have made many mistakes, but these I accept. I have made a great effort never to hurt anyone deliberately, and I do not think I have.

Integrity, truth and honesty have been my main guidelines, but they have been very costly, very costly indeed!

I have loved deeply and despaired deeply, but it has taught me understanding and tolerance.

Why does one fall in love? What did I want from a man? Warmth, availability, gentleness, goodness, a sense of humour, eagerness, companionship, friendship—maybe I have asked for too much, but I have tried to give the same in return, and never to take myself too seriously.

If in a marriage or a relationship you have found all these qualities, you must consider yourself fortunate.

My husband said that although he was the 13th Duke, he counted himself lucky. I am the wife of the 13th Duke, and I feel the same way.

My abiding joy has been my four children. They are healthy, well balanced, hard working and, by luck, good-looking.

Everyone told me when they were small that my way was no way to raise children. I tried to make them feel responsible for their lives from an early age and I believe I succeeded. Self-discipline and the absence of self-pity make you grow up very fast. When they were little, I used to pose problems like the following:

'All right,' I would say, 'your ball is on the roof. Choose what you want to do. Either you can go there and get it, and you may have no problem, or you may fall and break a limb and be four months in plaster, or even break your head and die. Alternatively, you can wait and ask the gardener to fetch it for you. The choice is yours.'

I have always been fascinated to see in the decision of so small a human being the behaviour of the man or woman to come.

It is very important to have a united family. I believe in the French idea for children, that they should respect their parents. Many English children do not have this respect, and I feel sorry for them.

When you have children, of course, you want them to love you, but it is a duty to prepare them for the world even if they dislike you for it. The world is a brute of a place.

I always laugh when friends say I have been lucky with my children, because it was not luck; it was really hard work plus plenty of love.

Socrates said in the fourth century B.C.: 'They have inexcusable manners, flout authority, have no respect for their elders. What kind of awful creatures will they be when they grow up?'

It makes me laugh. The French have a saying 'Plus on recommence plus c'est la même chose'—as often as you try again, so you get the same result.

Marriage, like bringing up children, is a business. I have learnt, and I am still learning, to compromise, to fit in with my husband's feelings and desires. I have worked hard on my marriage, for I want it to last until my dying day. If you do not work at it, it fails. There is no point in just hoping for the best.

Ian and I have been married nearly 14 years and known each other 17 years. We have worked together nearly as long. He returned home one day in a delighted mood, having just bought from the Spencer-Churchill sale a partner's desk that had been made for Warren Hastings at the end of the eighteenth century. It was huge—seven feet square. The ballroom had been transformed into an office, with Chinese wallpaper, gilded pine panelling and the famous Gainsborough 'Woodcutter and Milkmaid' above the chimney. When the desk was installed, my husband called me in and simply said. 'I shall sit here and you shall sit there, now let's work.'

Luckily one of my great strengths is an ability to delegate, to choose carefully the people to whom I give responsibility. Their background, looks, accent do not matter. It is whether they do the job well that counts. Another thing I learnt a long time ago, when making films, is to work with people I do not like, if I think their ability qualifies them for the job. My attitude has helped us to create new things, to move, and to be free, but it is essential when you are at the top to remember that if something goes wrong, the fault is yours, for you selected the person in charge.

When I told my husband that I would start an Antique Centre of the highest quality, he said 'You must be mad. We are an hour from London and nobody will come.' It took me nearly a whole summer, with a large group of helpers, to clear a corner of the magnificent stable block designed by Henry Flitcroft in 1747. Six shops were created inside the stable spaces and immediately rented. There was a big opening in September 1967. The venture was such a success that it was first enlarged to 16 shops, then 25, and now there are over 40, which is the full capacity.

Managing the Centre was a full-time business, and I had to find the right person. I had met Sylvie de Cardinal, whose sister Caroline was helping my daughter-in-law in her London antique shop. One weekend Fernanda asked if she could bring Caroline to an auction. On the Saturday afternoon Caroline was called to the telephone to learn that her sister Sylvie had lost the top of one of her fingers in an accident. I immediately made arrangements for Sylvie to see a surgeon, and I am pleased to say that the finger was repaired perfectly. For a time, however, Sylvie could not work properly, and she had also lost her handbag with all her money when she fainted following the accident. I therefore invited her to stay with us.

She was a nice steady responsible girl, and when she was better, I asked her to take over the Centre. She herself trained an assistant, Ivy Manning, who is now in charge, well liked and a model of efficiency.

I was to follow our success with the Antiques Centre by establishing the catering organisation with David, an even greater achievement, then by fighting the ghastliness of the plastic souvenirs by introducing the arts and crafts galleries and finally the exhibition centre. I gave myself totally.

I fell in love with a man who had a demanding mistress. I married him and fell in love with his mistress. She was Woburn Abbey.

In a marriage what matters is what you achieve as a couple; and it is important when you get older to have no regrets, to be able to look back with peace of mind.

I know I am sticking my neck out but I have very strong views about marriage. All my friends and family know them and it would be hypocrital not to acknowledge them.

Nothing makes me sadder than to see every week in our local paper all the smiling faces of the newly married couples—so often boys of 20 marrying girls of 18. I know that unless they are saints or incredibly mature, early marriage is likely to lead to catastrophe and I firmly believe that in the jet age, when travelling and moving fast from one point to another are part of one's daily life, and of course with nearly all young girls earning their living, the rules of marriage as known by our Victorian grandmothers have become completely obsolete.

I shall be misjudged for this statement but I believe that young people should become mature before marrying and having children, and they can only mature by living. The fact of marriage need have nothing to do with your love and devotion to a man or the care and tenderness you have for your children. When someone you cherish dies, there is grief and terrible sadness inside you, and wearing black clothes does not change your feelings. It is the same with marriage. It is not because you have a marriage certificate that you decide, for example to be faithful. Your decision is based only on the fact that you want to give yourself wholly and exclusively to the other person. Marriage is giving without taking, understanding and hoping to be understood. There is something desolate in an excess of love that is rejected.

Early in our marriage I established a formula: If you can always do what you don't want to do, and perhaps never do what you want to do, and still remain loving and happy, you have a successful marriage.

The future of marriage as such will be fascinating to watch, because we have entered the century of the peacock and of 'Women's Lib'. The French couturier Ted Lapidus invented Unisex, and Yves Saint-Laurent popularised it. Women have risen to be men in their thinking, behaviour and demands.

I would like to see injustice to women rectified but I love men and I find 'Women's Lib' ludicrous. I suppose that I did my own 'lib' years ago without knowing it, when I took my life in my own hands and went to work. Facts count, not words, chants and banners.

If women have conquered trousers, cigarettes, and top executive jobs, men have taken to using face cream, scent, and bright clothes. Homosexuality, bisexuality are in. I try to understand, to be fair. Is it the fault of the woman or the century?

I found it both moving and refreshing when Emlyn Williams spoke about his bisexuality on the Michael Parkinson television programme when his autobiography appeared. I suppose honesty, as opposed to hypocrisy, appeals to me anyway.

We shall see in the years to come what will happen, but I still think that when in doubt, look to nature. The male leads, the female follows, and I think that is the way it should be. Men are creators, women finishers.

But why when a foreign woman marries an Englishman, can she choose to become English, but if a foreign man marries an English girl, the reverse is not the case?

Looking back over my life, I remember with deep gratitude and affection the four men who, each in his own way, brought me joy and fulfilment.

It is a fallacy, I believe, to pretend that only one man counted.

Each human being has the ability to add to life his or her own special dimension—you change, they change. When you are two, you give away half of yourself, but you gain from the other person half of something new.

It was Michel who turned me from a neglected tomboy into a woman, from a child into a responsible human being. Ours was a young love that stood the test of the extraordinary years of war. He brought tenderness, courage and beauty into my life. For that he will always be present in my memory.

Astrology was used a great deal by the ancient civilisations, then with scientific knowledge it fell into disrepute, but in our Godless society it is once more in fashion. I have found great similarity of behaviour and life-patterns among people born under the same signs. Also I find people born in the summer more joyful than those born during the winter months.

Michel was born under the sign of Scorpio and I was born under the sign of Cancer. Scorpio people are supposed to dominate my sign of Cancer, and I know this is true, because I had for many years a secretary, Patricia Bain, also born under the sign of Scorpio, who absolutely ruled my life—but as she had very good judgment, I did not mind; in fact, I liked it.

Guy de Lacharrière was an intellectual love affair. He was my Scott Fitzgerald who took a raw, untrained brain and extended it to explore the world of literature and the arts. Without Guy's tutelage I would never have developed as I did. He gave me a thirst for knowledge, for new books to read, museums to visit, galleries to explore. Cultured, kindly Guy, with his fine brain, was my mentor. No woman could have wished for better. Of course I should have married him, as he was the only one whose love was totally selfless.

Guy was born under the sign of Aquarius. Cancer loves water, so probably that was what subconsciously attracted me to him and gave me fulfilment. People born under that sign are kind and good, two qualities I respect.

The tempestuous, brilliant Shelly gave me so much too. Ours was a raging, torrential love-affair, enacted across the globe, and covering many years. By chance he also led me into the film world as a producer, where I did some of my most rewarding work.

Shelly was a Sagittarian. People of this sign too, dominate Cancer women. They bend them to their will, which is all right as Cancer people are slave-minded—up to a point!

Lastly Ian, beguiling, wonderful Ian, so diverse, so funny—he combines many of the qualities of the others; Ian who asked me to marry him more times than any other man in my life; sweet, gentle Ian who took me from the man's world of business to change me back into a vulnerable woman; witty, amusing Ian who, with his concealed strength, transformed me from a high-powered film executive into the kind of wife he wanted—a wife for Woburn.

Ian is a Gemini, a true one. He has a completely dual personality.

Everyone should write his autobiography, because by probing inside your soul, you discover characteristics that you did not know existed.

I found two that astonished and troubled me, but the facts are there! I have never chosen a man; men have chosen me. Secondly I do not act, I react.

I often wonder who I am. I was born Nicole Schneider, but I lost that name when I married. I became Nicole Milinaire, and when I started working, it was my professional name as well. As I was possibly the first woman film-producer, the Press was excited and full of praise; I was called 'the girl wonder' in America and 'the female Mike Todd' in France.

Then I became the Duchess of Bedford, but that is not a name, it is a title. When I married my husband there were three

Duchesses of Bedford, my mother-in-law, Lydia and I. I remember that this completely confused an American who had been sent to Woburn by a mutual friend. He arrived at teatime, when all three Duchesses were in the room, and as he left, he turned to the butler with a very puzzled expression and asked: 'Which one is the real one?'

So not having a proper name that I can call my own until my dying day, I have chosen in this book to tell the story of Nicole Nobody.

Her story is part of the past, but what of her future?

Three years ago at Easter, we had dinner at Woburn with Robin—Ian's heir—and my cousin Marie-Thérèse and her daughters, who had just arrived from Paris to stay with us. After the coffee, the girls went to study. Marie-Thérèse and I went to look at some ballet on the television. When the programme was over I put my head through the double doors of the low-lit drawing-room. The fire was still red, the atmosphere felt congenial, and I did not wish to intrude on one of the rare meetings between father and son. I said goodnight to my cousin and went to bed.

I started to read, and about an hour later my husband entered looking rather pale, I thought, and he said: 'We are moving.' I looked at him questioningly. 'We are leaving Woburn. I'll explain later. I am tired now. Goodnight.' He kissed me, and turned over.

This sudden shattering news was never explained to me. My husband may appear gentle to the outside world—I know better; he is a Russell and proud to be, determined in his life and actions.

Months later I learnt that 1974 was to be the year of departure, but I was never told how or where, and I concluded that Ian probably did not know himself. All he said was: 'We shall go naked.'

It would be very unsettling, after so many years, having to make a new home, and a new life in a new country—but c'est la vie—that's life!

Time passed, and I put the imminence of our departure at the back of my mind, but it hit me last Bank Holiday Monday, at the end of the summer.

I had asked the night-watchman to awake me at 7 a.m. The

telephone rang and I stumbled out of bed, not asleep, not awake. I went to the kitchenette to make a hot cup of China tea, and returned to bed with my tray, which I put next to my pillow. Then I went to draw the curtains.

I was suddenly immensely sad. I stood by the window, straight, staring ahead at the park. I knew I would never see it again at the joyful end of the summer, and in the bluish light of the early morning when the dew is still on the leaves and when the sun is warm enough to transform it into an Impressionist haze.

We have three windows in our bedroom at Woburn. Through the one on the left I saw the clump of old black-trunked oaks, brilliant green on their crowning tops. Oaks look like human beings with legs and multiple arms, robust, happy to live, full of the joy of creation.

On the right, the view through the window is blocked by a mass of dark evergreen trees, ominous, forbidding, hateful, pine-trees as in a cemetery, conifers like death. On the left, there is hope, on the right despair.

Through the centre window, I saw my joie de vivre—a long sweeping expanse of brilliant green grass, sloping down to a lake surrounded by shocking-pink rhododendrons when in season, and going up again to another lake, the favourite of the swans.

In the centre stands a blue cedar, planted on the frail body of my miniature Yorkshire terrier, Rembrandt, better known as Goo-Goo. He was fierce, so he deserved a noble tree.

I looked too at the deer grazing, especially the breed I like best, the Père David.

The scene was peaceful. I was not. My cheeks were wet, my heart heavy. I knew that we would soon be off for a long journey to Australia for the opening of the Opera house in Sydney, with a slow return through the Pacific and the United States, where I would see my granddaughter Serafine in New York.

It would be winter when we returned: rain, fog, and no leaves, I would never see the glorious summer from our bed again. What of the future?

I wish I knew.

Index

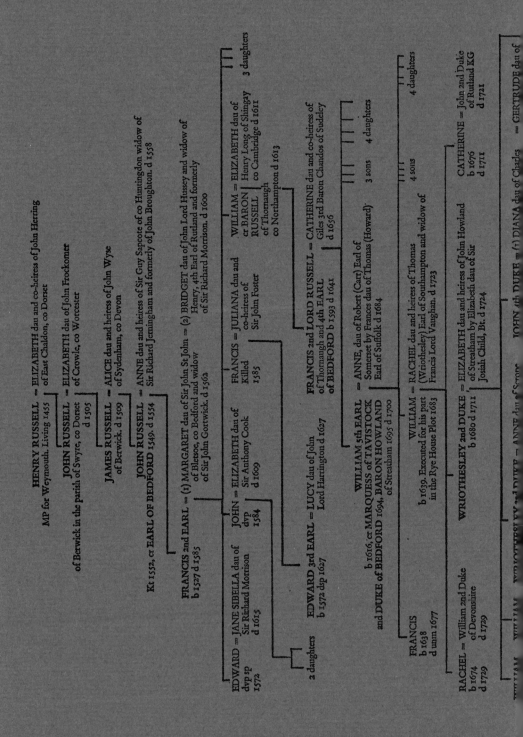